BEFORE CIVILIZATION

BEFORE CIVILIZATION

THE RADIOCARBON REVOLUTION
and PREHISTORIC EUROPE

COLIN RENFREW

ALFRED A. KNOPF   NEW YORK

1973

LIBRARY OF CONGRESS CATALOGING IN PUBLICATION DATA
Renfrew, Colin (date).   Before civilization.

1. Man, Prehistoric—Europe.   2. Megalithic monuments—
Europe.   3. Radiocarbon dating.   I. Title.
GN803.R46 1973   913.36'03   73–6552   ISBN 0-394-48193-3

MANUFACTURED IN THE UNITED STATES OF AMERICA

FIRST AMERICAN EDITION

For Glyn and Ruth

CONTENTS

1	Introduction	15
2	The Problem of Dating	20
3	The First Radiocarbon Revolution	48
4	The Tree-Ring Calibration of Radiocarbon	69
5	The Collapse of the Traditional Framework	84
6	Beyond Diffusion	109
7	The Enigma of the Megaliths	120
8	The World's First Stone Temples	147
9	The Beginning of European Metallurgy	167
10	The Emergence of Civilization in Europe	192
11	Stonehenge and the Early Bronze Age	214
12	Prospect: Towards a New Prehistory	248
	APPENDIX Radiocarbon Dating	257
	NOTES	273
	BIBLIOGRAPHY	281
	INDEX follows page	292

LIST OF PLATES

Eight pages of plates follow page 60.

1. The bristlecone pine: earth's oldest inhabitant

2. Megalithic tomb, La Roche-aux-Fées, at Essé in Brittany

3. The earliest stone temples: decorated doorway at Mnajdra in Malta

4. Marble flute-player from the Cycladic Islands of Greece, dated *c.* 2500 B.C.

5. Axe-adzes of copper from the Balkans, dated *c.* 4000 B.C.

6. Incised signs on a clay plaque or dish from Gradeshnitsa in Bulgaria, dated *c.* 4000 B.C.

7. Incised signs on a baked clay 'seal' from copper-age Karanovo in Bulgaria

8. Early bronze-age weapons and gold from the Bush Barrow, Wiltshire, England

9. Early bronze-age gold cup from a barrow at Rillaton, Cornwall, England

10. Round houses of the Louisiana Indians drawn in the 18th century A.D., resembling those of the British neolithic chiefdoms

11. Colossal stone burial platform in Tahiti, built in the 18th century A.D., comparable in scale with the great monuments of neolithic western Europe

12. The great stone rotunda of Stonehenge (Stonehenge IIIa)

LIST OF FIGURES IN THE TEXT

1. 4004 B.C. in the margin of the Authorized Version of the Bible   21
2. Dolmen at Pentre Ifan, Wales   32
3. Elliot Smith's map of the diffusion of 'heliolithic' cultures   34
4. Typological series of daggers by Oscar Montelius   38
5. Neolithic corbelled tomb in Brittany and the 'Treasury of Atreus' at Mycenae   40
6. Childe's chronological links for prehistoric Europe (map)   43
7. Logical structure of Childe's chronological system (diagram)   44
8. Simplified version of Childe's chronology (1957) for prehistoric Europe   45
9. Traditional view of the diffusion of passage graves (map)   46
10. Libby's use of Egyptian radiocarbon dates as a check of the validity of the radiocarbon method   53
11. Radiocarbon dates for the spread of farming to Europe   64
12. Differences between the traditional and radiocarbon chronologies for the neolithic in Europe and the Near East   65
13. First use of tree-ring dating to check radiocarbon dates   73
14. Calibration chart for radiocarbon dates   75
15. Bastioned fortifications in Spain and the Aegean   87
16. Comparison between early Balkan and east Mediterranean signs   92
17. Faces on pot-lids from Vinča and Troy   94
18. The traditional and calibrated radiocarbon chronologies for the Balkans compared   96–7
19. Grave finds from the Bush Barrow in Wessex   100
20. The chronological 'fault line' (diagram)   104
21. The 'fault line' in Europe (map)   105
22. Simplified table of the new chronology for Europe   107
23. Passage grave at Newgrange, Ireland   121
24. Plan of gallery grave at Essé, Brittany   124
25. Distribution of neolithic chambered tombs in Europe (map)   125
26. Long dolmen at Valdbygaards, Denmark   127
27. Use of a crib to raise a megalithic lintel   130
28. Corbelled passage grave at Er-Mané, Carnac, Brittany   131
29. Distribution and territories of megalithic tombs in Arran, Scotland (map)   133

30. Distribution and territories of chambered tombs in Rousay, Orkney (map) 136
31. Plan of the Ġgantija temples, Maltese islands 148
32. Relief spirals at the Tarxien temple, Malta, compared with spirals from Mycenae 150
33. Distribution and territories of temples in the Maltese islands (map) 154
34. Schema of chiefdom descent and territorial division 157
35. View and section of image *ahu*, Easter Island 161
36. Tribal territories on Easter Island (map) 163
37. Important copper age sites in the Balkans (map) 168
38. The Tartaria tablets 177
39. Interior of a Hopi house, south-western United States 184
40. *Rongo rongo* writing of Easter Island 185
41. Plan of the Late Minoan palace at Knossos in Crete 194
42. Reconstruction of the courtyard of the palace at Mycenae 195
43. Tablet with Minoan Linear B inscription 196
44. Plan of the early bronze age citadel at Troy 206
45. Population growth in the prehistoric Aegean 207
46. Diagram of Stonehenge III 217
47. Diagram of Stonehenge I with alignments 221
48. Faience beads from early bronze age Britain 224
49. Distribution of 'causewayed camps' and long barrows in neolithic south Britain: the emergence of embryo chiefdoms 229
50. Reconstruction of wooden rotunda at The Sanctuary, Avebury, south Britain 232
51. Eighteenth-century plan of rotunda of Cherokee Indians 235
52. Diagram of roofing of Creek Indian rotunda 236
53. Comparison between Hopi horizon calendar and alignments in British prehistoric stone circles 238
54. Maya astronomical observatory at Uaxactun, Guatemala 240
55. Chiefly burial at Leubingen, East Germany 246
56. Half-life decay (diagram) 256
57. Statistical variation in radiocarbon determinations 259
58. Calibration curve by Professor H. E. Suess 266–7

ACKNOWLEDGMENTS

I am very grateful to Miss Clare Draffin for her care in handling my text; and to the following for permission to reproduce the following figures and plates:

Fig. 3 – Manchester University Press, from *The Migrations of Early Culture* by G. E. Smith; Figs. 5, 15, 17 and 32 – from 'Carbon 14 and the Prehistory of Europe' by Colin Renfrew, and 'The Tartaria Tablets' by M. S. F. Hood. Copyright © 1971, 1968 by *Scientific American*, Inc. All rights reserved; Figs. 9 and 24 – Dr Glyn Daniel; Fig. 10 – reprinted from *Radiocarbon Dating* by Willard Libby by permission of The University of Chicago Press, Copyright 1952, University of Chicago; Figs. 11 and 12 – Professor J. G. D. Clark; Figs. 19 and 55 – Stuart Piggott; Fig. 27 – Hamish Hamilton Ltd and Professor R. J. C. Atkinson, from *Stonehenge* by R. J. C. Atkinson; Fig. 28 – Dr Jean L'Helgouach, from *Les sépultures mégalithiques en Armorique;* Fig. 31 – Professor J. D. Evans; Fig. 34 – from Marshall D. Sahlins, *Tribesmen,* © 1968, p. 25, reprinted by permission of Prentice-Hall, Inc., Englewood Cliffs, New Jersey; Fig. 39 – Methuen & Co. Ltd, from *Habitat, Economy and Society* by C. D. Ford; Figs. 41 and 42 – Hirmer Verlag München, from *Crete and Mycenae* by S. Marinatos; Fig. 43 – New American Library, Inc., from *The Palace of Minos* by Sir Arthur Evans; Fig. 44 – J. Mellaart; Figs. 46 and 47 – Souvenir Press Ltd and Doubleday & Co., Inc., from *Stonehenge Decoded* by G. Hawkins; Fig. 50 – Edinburgh University Press and Stuart Piggott, from *Ancient Europe* by Stuart Piggott; Fig. 54 – reprinted from *The Ancient Maya*, Third Edition, by Sylvanus G. Morley, revised by George W. Brainerd, with permission of the publishers, Stanford University Press. Copyright © 1946, 1947 and 1956, by the Board of Trustees of the Leland Stanford Junior University; Fig. 57 – The Royal Society and Harold Barker; Fig. 58 – Almqvist & Wiksell Forlag AB and Professor H. E. Seuss, from 'Bristlecone pine calibration of the radiocarbon time scale 5200 B.C. to the present', by H. E. Seuss, published in *Radiocarbon Variations and Absolute Chronology: Proceedings of the Twelfth Nobel Symposium* edited by I. U. Olsson.

Plate 1—British Broadcasting Corporation; Plate 2—Jos le Doaré; Plate 5—Mr L. Morley; Plate 6—Mr Bogdan Nikolov; Plate 7—Dr G. I. Gorgiev; Plate 8— Devizes Museum and the Wiltshire Archaeological and Natural History Society, and British Museum; Plate 9—British Museum; Plate 10—The Peabody Museum, Harvard University; Plate 12—Mrs Edwin Smith; endpapers—Dr R. Galović.

BEFORE
CIVILIZATION

Introduction 1

The study of prehistory today is in a state of crisis. Archaeologists all over the world have realized that much of prehistory, as written in the existing textbooks, is inadequate: some of it quite simply wrong. A few errors, of course, were to be expected, since the discovery of new material through archaeological excavation inevitably leads to new conclusions. But what has come as a considerable shock, a development hardly foreseeable just a few years ago, is that prehistory as we have learnt it is based upon several assumptions which can no longer be accepted as valid. So fundamental are these to the conventional view of the past that prehistorians in the United States refer to the various attempts to question them, to attempt the reconstruction of the past without them, as 'the New Archaeology'. Several commentators have spoken recently of a 'revolution' in prehistory, of the same fundamental nature as a revolution in scientific thinking.

It has been suggested, indeed, that the changes now at work in prehistory herald the shift to a 'new paradigm', an entire new framework of thought, made necessary by the collapse of the 'first paradigm', the existing framework in which prehistorians have grown accustomed to work. Certainly in Europe the conventional framework for our prehistoric past is collapsing about our ears. At first sight the problem appears to be one of dating, of establishing a chronology for the different monuments and remains from prehistoric Europe. But, as we shall see, the underlying difficulty is much more serious, and springs from our whole approach to the prehistoric past. For it turns out that what at first seemed a minor inconsistency in the chronology of prehistoric Europe betrays a serious flaw in archaeological theory in general which has far wider repercussions.

Most of us have been brought up to believe, for instance, that the Pyramids of Egypt are the oldest stone-built monuments in the world, and that the first temples built by man were situated in the Near East, in the fertile land of Mesopotamia. There, it was thought, in the homelands of the first great civilizations, metallurgy was invented. The knowledge of working in copper and bronze, like that of monumental architecture and many other skills, would then have been acquired by the less advanced inhabitants of surrounding areas, and gradually have been diffused over much of Europe and the rest of the Old World. The early prehistoric monuments of western Europe, the megalithic tombs with their colossal stones, would document one very striking instance of this diffusion of ideas. In Britain, we have similarly been led to believe that the riches of our early bronze age and the sophistication of Stonehenge itself reflect, in a comparable way, the inspiration of the more sophisticated world of Mycenaean Greece.

It comes, then, as a shock to learn that all of this is wrong. The megalithic chamber tombs of western Europe are now dated earlier than the Pyramids—indeed, they rank as the earliest stone monuments in the world—so an origin for them in the east Mediterranean seems altogether implausible. The impressive temples of Malta are now set before any of their Near Eastern counterparts in stone. Copper metallurgy appears to have been underway in the Balkans at an early date—earlier than in Greece—so that it may have developed quite independently in Europe. And Stonehenge was, it seems, completed, and the rich early bronze age of Britain well under way, before the Mycenaean civilization of Greece even began. In fact Stonehenge, that remarkable and enigmatic structure, can now be claimed as the world's oldest astronomical observatory. The traditional view of prehistory is now contradicted at every point.

Already, twenty years ago, the new scientific technique of radiocarbon dating brought archaeologists several surprises. But it did not challenge the basic assumptions underlying what they had written: the position of the ancient civilizations of Egypt and Mesopotamia as the innovators, illuminating the rest of the Old World with the radiance of their culture, was not challenged. Today the second radiocarbon revolution, based on recent advances in tree-ring dating, has undermined these assumptions. Indeed, it is bringing down the whole edifice of links and connections that were so laboriously built up by scholars over the last fifty years in order to date and make intelligible our prehistoric past.

The new dating strikes what seems a decisive blow at the whole framework of thought which has dominated archaeological discussion until very recent times. This influential outlook, the so-called diffusionist view, held that nearly all the significant advances in prehistoric European culture, and especially in technology, were brought about by influences, by the diffusion of culture, from the Near East. It was hardly thought possible that impressive monuments, such as the megalithic tombs or Stonehenge, could have a purely European origin. And although the diffusionist doctrine had already come under attack before the new and conclusive advances in dating, most archaeologists were content to follow the very distinguished prehistorian Gordon Childe when he summed up the essential theme of European prehistory as the story of 'the irradiation of European barbarism by Oriental civilization'.[1]

The new dating helps us to see that we have been underestimating those creative 'barbarians' of prehistoric Europe. It now seems that they were erecting monuments in stone, smelting copper, setting up solar observatories and doing other ingenious things without any help from the east Mediterranean. This is not to say that they were 'civilized' in the strict archaeological usage of the term: they did not yet live in cities or keep elaborate written records. In this sense, they were indeed barbarians, but very much more creative and productive ones than has been realized. They are not to be dismissed as uncouth yokels on the remote Atlantic fringe of Europe, far removed from the so-called 'hearthlands' of the civilized world.

This new development is exciting for European prehistory, but its implications go far wider. It implies more than a reassessment of the origins of the European megalithic tombs, more even than a change in the picture of the relationship of prehistoric Europe to the Ancient East. For if the procedures and assumptions used to build up this single, if important, piece of prehistory are wrong, then they are wrong for the rest of prehistory as well, at all places and all times.

In North America, for instance, it has often been assumed, in a rather similar way, that the advances in the south-eastern States – in the Burial Mound and Temple Mound cultures – were due to 'influences' from the great civilizations of Mesoamerica, and sometimes even that these were in turn the result of contacts across the Pacific, with the earlier civilizations of the Old World. And often the assumption has been made that the development of agriculture in the Far East, or of metallurgy, both developments apparently occurring later there than in the Near East, must therefore be the consequence of diffusion. Today such ideas are coming increasingly into question.

We are led now to examine afresh the whole notion of the 'diffusion of culture', and to reopen the debate which dominated prehistoric archaeology in the nineteenth century and the first half of the twentieth, between the diffusionists on the one hand, and the evolutionists on the other.

Glyn Daniel has recently traced the development of these two sets of ideas. On the one side were scholars like Worsaae and Montelius who believed that most of the important innovations and advances in human culture occurred only once and were transmitted by contact to other areas. And on the other side were evolutionists such as Gabriel de Mortillet who believed that similar developments in different places were due to 'the like working of minds under like conditions', the products of a universal process determined by the very nature of man. As we shall see, the diffusionists prevailed, and since 1925 European prehistory, and much of world prehistory, has been written in very much the diffusionist terms set down by Oscar Montelius at the beginning of this century.

At first sight the sudden collapse of the diffusionist framework for Europe might tempt us to revert to an evolutionist viewpoint. But this is no longer adequate. For to ascribe all progress everywhere to innate properties of the mind of Man is to give an explanation so general as to be meaningless. Unless we have some independent means of discovering these properties, and of testing whether they do indeed govern cultural changes and developments, the theory says little more than that everything that has happened in human history is to be seen as the logical outcome of man's mental structure. This view is about as helpful as the proposition advanced by Voltaire's Dr Pangloss, that we live in 'the best of all possible worlds'.

In order to disentangle ourselves from this old and arid debate, it is sufficient to see that 'evolution', applied to human culture, need imply little more than gradual development without sudden discontinuity. We would all agree, moreover, that ideas and innovations can be transmitted from man to man and from group to group, and that this is a fundamental distinction between biological and cultural evolution. All this is perfectly acceptable, but it does not supply us with any useful or valid explanatory principle.

In rejecting both evolution and diffusion as meaningful explanatory principles, we are rejecting much of the language in which conventional prehistory has been written. For both localized evolution and more general diffusion were essential components of the first paradigm, the general language and framework of the prehistory built up in the century following the publication of Darwin's *Origin of Species* in 1859, and the demonstration of the antiquity of man – that man has a prehistory extending back far before the biblical Creation – in the same year.

The old order, then, is changing, and the task of the New Archaeology today is to construct a more effective way of speaking about the past, a new language implying fresh models of the past – a new paradigm. Until we can do this, we shall have simply shown up some shortcomings in the traditional view without demonstrating that something better might be put in its place. And, as the American anthropologist Julian Steward remarked: 'Fact-collecting of itself is insufficient scientific procedure; facts exist only as they are related to theories, and theories are not destroyed by facts – they are replaced by new theories which better explain the facts. Therefore, criticisms ... which concern facts alone and which fail to offer better formulations are of no interest.'[2]

The first part of this book tells the story of the rise and fall of the first paradigm in European prehistory – the diffusionist view – and in particular its collapse under the influence of the new and revised radiocarbon dating. Indeed (despite Steward) the new facts alone do appear sufficient in this case to destroy the old theory. The second part, from Chapter 6, tackles some of the questions which at once arise – for if barbarian Europe did not acquire its important innovations from the Near East, how did they come about? To answer this question fully would be to rewrite the whole of European prehistory, and this necessary task will require years of work by many scholars. An attempt is made here to show that it is at least a legitimate aim, and to indicate the lines along which work is now proceeding that will one day offer a more adequate image of the past.

2 The Problem of Dating

How old is old? The question is certainly not a new one; indeed, it was already being asked by the ancient Egyptians. Well before 2000 B.C. they were taking great care to list their kings, and the duration of the reign of each, so that an accurate chronology could be maintained. So too were the Chinese, the ancient Assyrians, and many early civilizations. This same desire for a calendar, for some way of reckoning and making intelligible the mysterious and intangible passage of time, is reflected in many human societies. The Maya of Mexico, for instance, went to considerable pains to bring the chaos of the world into rational order by means of a meticulously accurate calendar (cf. Fig. 54). And there is no doubt now that our own Stonehenge is a solar observatory and calendrical device some 4,000 years old.

The archaeologist faces much the same problem of measuring the passage of time, but his task is made more difficult since the desired chronology must order past events and not serve simply as a calendar for the present. Dating is crucial to archaeology. Without a reliable chronology the past is chaotic: there is no way of relating or ordering people, events and cultures into the coherent narrative which the prehistorian seeks to construct.

Until a century ago, before the development of scientific dating methods, there seemed no way of piercing the obscurity of the unimagined centuries before the beginning of written history. Simple stone tools and other relics were frequently found, dimly hinting at long periods of human life in the unrecorded past, but while no means was available for measuring those remote centuries there could be no serious investigation of prehistory, and indeed no such subject of study. It is significant that the term 'prehistory' itself was not used until 1851. The Danish archaeologist Rasmus Nyerup, writing in 1806, was not being unduly pessimistic when he said: 'Everything which has come down to us from heathendom is wrapped in a thick fog; it belongs to a space of time which we cannot measure. We know it is older than Christendom, but whether by a couple of years or a couple of centuries, or even by more than a millennium we can do no more than guess.'[3]

The European solution to this yawning void in human understanding was, until the nineteenth century, just the same as that of most earlier cultures: to rely on myth. The ancient Egyptians, the Maya, the Classical Greeks, all had their own version of the beginning of things, and the Bible likewise supplied a circumstantial account of the 'first morning of the first day'. The long genealogies of the sons of Adam, given in the Book of Genesis, permitted—when taken literally in a fundamentalist way—a reckoning in terms of generations back from the time of Moses to the Creation. The seventeenth century Archbishop Ussher set the date of the Creation at 4004 B.C., a later scholar fixing it with remarkable precision on October 23rd of that year, at nine o'clock in the morning. This convenient fixed point, printed in the margin of the Authorized Version of the Bible (Fig. 1), gave scholars an inflexible boundary for early human activity, a starting point for prehistory and the world.

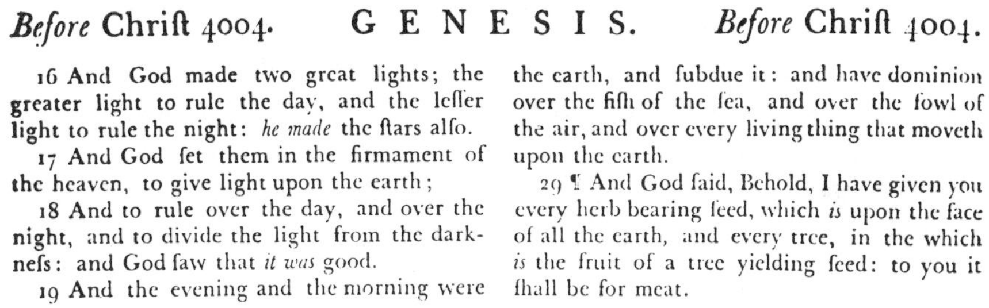

Before Chrift 4004.   G E N E S I S.   *Before* Chrift 4004.

16 And God made two great lights; the greater light to rule the day, and the leſſer light to rule the night: *he made* the ſtars alſo.

17 And God ſet them in the firmament of the heaven, to give light upon the earth ;

18 And to rule over the day, and over the night, and to divide the light from the darkneſs : and God ſaw that *it was* good.

19 And the evening and the morning were

the earth, and ſubdue it : and have dominion over the fiſh of the ſea, and over the fowl of the air, and over every living thing that moveth upon the earth.

29 ¶ And God ſaid, Behold, I have given you every herb bearing ſeed, which *is* upon the face of all the earth, and every tree, in the which *is* the fruit of a tree yielding ſeed: to you it ſhall be for meat.

FIG. 1. Marginal note in the Authorized Version of the Bible setting the Creation at 4004 B.C., as calculated by Archbishop Ussher in the seventeenth century.

Nor was this belief restricted to the credulous or the excessively devout. No less a thinker than Sir Isaac Newton accepted it implicitly, and in his detailed study of the whole question of dating, *The Chronology of Antient Kingdoms Amended*, took the ancient Egyptians severely to task, since they had set the origins of their monarchy before 5000 B.C., and 'anciently boasted of a very great Empire under their Kings ... reaching eastward to the Indies, and westward to the Atlantic Ocean; and out of vanity have made this monarchy some thousands of years older than the world'.[4] This criticism was meant literally: for an educated man in the seventeenth or even the eighteenth century, any suggestion that the human past extended back further than 6,000 years was a vain and foolish speculation.

It took two great intellectual advances before history could be set free from this very restrictive model of the past. Both are now so fundamental to our thinking that it is hard to appreciate their daring a hundred years ago.

In the year 1859, two Englishmen, the geologist Joseph Prestwich and the antiquarian John Evans, made a historic journey. It resulted in the general recognition of a concept basic to the study of prehistory: the antiquity of man. For some years British antiquaries had been excavating in the caves of Devon, finding stone tools together with the bones of extinct animals. These finds seemed to imply that man had been active on earth long before 4004 B.C., and their significance was hotly disputed as reflecting adversely upon the literal truth of Holy Writ. At the same time, Boucher de Perthes, a customs official at Abbeville in north France, had been excavating in the gravels of the River Somme, and finding hand-axes (of what is today termed the old stone age, or palaeolithic period) associated with the remains of extinct animals. He argued for the very great antiquity of his finds, and Prestwich and Evans, who went across to France to see the discoveries, were persuaded by them. Prestwich read a paper to the Royal Society announcing the significance of the finds, and Evans, in a paper delivered to the Society of Antiquaries, said: 'This much appears to be established beyond doubt, that in a period of antiquity remote beyond any of which we have hitherto found traces, this portion of the globe was peopled by man.'[5] This idea was generally accepted, and the way was now open for research into the nature of this remote period and its chronology.

The second great intellectual advance making possible the study of prehistory was the theory of evolution. In the same year, 1859, as Prestwich and Evans announced their acceptance of the antiquity of man, Charles Darwin published his *Origin of Species*. For the first time the development of the living world was presented as a continuous process which could be studied and understood. Darwin did not at first stress the position of man in his evolutionary picture, although the implication was already there that man too developed as part of this same process. With his *Descent of Man*, published in 1871, the theory was complete: a new model of human origins had been constructed which could replace the fundamentalist biblical one. Man was not a unique creation at the hand of God, but the product of a long evolutionary process; he evolved from the same humble marine ancestors as the rest of the animal kingdom. The study of prehistory now took its place among the other humanist disciplines as a valid approach to the understanding of man and his place in the world.

Towards systematic dating

A vast new perspective was opened up by these advances. A whole uncharted span of time during which man inhabited the earth, and yet left no written records, was revealed. The archaeologist was faced with the task of building up an account of the past on the basis of the monuments and the artifacts alone, without any kind of written narrative.

The recently developed science of geology offered a first approach. Geologists, in ordering their discoveries, already used the idea of stratigraphic succession, the principle that when successive layers or strata are observed in position, the underlying ones are the earliest. Using this principle, and the characteristic remains of extinct plants and animals within the strata – the type fossils – a succession of geological periods or epochs was established and gradually extended to cover the world as a whole. Archaeologists realized that the layers of deposit on archaeological sites could be studied in the same way, and that for each site a coherent sequence of occupation could be worked out in terms of the successive strata. The stratigraphic method remains today the essential basis for archaeological excavation. By allowing the successive layers, and the finds in them, to be set in chronological order, it provides the first necessity for effective dating: a sound sequence. But this is, of course, only a relative chronology: it establishes sequence, but not absolute date. Layer A can be shown to be older than Layer B, but this does not indicate the precise age or duration of either.

The second conceptual tool of the early archaeologists was the Three Age System, put forward by the Danish antiquary Christian Thomsen as early as 1819. It at once became the basic method by which museum curators and antiquaries set their collections in order. J. J. A. Worsaae,

Thomsen's successor as Keeper of Antiquities in the National Museum in Copenhagen, described it as 'the first clear ray ... shed across the universal prehistoric gloom of the North and the world in general'.[6] It proposed the division of the prehistoric past into three ages, of stone, bronze and iron. The stone age was later divided into an old (palaeolithic) and a new (neolithic) period, where chipped stone tools and polished stone axes respectively were the most characteristic finds. This theoretical subdivision, accomplished through the study and classification of museum collections, was demonstrated in practice by Worsaae. He showed stratigraphically that finds of bronze were indeed later than the period when stone alone was used. This simple system allowed archaeological finds anywhere in Europe to be placed in their approximate period, and despite all subsequent advances, and several criticisms, 'palaeolithic', 'neolithic', 'bronze age' and 'iron age' are still used today as convenient general terms.

Here again was a method highly effective in arranging finds in terms of a relative chronology. But it did not date them in years. This now became a central problem for European prehistory.

Geological methods of a different kind offered some hope of dating 'absolutely'. Firstly, it was possible to observe the present rate of deposition in the sediments at the bottom of lakes and rivers. Assuming that these rates had remained roughly constant, geologists could estimate how long the processes had been in operation in particular cases, and thus date the beginning of the formation of various deposits. This method was used in 1909 by the geologists Penck and Brückner. Using evidence from the Swiss lakes, they were able to calculate the length of the ice age as about 600,000 years. Sir Arthur Evans, whose excavations brought to light the Minoan civilization of Crete, employed the same principle in estimating the date of the first neolithic settlement at Knossos in Crete. He was able to calculate the rate of deposition of the strata which accumulated there as a result of human occupation during Minoan (bronze age) times, since the duration of the Minoan period was known through cross-dating with Egypt. Having obtained a figure of three feet per millennium, and assuming the same rate for neolithic times, Evans used the great depth of deposit to suggest a date between 12000 and 10000 B.C. for the first neolithic settlement. The weakness of the method, however, is the untested assumption that the rate of deposition has always been a constant one.

A more sensitive and ingenious technique was developed in Sweden in 1912 by the Baron de Geer. He studied the annual deposits of sediment, called 'varves', left by the spring meltwaters of glaciers. Extensive deposits of varves are found in Scandinavia, and by comparing them carefully de Geer was able to build up a succession of varves extending back in time to the end there of the last ice age, which can thus be set about 10,000 years ago. There were – and remain – problems in tying in the more recent varves with well-dated historical events, so as to give a modern fixed point from which the chronology could be extended earlier and earlier back in time. And of course varves are found only in areas on the fringe of glaciers or ice sheets. But the beauty of the method is that it gives a result directly in years, since varve deposition is an annual event. De Geer's work remains of real value today.

Another approach to absolute dating is a purely mathematical one: the calculation of the climatic effects on earth of small changes in its orbit round the sun. The Jugoslav astronomer M. Milankovitch developed, in the 1920s, the theory that the successive ice ages were the consequence of changes in the quantity of solar radiation reaching the earth as a result of orbital changes. He was able to calculate how and when these changes in orbit occurred, and hence reach an estimate for the duration of the ice age of around 600,000 years. But the validity of his reasoning in general is now widely called into question.

Before the development of dating techniques such as radiocarbon dating, based on radioactive isotopes, the so-called 'radioactive clocks', methods such as the three just described were the only ones available for setting absolute dates, in calendar years, for man's early occupation of the earth. But while these procedures were useful enough for the old stone age, they were really of very little use after its end around 8000 B.C. Not only were there few geological events at all after that date, but the accuracy of these methods was not good – and while you can give or take a thousand years or so when dealing with finds 100,000 years old, such an error becomes proportionately larger and more serious if they are only 4,000 or 5,000 years old.

Until the discovery of radiocarbon dating, therefore, there was really only one reliable way of dating events in European prehistory after the end of the last glaciation around 8000 B.C. – only one way, that is, to date the neolithic, bronze age and iron age periods. This was by the early records of the great civilizations, which extended in some cases as far back as 3000 B.C. The records of the Greeks did not go back before the first millennium B.C., but in Mesopotamia the Assyrians and their predecessors the Sumerians left records of kings and dynasties extending back well before 2000 B.C. The Egyptian king lists go back to the First Dynasty of Egypt, a little before 3000 B.C. Before that, there were no written records anywhere.

Here, then, was one fixed point in the uncertain world of the prehistoric past. To date prehistoric Europe it was necessary to relate it, and its culture succession, to the historical chronologies of Egypt and the Near East. This was just what Sir Isaac Newton had tried to do (when he berated the ancient Egyptians for their 'vanity'). And without the mental straitjacket imposed by the biblical dating, scholars were now free to interpret the evidence as they saw fit. In 1878 Jacob Worsaae published a chronological table in a book which represents perhaps the first systematic effort to establish the chronology of prehistoric Europe on a logical basis. He set the neolithic period of northern Europe from 2000 to 1000 B.C., and the early bronze age from 1000 to 500 B.C., assuming that the cultures of the Mediterranean were more highly developed, so that the dates for Europe could be set a little later. Subsequent chronologies put these dates a good deal earlier, but already the problem was being tackled in a methodical way.

Until the advent of radiocarbon dating, most scholars followed much the same procedure. The calendars of Egypt and the Near East were gradually understood more completely, and the links between Europe and the Near East more intensively studied. It is to these two problems that we must now turn.

The chronology of Egypt

The chronology for early Egypt depends entirely upon the records left by the Egyptians and written in their own language and script. Not until the decipherment of this script in the nineteenth century was any real progress possible in dating Egyptian civilization.

Several Egyptian historical documents have been preserved: the most useful are the royal annals, which name the kings of Egypt in order of succession and record the length of their reigns. Groups of kings are collected together in 'Dynasties', 31 in number, which cover the entire Egyptian kingdom from its early beginnings to the time of the conquest of Alexander the Great in 332 B.C. The Palermo Stone is one of these documents that allow the Egyptian royal succession to be reconstructed. It dates from the time of the Fifth Dynasty of the Egyptian kings (now set around 2400 B.C.). The Turin Royal Canon is a further long inscription on papyrus, now in fragmentary condition, which dates from about 1300 B.C. When complete, it gave a list of kings with the lengths of their individual reigns. By good fortune the fragment giving the total for the period from the beginning of the First Dynasty to the end of the Eighth has been preserved, giving a total of 955 years for this time span, a crucial figure for the modern reconstruction.

The inscriptions which record astronomical events are of central importance for the modern interpretation. The Egyptians used a calendar of 365 days, and in the ideal year, the first day of the year coincided with the first day on which the dog-star Sothis (known today as Sirius) could be seen on the eastern horizon, just before the rising of the sun. This is known as a 'heliacal rising' of Sirius. Dr I. E. S. Edwards has explained well how these early astronomical records can be used today to give a highly accurate date, in terms of our own calendar, in years B.C. to the events they record.

> Since the dynastic Egyptians never introduced a leap year into their civil calendar, New Year's Day advanced by one whole day in relation to the natural year in every period of four years. As a result of this displacement, New Year's Day and the day on which Sothis rose heliacally actually coincided for no more than four years in every period of approximately 1,460 years (i.e. 365 x 4), the so-called Sothic cycle.
>
> By a fortunate chance the Roman writer Censorinus tells us that New Year's Day on the Egyptian civil calendar and the day on which Sothis rose heliacally coincided in A.D. 139, and by a simple arithmetical calculation it follows that this coincidence occurred previously in approximately 1322, 2782 and 4242 B.C. or more precisely 1314, 2770 and 4228 B.C. These are the first years of the three Sothic cycles which concern us.[7]

Several inscriptions record astronomical events. The earliest and most important of these refers to the seventh year of the reign of King Sesostris III, of the Twelfth Dynasty. In this year a heliacal rising of the star Sothis was recorded on the sixteenth day of the eighth month of the civil calendar. This gives us exactly the information needed to calculate the time taken to displace the calendar from the original coincidence of New Year's Day with the heliacal rising of Sothis at the beginning of the appropriate Sothic cycle in 2770 B.C. The date in question corresponds to 1872 B.C., so that the reign of Sesostris III is now set with some confidence from 1878 B.C. to 1843 B.C.

This is, in fact, the earliest fixed calendrical date in human history. And while some uncertainties of detail makes possible an error of a decade or so, it is a date which Egyptologists accept with considerable confidence. Using the information from the annals, the end of the Eighth Dynasty, with which the so-called 'Old Kingdom' of Egypt terminated, may be set at 2160 B.C. As we have seen, the Turin Royal Canon reports a total duration for the Old Kingdom of 955 years. Some scholars think this may be inaccurate by a couple of centuries or so, but if the figure is accepted, the beginning of the Old Kingdom of Egypt – the founding of Egypt's first historic dynasty – can be set close to 3100 B.C.

King lists and other records are also preserved from Mesopotamia, but unfortunately many of them are later copies of the original texts. The Mesopotamian chronology is less reliable than the Egyptian, and it does not go back so far.

This date of 3100 B.C. thus sets the limit of recorded history. No earlier dates can be obtained by calendrical means, and indeed the dates cannot be regarded as reliable before 2000 B.C. There is thus a theoretical limit beyond which the traditional chronology for Europe, based, as it was, ultimately on Egypt, simply could not go. Any dates before 3000 B.C. could be little more than guesswork, however persuasive the arguments and the evidence after that period.

Cross-dating

Once the chronology of ancient Egypt has been established, it can be used to date any neighbouring lands which had direct trading links with Egypt. The method is known as 'cross-dating', and it depends on the recognition, in the region to be dated, of actual imports from the land whose chronology we know – in this case, Egypt. It was first employed by the great Egyptologist Sir Flinders Petrie, who managed to date the bronze age of Crete and Greece in this way.

He recognized as 'Aegean' – that is to say, as originating in Greece or Crete, in the Aegean Sea – some of the pottery found in his excavations at Kahun in Egypt, in contexts which could be dated around 1900 B.C. Then in 1891, he visited the important prehistoric Aegean site of Mycenae, on the Greek mainland, to follow up this clue. There he recognized actual Egyptian imports which could be dated around 1500 B.C. Petrie had thus established two synchronisms, both useful for dating prehistoric Greece. He had identified Aegean (actually Cretan) pottery in a datable Egyptian context, as well as datable Egyptian material in Greece in association with Aegean finds. The Cretan pottery must obviously have been manufactured at a date at least as early as that of its findspot in Egypt. Equally the datable Egyptian finds in Greece could not have got there, or been buried with Aegean material, before their date of manufacture in Egypt. In this way a narrow, well-defined time range could be set up for the Aegean material, using the known dates of the Egyptian material.

By this double link, or cross-dating, Petrie was able to put the dating of the Mycenaean civilization of prehistoric Greece on a sure basis for the first time, linking it to the chronology for Egypt. This was a major advance for Europe, and Petrie's achievement still stands in its essentials to this day.

The earliest Egyptian finds which have any relevance for Europe are some thirty or so Old Kingdom and Predynastic stone vases which have been found in Crete. They give the only possibility of establishing a calendrical chronology for Early Minoan Crete in the third millennium B.C. Different scholars have unfortunately interpreted the evidence very differently: Sir Arthur Evans began the Early Minoan period in 3400 B.C., while Sinclair Hood has set its beginning as late as 2400 B.C. After a comprehensive survey of all the evidence, Peter Warren has suggested a date of 3000 B.C. for the beginning of the Early Minoan period, and this is very probably right to within a century or two. There is more agreement about the dating of the first palaces of Crete at the beginning of the Middle Minoan period around 2100 B.C.

These dates, of around 3000 B.C. for the beginning of the Early Minoan culture, and around 2100 B.C. for its end, are based on actual and undoubted imports, and however few these may be, do give a foundation for Aegean chronology. By similar although less certain reasoning, the beginning of the First City at the famous early bronze age site of Troy has been set by Carl Blegen around 3000 B.C. This could be in error by a couple of centuries or more, but the various Aegean imports at Troy suggest that it is fairly sound. The method of cross-dating thus allows the Aegean to be brought reliably, although perhaps not very precisely, into the reach of the Egyptian calendrical chronology.

The idea of diffusion

These dates for early Crete and mainland Greece are based on finds of actual Aegean exports to Egypt, and Egyptian ones to the Aegean. They are therefore reliable: they do not depend on any assumptions about contacts or influences, since the contacts are undoubted. Ideally, if Egyptian exports were found in the rest of Europe, this cross-dating method could have been used for the chronology of Europe as a whole. Or indeed if actual objects of bronze age Cretan or Greek manufacture were widely found in Europe, a network of reliable links could be built up, ultimately stretching back to the historically established chronology of Egypt.

Unfortunately Egyptian exports did not go beyond the east Mediterranean and the Aegean until Classical times, nor are there sufficient finds in Europe of Aegean origin to make such cross-dating possible. If prehistoric Europe was to be dated at all, it was necessary instead to make an important assumption, which at the same time seemed to explain very satisfactorily many of the apparent similarities between the monuments and finds of Europe and those of the early civilizations of the east Mediterranean. Although its crucial significance was not widely appreciated at the time, it conditioned most of what was written about European prehistory for nearly a century.

This single and simple assumption was that the chief advances in the prehistory of Europe were the result of influences from the Near East, brought either by migrating peoples or by the peaceful process known as diffusion where contact between adjacent areas is accompanied by the transmission of new ideas and discoveries. The past was seen in terms of groups of people, of tribes and ethnic units, much as the anthropologists had come to speak of living groups in different parts of the world—the Kwakiutl of north-west America, for instance, or the Bushmen of Africa. Successive generations of archaeologists, influenced by this approach, came to think of their prehistoric cultures—defined, of course, by the tools and artifacts found—as distinct ethnic groups, and these became the focus of study. As the leading scholar Gordon Childe wrote of prehistoric archaeology in 1957: 'It aimed at distilling from archaeological remains a pre-literate substitute for the conventional politico-military history, with cultures instead of statesmen as actors, and migrations in place of battles.'[8] Prehistory was seen as a kind of global chessboard, with the various cultures as pieces shifting from square to square. The task of the archaeologist was simply to plot the moves—or, in other words, trace the path of the 'influence' as new ideas were diffused.

Nobody could prove this assumption of the diffusion of culture—without an independent dating system that would hardly have been possible. Precisely because the assumption was itself necessary to establish the dating, any demonstration of such diffusion was inescapably based upon a circular argument.

Perhaps the first serious consideration of the problem of diffusion, as it concerns European prehistory, was a treatise by James Fergusson, *Rude Stone Monuments in all Countries: their Age and Uses*, in which he discusses the origin of the prehistoric 'megalithic' tombs (Fig. 2) of western Europe. He sets the origin of megalith building in India, in pre-Roman times; from there the idea was carried westward to north Africa, and then to Europe. Fergusson assumed that the megalithic tombs of Europe and Asia are similar because they were made by a single 'race' or 'people':

> From shortly before the Christian era, till the countries in which they are found become entirely and essentially Christian, the use of monuments seems to have been continual, wherever a dolmen-building race—or, in other words, a race with any taint of Turanian blood in their veins—continued to prevail.[9]

Fergusson justified his comparison of the megaliths of the east with those of the west in what was a very frank admission: 'If anyone cares to insist that there was no connection between the two, he deprives himself of one of the principal points of interest in the whole enquiry.'[10] This is a key statement, very revealing of the diffusionist position, where the preference of the observer rather than the evidence itself sometimes appears to dictate the conclusion reached.

Oscar Montelius, who succeeded Thomsen and Worsaae as Scandinavia's leading antiquary, used this basic idea of the diffusion of culture from a single source when he formulated his own position, achieving what was really the first coherent view of European prehistory. He began his book *Der Orient und Europa* (*The Orient and Europe*) with this assertion:

> At a time when the people of Europe were, so to speak, without any civilisation whatsoever, the Orient, and particularly the Euphrates region and the Nile valley, were in enjoyment of a flourishing culture ... The civilisation which gradually dawned on our continent was for long only a pale reflection of Oriental culture.[11]

FIG. 2. A dolmen (simple megalithic burial chamber) at Pentre Ifan, Wales, from James Fergusson's *Rude Stone Monuments* (1872).

Montelius never really questioned the validity of this basic premise, and his closest examination of it, once again in relation to the megalithic tombs, seems today stronger in polemic than logic:

> One does not have to probe deeply into the study of the ... conditions here in the north during the stone age ... to see that the original homeland of the dolmens cannot be sought in north Europe.

They could not have spread from here to the southern shores of the Mediterranean, to Palestine and to India. The entire discussion here shows that this would be absurd. So powerful a movement, able to influence the burial customs of so many and widely distributed peoples, simply cannot have originated here, thousands of years before our era. It is indeed remarkable enough that, originating in the Orient, it should already have reached us here at so early a date.[12]

Montelius's approach, which was based on a very detailed knowledge of the finds from prehistoric Europe, was, however, sober and scholarly when contrasted with that of Sir Grafton Elliot Smith, who carried the theory of diffusion to its logical extreme, and indeed beyond. While Professor of Anatomy at Cairo in the 1920s, he became fascinated by the civilization of ancient Egypt, and gradually became convinced that all the civilizations of the world, and indeed all human progress, were due to travelling Egyptians, whom he termed 'The Children of the Sun'. He wrote:

> Practices such as mummification and megalith building present so many peculiar and distinctive features that no hypothesis of independent evolution can seriously be entertained in explanation of their geographical distribution. They must be regarded as evidence of the diffusion of information, and the migration of the bearers of it, from somewhere in the neighbourhood of the east Mediterranean, step by step out into Polynesia and even perhaps beyond the Pacific to the American littoral.[13]

This is much more sweeping diffusionism than that of Montelius, or even of Fergusson. For Fergusson, already in 1872, had seen the potential conflict between theories of diffusion and independent invention. And in an interesting statement that foreshadows much of the later discussion between evolutionists and diffusionists, he stopped short of trans-Atlantic contacts:

> No one will, I presume, contend that there was any direct communication between Europe and the west coast of South America before the time of Columbus. Yet there are similarities between the masonry of the Peruvian monuments and those of the Pelasgi [i.e. Mycenaeans] in Greece and Tyrrheni [i.e. Etruscans] in Italy which

are most striking, and can only be accounted for at present on the assumption that nations in the same stage of civilisation, and using similar materials, arrive nearly at the same results.[14]

With the grandiose theories of Elliot Smith, however, the way was open for all manner of imaginative derivations for the civilization of the Americas: pyramids, mummification, gold work, art styles, tattooing, the swastika, the use of pearls and conch-shells, trumpets, the worship of serpents, stories of dwarfs and giants – all became grist to the diffusionist mill. All were taken as indications of the migrations of these wandering

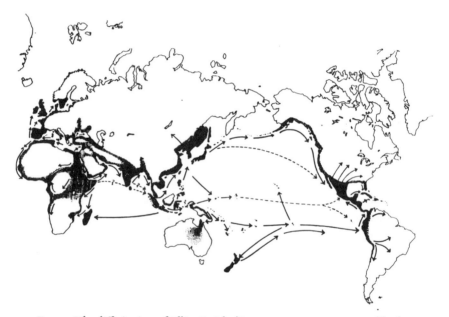

FIG. 3. The diffusionism of Elliot Smith: 'An attempt to represent roughly the areas more directly affected by the "heliolithic" culture complex, with arrows to indicate the hypothetical routes taken in the migrations of the culture bearers who were responsible for its diffusion.' Note that all the diffusion starts from Egypt. From *The Migrations of Early Culture* (1929).

Egyptians and their culture, termed 'heliolithic' (Greek *helios*, sun; *lithos*, stone) in view of the combination of sun-worship and megalith building supposedly manifested by its adherents. 'To these practices', wrote Elliot Smith, 'one might add a large series of others of a character no less remarkable, such for example, as circumcision, the practice of marriage, the curious custom known as the *couvade*, all of which are distributed along the great "heliolithic" pathway and belong to the great culture-complex which travelled with it.'[15] The path of the global spread of the 'heliolithic' culture was plotted by Elliot Smith in maps, where all the arrows start, ultimately, from Egypt (Fig. 3).

This extraordinary and imaginative web of ideas which has survived to inspire Thor Heyerdahl's recent crossing of the Atlantic in *Ra*, a papyrus boat modelled upon those of the ancient Egyptians, has very properly been dismissed as 'academic rubbish' by Glyn Daniel on the ground that it 'neglected all semblance of scientific method'.

At the other extreme, as it were, a number of European scholars shared a view, almost precisely the opposite and no less extravagant. Their leader was Gustav Kossinna, who in 1912 published a book in which the primacy of German prehistory over that of the rest of Europe was heavily stressed. Entitled *Die Deutsche Vorgeschichte eine Herrvoragend Nationale Wissenschaft* ('German Prehistory, a Supremely National Science'), it anticipated disquietingly some of the excessively nationalistic views of the Nazi era, twenty years later. Kossinna reversed the direction of the arrows on the diffusionist map. Writing now originated in Europe and metallurgy was independently invented there. The megaliths of north Europe were still related to those of the Mediterranean and the Near East, but now they were the product of heroic Indo-European people ('Indo-Germanic' in Kossinna's vocabulary) who supposedly carried their language and their burial practices out with them from their German homeland:

> The Germans were a heroic people and have always remained so. For only a thoroughly manly and efficient people could have conquered the world at the end of the Roman empire.
>
> And how was it two to three thousand years earlier? ... The great folk movements then went out, in the third millennium B.C., from north-central Europe, from this side of the Baltic and beyond, and then further, from the middle and lower Danube, populating all Europe, and especially southern Europe and the Near East, with the people who speak our tongue, the language of the Indo-Germans. Everywhere people of central European blood became the ruling class ... and imprinted at least our language, as an external symbol of the world-historical vocation of our race, indelibly upon those lands.[16]

Kossinna's chauvinism led directly, and knowingly, to racism – Hitler is quoted at length in the 1941 edition of the book. Himmler was glad to use such arguments to give intellectual backing to Nazi policy, and is reported to have pronounced: 'Prehistory is the doctrine of the eminence of the Germans at the dawn of civilisation.'

(In our own time, perhaps only the official Rhodesian view is comparably chauvinistic in its reluctance to accept that the great stone ruins at Zimbabwe were built, as most competent archaeologists now hold, without the inspiration or aid of Eurasian architects or craftsmen.)

It was largely a very natural revulsion from the extreme racism of Kossinna which led Gordon Childe to favour an approach that Glyn Daniel has termed 'modified diffusionism'. Childe did more than any other to maintain a balance and further the international approach on the foundations laid down by Montelius. These foundations were, as he conceded, frankly diffusionist, and writing in 1939, he pointed out that Montelius's initial statement in *The Orient and Europe*, quoted above, could be 'resolved into five propositions treated as axioms':

(1) Civilisation in the Orient is extremely ancient.
(2) Civilisation can be diffused.
(3) Elements of civilisation were in fact diffused from the Orient to Europe.
(4) The diffusion of historically dated Oriental types provides a basis for bringing prehistoric Europe within the framework of historical chronology.
(5) Prehistoric European cultures are poorer than contemporary European cultures, i.e. civilisation is later in Europe than in the East.[17]

This splendidly clear statement by Childe sets out very fairly the essence of Montelius's thinking, and indeed of his own. It brings out into the open the often-overlooked assumptions which underpin the textbook accounts of European prehistory, while avoiding all the extravagances of Elliot Smith or of Kossinna. In these assumptions the problem of dating the past is inextricably mixed with the problem of the origin of the finds. If you accept that megaliths and metallurgy came from the Orient to Europe either by diffusion or by the migration of groups of people, then you have both an explanation for them and a means of dating them. If you deny such diffusion you have a void, with no possibility of dating these things (since only the Near East offers a historical chronology), and very little of explaining them. So at any rate it seemed until recently. It was natural, therefore, that early prehistorians should choose the first alternative, and opt for diffusion.

The typological method and the chronological framework for Europe

As we saw, the first step in the dating of prehistoric Europe was the dating of prehistoric Crete and Greece by cross-dating, through direct contacts, with the historic civilization of Egypt. The next important step was the extension of this chronology to the rest of prehistoric Europe. In the absence of direct contacts, this had to be done on the basis of the similarities between the monuments and finds of Europe and those of the east Mediterranean, interpreted in the light of the diffusionist assumptions just discussed. Without the assumption that the finds of Europe were related to those in the Aegean and Near East, no chronological relationship was possible; and without assuming the direction of influence (that the finds came *from* the Near East *to* Europe) it was not possible to say which were earlier.

As well as setting out his basic diffusionist premise clearly, Montelius gave a great deal of thought to the other principles of chronology, and in 1903 he published a book on the *methods* by which the prehistoric past could be dated — one of the very first such works in archaeology. In it he presented the details of his typological method, which used the principle of diffusion. This method may not have been Montelius's own invention, but he was the first to apply it both widely and systematically. He observed that a specific tool type — a bronze axe, for instance, or a dagger — developed slowly with the passing of years, so that each newly developed form differs only slightly from its immediate predecessor. By arranging like with like in a continuous series among the various prehistoric finds, the whole development of such a type can be reconstructed using this principle (Fig. 4). Moreover, where closely similar developments are seen in other areas, the two series may be termed 'parallel', even if one or two of the forms are missing. For Montelius, a parallel evolution in two adjacent areas implied the spread of ideas and innovations from one

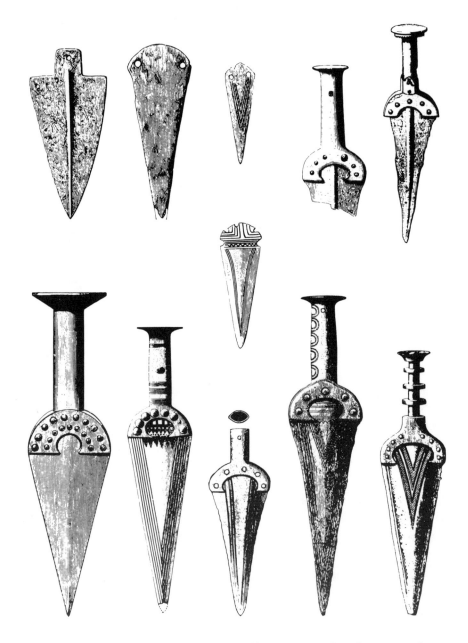

FIG. 4. A typological series, as constructed by Oscar Montelius: the copper and
bronze daggers of prehistoric Italy.

to the other—in Europe generally from south to north. Closely similar forms could thus be used as a guide to dating.

Montelius focused his attention on two of the most striking developments in European prehistory: the megalithic collective burial tombs of neolithic Europe—Fergusson's 'rude stone monuments'—which had already (as we have seen) been the subject of much speculation; and early developments in the working of copper and then bronze in the succeeding period. To the considerable mass of comparative information that previous scholars had built up, Montelius applied the Three Age division of Thomsen and Worsaae, putting the megalithic tombs firmly in their neolithic setting, which earlier workers had failed to do. He no longer insisted that these impressive monuments were the work of a single 'people' or 'race'; but he accepted that they were related in origin, and gave first place to the monuments of the Orient, the 'dolmens' of Syria and Palestine. He envisaged a diffusion of the practice of collective burial along the coast of north Africa to Spain and Portugal (Iberia) in the fourth millennium B.C. (i.e. between 4000 and 3000 B.C.) 'if not earlier', reaching northern Europe early in the third millennium. The new 'passage grave' tomb form would have been transmitted along much the same path at a later date. A rather similar set of arguments explained the development of metallurgy in Europe through diffusion from the Near East, via Greece.

In the first edition of *The Dawn of European Civilisation* (1925), Gordon Childe put forward a chronological framework firmly based on this scheme proposed by Montelius; and in his later writings, it was elaborated with a masterly wealth of detail. The sometimes rather arid and algebraic comparison of artifacts of the typological method was replaced by a much more comprehensive consideration of the developments in each region and each individual culture, but the basic framework was essentially the same: the megalithic tombs were dated on the basis of their origin, through Aegean influence, in Iberia, and the techniques of metallurgy and the metal types themselves were dated on the basis of their assumed spread from the Near East to Italy and the Balkans, and so to the rest of Europe.

In the first *Dawn*, Childe emphasized above all the key position of Iberia in the origins of megalithic architecture. He accepted that the initial idea of building simple megalithic tombs or 'dolmens' probably reached Portugal from the east Mediterranean, and was carried on to

Brittany, Ireland and Denmark. Then, a little later, around 2500 B.C., actual colonists arrived in Iberia and set up trading stations, introducing metallurgy and building the first tombs with a corbelled drystone vault (Fig. 5), which is seen also in Brittany, Ireland and Scotland. 'Thus there arose in the Iberian peninsula a veritable counterpart of the maritime civilisation of the Aegean, albeit infused with original elements.'[18] Trade and other contacts, Childe argued, carried the knowledge of metallurgy, corbelled construction and other new ideas through all western Europe to Scandinavia. The supposed contacts between Iberia and the Aegean thus

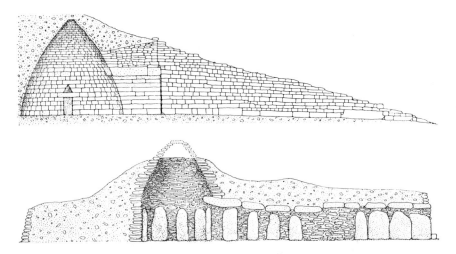

FIG. 5. Neolithic corbelled tomb at Île Longue, Brittany (*lower*), and the 'Treasury of Atreus' at Mycenae, dated to *c.* 1500 B.C. (*upper*). At first the Breton tombs were dated to the same period. Montelius and then Childe set them earlier.

formed the first essential link in Childe's picture of the diffusion of culture from the east Mediterranean to Europe. Using the same logic as Montelius, he was able to extend to Iberia the chronology established for Crete, which was itself based on that for Egypt: the first Iberian passage graves were set after 2700 B.C., which was the date ascribed to the earliest collective tombs in Early Minoan Crete.

The importance of the Danube as the second major thoroughfare for Oriental influences upon Europe was brilliantly expounded four years after the first publication of *The Dawn*, in *The Danube in Prehistory*. Like

Montelius, Childe argued that the techniques of metallurgy spread from the Near East and could be dated on the basis of this connection. However, he broke new ground in suggesting that the development of metallurgy in the Balkans (Bulgaria, Romania and southern Jugoslavia) was perhaps the earliest in Europe.

Childe was greatly impressed by the deep deposits of stratified material at the great site of Vinča near Belgrade on the middle Danube. He was influenced, too, by Sir Arthur Evans's chronological divisions for the Minoan civilization of Crete, based on the even longer stratigraphy at Knossos. So he applied the system of the latter to the material of the former. In a paper delivered to the Society of Antiquaries in March 1924 he divided the prehistoric sequence of the Danube area into four periods, later extended to seven, and dated these on the basis of supposed contacts with the Aegean. The location was different – this was the Balkan region instead of Spain – but the basic argument was the same as before. The most relevant site in the Aegean was ancient Troy, where five successive 'cities' of the early bronze age and a couple of later ones underlay the Troy of Mycenaean times immortalized in the *Iliad* of Homer. Several finds at Vinča were so like those of early Troy as to suggest the two were contemporary or 'synchronous'. These 'synchronisms' were of fundamental importance for Europe as a whole.

> Taken as a whole, the 'Aegean' features in the culture of Vinča I are too fundamental and far-reaching to be the result of mere external relations or cultural borrowing. The whole civilisation is saturated with 'Aegean' elements; south-eastern elements are interwoven into its innermost existence ... It would be vain to seek to localise the original starting point of the first colonists ... Rather we should regard Troy II and Vinča I as separate branches put forward by one ancestral trunk whose roots spread to Crete and Mainland Greece and across Asia Minor.[19]

This basic link allowed Childe to date Vinča, and hence give an early fixed point for the whole chronology of continental Europe. Vinča and its contemporary in what are now Bulgaria and Romania, the Gumelnitsa culture, were dated to the same time as the Second City of Troy, around 2700 B.C. (Fig. 8). The evidence on which Childe based this dating is reviewed in more detail in Chapter 5.

Childe's third major element in the chronological structure was of later date. He saw that the early bronze age of central and northern Europe, with its rich princely burials, possessed a number of exotic features not unlike those of the Mycenaean culture of Greece. At Mycenae the rich Shaft Graves, dated around 1600 B.C., had contained numerous swords, a wealth of gold, and quantities of amber beads which must have been imported from the Baltic area; and in north Europe, notably in the Wessex area of Britain, the princely burials in dagger graves were sometimes furnished with gold objects and frequently contained amber beads. Indeed the burials of south Britain – the so-called Wessex culture – seemed to furnish a number of indications, such as the faience beads (described in Chapter 5), of direct contact with the Mycenaean world. Childe concluded that the early bronze age of Europe was dependent on, and therefore later than, the Mycenaean civilization. As he wrote in his last book, published in 1958:

> While a distinctive bronze industry was being established around the Aegean, a neolithic economy still persisted north of the Balkans, the Alps and the Pyrenees. The Early Aegean Age corresponds in time to parts at least of Middle or Late Neolithic in Temperate Europe. But at least during the latter period, ripples generated by the Urban Revolution were already disturbing the self-sufficiency of the peasant communities. At the same time 'political events' – migrations and conquests – were preparing the sociological foundations for a Bronze Age economy.[20]

On this basis, the early bronze age Wessex culture was set around 1400 B.C., well after the beginning of Mycenaean civilization around 1600 B.C. The whole question of the British early bronze age, and of Stonehenge (which is generally set in the same period), is discussed in Chapter 11; its particular interest here is the way it was used to help build up a coherent structure for the dating of Europe.

European chronology, and hence the whole sequence of events that prehistorians reconstructed, was built on these three crucial links. Spain and the Balkans were both dated on the basis of supposed contacts with the Aegean. France and central Europe could then be tied in with their respective neighbours to the south. So, by a series of chronological steps, the whole of Europe was brought into contact with the world of the

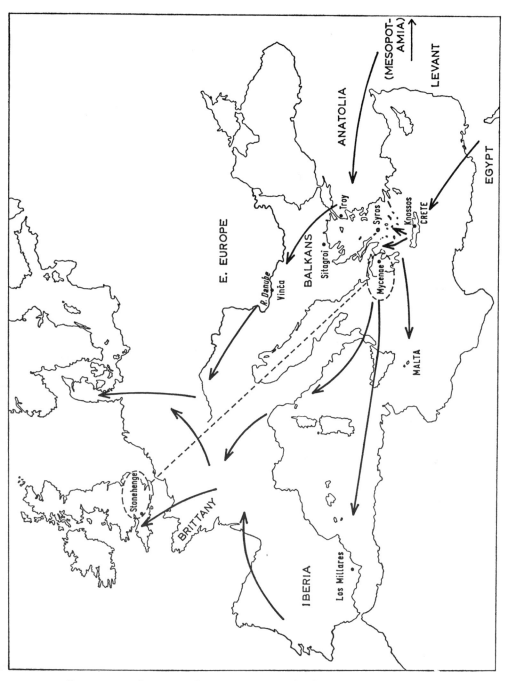

FIG. 6. Map of Europe with arrows indicating the chronological links used by Childe to date prehistoric cultures, by reference to the historical calendars of ancient Egypt and Mesopotamia.

Aegean and the east Mediterranean in general (Fig. 6). Since the absolute chronology of Egypt and the Near East had by then been worked out satisfactorily, the whole of Europe could be dated too.

The logical structure of Childe's thinking can be set out in diagrammatic form (Fig. 7). The various links form a chain of chronological connections stretching across Europe.

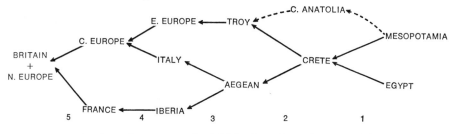

FIG. 7. The logical structure of Childe's chronological system (cf. Fig. 6).

The chronology was first comprehensively and systematically set out by Childe and Miles Burkitt in their 'Chronological Table of Prehistory' published in 1932. A revised version was incorporated into subsequent editions of *The Dawn*. Figure 8 shows five columns from the latest edition (1957). Although this looks complicated, with its detailed succession of culture names for each area, it does in fact rest on the three links discussed. The Iberian passage graves, with their connection with Early Minoan Crete (contemporary with the Early Helladic II culture of Greece), are set after 2700 B.C. Vinča and its contemporary Gumelnitsa culture begin at about the same time, which is also the period of Troy II. These are the first two links. We may note that at this time in Britain the first megaliths (indicated as 'Severn–Cotswold') are seen, as they first reach Britain from Iberia. The early bronze age Wessex culture is set around 1400 B.C., comfortably after the beginning of the Mycenaean civilization. Faience beads of segmented form, like those of the Wessex culture, are also found in the early bronze age El Argar culture of Spain, and they supposedly establish a chronological link with the Aegean. The rest of the table is fitted round these synchronisms, since the culture sequence in each individual region – the relative chronology – is well known.

As we have seen, there are no calendrical dates anywhere before 3000 B.C. In consequence the neolithic period in the Near East, and its earlier phases in Europe, could not reliably be dated by the conventional method.

Montelius set the beginning of the neolithic period in northern Europe well before 3000 B.C., and Sir Arthur Evans put the inception of the Cretan neolithic before 8000 B.C. But these bold estimates seemed too early to Childe and most of his contemporaries. In 1932, Childe placed the beginning of the Balkan neolithic around 2700 B.C., and that of Britain and Scandinavia around 2400 B.C. Only Crete was set earlier, in the fourth millennium B.C. This short chronology for the European neolithic, which depended essentially on the view that the passage graves of Iberia, and the megaliths of Europe in general, originated in influences from the Aegean early bronze age, was followed by most writers. The slightly earlier dates indicated in the 1957 table (Fig. 8) already show the influence of radiocarbon dating.

Until the advent of radiocarbon, the chronology put forward by Childe and modified slightly in later editions of *The Dawn* was almost

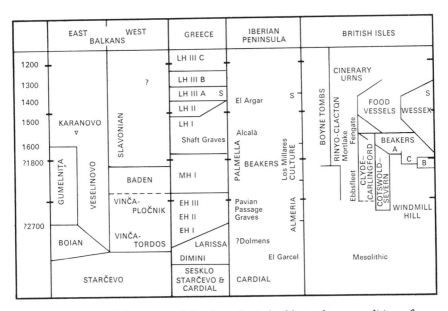

FIG. 8. Simplified version of the chronological table in the 1957 edition of Gordon Childe's *Dawn of European Civilisation.* (Note that Vinča and Gumelnitsa in the Balkans are contemporary with Troy and EH II. The first passage graves in Spain and the early Cotswold–Severn megaliths in Britain begin at the same time—the period of the first Cretan round tombs. Wessex is set around 1450 B.C. by reference to the developed Mycenaean culture, LH IIIA.) 'S' indicates segmented faience beads.

universally accepted. The chronology was further refined, and many scholars devoted detailed studies to particular aspects of it. Indeed, it became possible to dispute a matter of only fifty years when dealing with dates around 2000 B.C. This presents, then, a sketch outline of European prehistoric chronology, as it appeared up to about 1950.

FIG. 9. The modified diffusionism of Gordon Childe and his successors: a map illustrating the origins and diffusion of passage graves, published by Glyn Daniel in 1941. All the passage graves are seen as derived ultimately from the Cretan round tombs.

Childe's whole view of European prehistory has been widely followed. His theory for the megalithic tombs, for instance, was further developed and refined by Glyn Daniel, and well illustrated in a map published in 1941 (Fig. 9). Indeed this view has become firmly established in all the important textbooks. As Grahame Clark wrote in 1969, in the second edition of his *World Prehistory*, the most recent authoritative survey:

It is hardly possible to doubt that it was from the Aegean area that the rite of collective burial, associated with belief in a mother goddess, spread widely over the Middle and West Mediterranean, or that this was associated with the voyages of exploration and prospecting already hinted at ...

The diffusion of collective burial and of megalithic tomb-construction in the west, and the rise of copperworking in central Europe and north Italy ... are only symbols of the influence exerted from the Aegean towards the close of its Early 'Bronze' Age on the still predominantly Neolithic peasantries of barbarian Europe.[21]

This statement fully endorses the pattern established by Childe in 1925 of the development of European prehistory. In the next three chapters we shall see how this agreeably logical picture has been completely disrupted, first by the introduction of radiocarbon dating, and more especially by its calibration through tree-ring studies.

3 The First
Radiocarbon Revolution

Radiocarbon dating came as a godsend to archaeology. For the first time, the prehistorian could hope to date his finds, both accurately and reliably, by a method that made no archaeological assumptions whatsoever.

The first radiocarbon dates were announced by Willard F. Libby in New York in 1949. The potentialities of the method caused an immediate sensation: all that was needed was a couple of ounces of charcoal or some other organic material buried at the time in question, and science would do the rest.

Sir Mortimer Wheeler has related how excited he felt when told about it. He was in the company of Crawford, the founder and first editor of the British journal *Antiquity*, a man – like Wheeler – with a vivid archaeological imagination:

> We talked ... as we walked across Oxford one night in 1949 after an evening in the Senior Common Room of Christ Church. There Lord Cherwell, who had just come back from America, told us for the first time of the new radiocarbon method of dating ancient organic substances – probably the first occasion on which this tremendous discovery was mentioned in this country, at any rate to an archaeologist. I remember how Crawford's eyes lighted up as the conversation proceeded, and how under his breath he whispered to me 'It's a scoop'. And so it was. It made the next editorial in *Antiquity* and opened a new era.[22]

Principles of radiocarbon dating

Radiocarbon dating was made possible by developments in atomic physics. This is a field with which archaeologists are not, in general, familiar (until recently most of them have had a training in humanities rather than science), and it is, perhaps, for this reason that the working of

48

radiocarbon dating has been persistently misunderstood, or more frequently not understood at all. The whole thing has often been regarded as a mysterious boffinry, best left to the scientists in their laboratories. Yet the basic principles of the method are delightfully and ingeniously simple: so that, while the actual radiocarbon determinations are conducted by the professionals, it is easy for anyone to grasp what they are doing. Here the basic principles are presented in outline, but for those who would like to know something more, the method is discussed in greater detail in the Appendix.

In the early decades of this century, when the whole field of atomic physics was first investigated, it was discovered that the earth is constantly being bombarded by small, sub-atomic particles possessing a very high energy. These particles have their origin outside the solar system, so the bombardment was termed *cosmic radiation*. The particles are, of course, so small that they are normally only detectable by the methods of atomic physics, but they have important effects.

When they come into contact with the earth's atmosphere, they set off a number of atomic reactions. One of these results in the production of small quantities of radiocarbon in the atmosphere, chiefly at high altitude. *Radiocarbon* is simply a rare variety of the very common element carbon which is present in the atmosphere (largely as the gas carbon dioxide, and a fundamental constituent of all living things, both plants and animals). Radiocarbon, or carbon-14 (often written ^{14}C, or C-14), behaves chemically in just the same way as ordinary carbon, carbon-12. But it is a little heavier, the atoms weighing fourteen units instead of the usual twelve. Such varieties of a single element, behaving chemically in the same way, but having different atomic weights, are known as *isotopes*. Carbon-14 is a rare isotope of carbon, there being only about one atom in the earth's atmosphere for every million million atoms of the common isotope, carbon-12.

The carbon-14 atoms in the atmosphere combine chemically with oxygen in the ordinary way, giving carbon dioxide, and are distributed throughout the earth's atmosphere in the same manner as carbon-12 atoms, likewise in the form of carbon dioxide. This is taken up by plants during the process of photosynthesis by which they form their structure: all of their carbon comes from the carbon dioxide in the air, and is taken up in this way. The animals of the earth eat plants, or other animals which eat plants, forming a complicated food chain in which all the carbon ultimately derives from the carbon dioxide of the atmosphere. And the carbon in the bodies of both animals and plants contains the same tiny proportion of carbon-14 atoms as does the atmosphere. This is the first important point.

Secondly, carbon-14 differs from the common isotope, carbon-12, in being *radioactive*. That is to say that at a slow and absolutely constant rate it decays spontaneously, giving off an electron – a tiny, sub-atomic particle – and changing to a different element, nitrogen. This radioactive decay takes place at a known rate, in such a way that half of a given sample of radiocarbon has disappeared after a time of about 5,500 years. The details of the decay process are less important to the dating method than the simple fact that it happens, and happens in a regular, intelligible way. It is taking place slowly everywhere that carbon-14 is to be found: in the air, dissolved in the sea, and in plants and animals, both living and dead.

The loss of carbon-14 through radioactive decay, and the creation of it through cosmic radiation, set up a balance. The net amount created in the atmosphere over a given period of time by cosmic radiation is exactly balanced by the loss over that time through radioactive decay, all over the world. So that the proportion of carbon-14 to carbon-12 in the atmosphere is neither increased by the cosmic radiation nor reduced by the radioactive decay, but stays constant – a uniform and small fixed proportion. It is picked up in this same proportion by living plants and animals, so that in all living things there is this same fixed small proportion of carbon-14.

But when a plant or animal dies, it drops out of the food chain by which it used to take up carbon, including carbon-14. It becomes a closed system. The radiocarbon in its structure decays radioactively, but is no longer replenished: the old balance is no longer maintained. From the time of the organism's death, its proportion of carbon-14 is declining slowly and at a fixed, known rate.

The beautifully simple principle of the radiocarbon method is to measure what proportion of radiocarbon is left in a sample whose age is to be determined. We know the initial proportion when it was living, since this is a constant figure through time. When we know the proportion left in the sample now, we can calculate how long the radioactive decay process has been going on. This is the same thing as the age since death of the sample; when we know this, we have dated it.

The task of the archaeologist, therefore, is to find suitable samples for radiocarbon determination, well stratified in the levels which he wishes to date. In theory, any organic material – any material of plant or animal origin – will do, since it will have had the usual proportion of radiocarbon built into it with the rest of the carbon of the body during life. After death the animal or plant will have undergone some chemical decay, but the proportion of radiocarbon to ordinary carbon in what is left will not have been affected by these chemical processes, but only by the radioactive decay of the carbon-14 with the passage of the years.

In practice, wood charcoal is very suitable, being almost pure carbon. But of course there is always the risk that the wood may already have been old when it was burnt and buried, so that the carbon date – which gives the date when the sample was alive – might not reliably date the archaeological level itself. Carbonized seeds – cereal grain, or beans or peas or whatever – are still more suitable, since they will only have been a year or two old at most when they were partially burnt and thus carbonized. Quite a small quantity of such suitable material will suffice – twenty grams is plenty.

Bones can also be carbon-dated in the same way, but a larger quantity is usually needed – about 300 grams – since bone is not pure carbon, and laboratories have found that the best results come from a radiocarbon determination on the collagen contained in them, which has first to be extracted. Seashells too can be used, although there have been doubts about some of the dates they have yielded. And indeed a whole range of materials – wood, peat and so forth – can be carbon-dated, but some of these run the risk of contamination by material of more recent origin – fungus may have grown on the wood, for instance – and so may not be ideal.

In each case, the sample has to be destroyed in the analysis. It is first of all carefully cleaned, and every attempt is made to extract any contaminating components. The problem is then a chemical one – of extracting the carbon from the sample and converting it to a form where it can be passed into the assemblage of counters for its radioactivity to be measured. In some cases, this is done by burning the sample in a current of pure oxygen, to give carbon dioxide which is either used directly, or converted chemically to acetylene, which has the advantage that it can be handled in liquid form. Some further detail as to how the activity of the sample is measured in the laboratory is given in the Appendix.

Even when these routine procedures are followed, there are still several problems that need to be considered. There are problems of contamination, when either older or more recent organic material has become mixed with the plant or animal remains of the period to be dated. And naturally the samples must belong to the time in question: if they were already old when buried, the determination will yield their date of formation rather than the date of burial. There is an age limit as well: samples more than 60,000 years old cannot be dated by this method, as by then the radiocarbon remaining in the sample is too weak to measure. Nor is the accuracy as great as one might wish. An error of a couple of centuries was common in the early days, and the method may be of little help where a more accurate historical chronology is already available.

Radiocarbon dating is not only subject to errors; like all scientific procedures, it depends on definite assumptions, and these must be understood if the method is to be used properly.

Firstly, it is assumed that the radioactive decay of radiocarbon will take place in a regular way, quite unaffected by physical or chemical conditions such as temperature or contact with the air, and also that the decay rate is known. This is a fundamental principle of modern physics.

Secondly it is assumed that the samples to be dated have not been contaminated since their death, so that the proportion of carbon-14 to carbon-12 has not been changed, other than by the steady process of radioactive decay. This depends on the careful collection of samples by the archaeologist in the field.

The third assumption is that the small proportion of radiocarbon in all living things at a given time is, in fact, a constant, and that it does not vary from place to place, or among different species. This too is found in practice to be broadly justified.

And finally it is assumed that the concentration of radiocarbon in the earth's atmosphere has remained constant through time. If this is so, by measuring the proportion of radiocarbon present in living things today we can obtain a valid value for the proportion that the sample contained when it was alive.

These are the assumptions on which the radiocarbon method rests, together with the knowledge that we can measure accurately in the laboratory the proportion of radiocarbon still present in the sample to be dated. In the early development of the method, its results were not so accurate as to reveal discrepancies which might call these assumptions into question. Libby put the whole method effectively to the test in 1955, when he published a graph showing the known historical age of selected samples (mostly from Egypt) against the radiocarbon dates obtained for them (Fig. 10). In general, the radiocarbon dates fell close to the predicted historical dates, and the method was, in its broad outlines, confirmed.

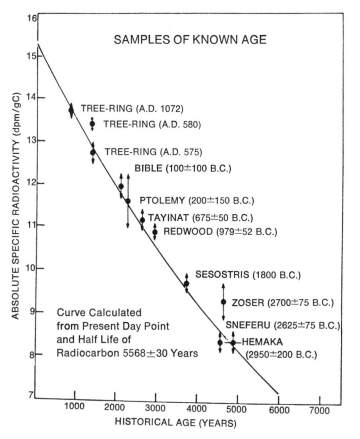

FIG. 10. Willard Libby's check of the basic soundness of the radiocarbon method. Observed radioactivities of historically dated samples are plotted against the curve, which shows the predicted values. The good agreement was confirmation of the validity of the method. (*After W. F. Libby*)

In recent years, however, it has become clear that the fourth assumption on which the method depends is not quite correct. That is the reason for the upheaval caused by the tree-ring calibration, discussed in Chapters 4 and 5.

In using radiocarbon dates it is important to realize that each has associated with it a standard error (or standard deviation), expressed in the form of 'plus and minus' after the date, for example 3650 B.C. ± 60. This is a statistical expression, and it does not mean that the date must lie within sixty years of the date given, merely that it has a 66 per cent chance of doing so, and a 95 per cent chance of lying within twice the standard error – in this case 120 years. Many misunderstandings have arisen over this, and it is a mistake to suppose that radiocarbon dates are more accurate than they claim to be. It is also important to note whether the date is expressed in years B.C. or years B.P. (Before Present), and to ensure that there is no confusion about the half-life (the figure expressing the decay rate of radiocarbon) used to calculate the date (see Appendix). The detailed comparison of radiocarbon dates involves the use of statistical procedures. This does not make them mysterious or uncertain in any way; like all scientific data, they simply have to be interpreted properly. Today this means taking into account the tree-ring calibration discussed in Chapter 4.

The first radiocarbon controversy

To start with, there were only a few radiocarbon dates – Libby's laboratory in Chicago produced the first list in 1950. In 1951 the Pennsylvania laboratory was set up, to deal exclusively with samples from archaeological sites. Then in 1953 came the first European publication of dates, from the Copenhagen laboratory. Soon there were many laboratories; and today there are about seventy. In 1960 Willard Libby, the pioneer of the method, received the Nobel Prize for Chemistry for his contributions. The laboratories produced a steady flow of dates, and archaeologists were delighted with the scientists who had put the remarkable new techniques at their disposal.

The honeymoon period, however, was a brief one. Very soon, archaeologists found that the dates obtained did not tally with their expectations. The trouble came in the Old World, in Europe and the

Near East, because it was here that archaeologists had already, in pre-radiocarbon days, put forward firm chronologies. In the New World the dates were breaking virgin ground: there was less for them to contradict, and consequently much less heart-searching.

The first revelation was the extreme antiquity of farming, and even of urban settlement, in the Near East. Before the discovery of radiocarbon, the early farming villages of the Near East were generally dated in the later fifth millennium B.C. (c. 4500 to 4000 B.C.). The growth of towns was set in the later fourth millennium (c. 3500 to 3000 B.C.), leading to the growth of states and full-scale civilization in the third millennium B.C. The first three published radiocarbon dates for an early village farming site – Jarmo in Iraq – fitted this picture fairly well, ranging from 4800 B.C. to 4600 B.C., with a standard deviation of 300 years. But then in 1956 came the publication of dates from Jericho in Palestine, whose walls, according to the legend, had been destroyed by Joshua's trumpet in biblical times. A large, fortified 'proto-urban' settlement was being excavated, in much lower pre-biblical levels which had flourished at a time before the use of pottery was known, and astonishingly early dates of 6250 ± 200 B.C. and 5850 ± 200 B.C. were obtained. The excavator, Kathleen Kenyon, and her scientific collaborator wrote: 'It becomes evident that the pre-pottery Neolithic city of Jericho is not only the oldest city in the world but the oldest Neolithic settlement so far known.'[23] The use of the word 'city' was not a happy one, for pre-pottery neolithic Jericho was not really a city, with the internal organization which that implies, but simply a large fortified village. The real surprise was that this early farming site should be dated so fantastically early, fully 1,500 years earlier than expected.

To some excavators – especially those whose early farming communities were not so early – these dates seemed doubtful. Professor Robert Braidwood, the leading American worker in the field and the excavator of Jarmo, who in 1951 had published a report entitled 'Discovering the World's Earliest Village Community', was engagingly frank about his reactions to the new dates. He wrote: 'In consequence, people have been looking at me – as the excavator of Jarmo – with that look which is usually reserved for bridegrooms left waiting at the church. My reaction, both in terms of what I know of the comparative archaeology of the Near East and of cultural process in general is – in pure Americanese – that it doesn't figure.'[24] He felt it necessary to point out that 'the radioactive method of dating still had many difficulties', and he deplored 'the well-known bandwagon phenomenon for generally earlier dates' which he feared would follow.

In a sense, of course, Braidwood was right: two dates alone are not sufficient to establish any conclusions finally. But Kathleen Kenyon was not anxious to relegate Jericho to 'a mere 5000 B.C.', and in her reply to Braidwood, reminded him 'that he *was* suffering from jaundice when he visited Jericho'. She wrote: 'The main disagreement between us lies in the fact that Professor Braidwood's thesis is that Jericho must fit into the chronological and developmental framework of the early villages known. Mine is that it lies outside it.'[25]

Although Braidwood's caution was justified at the time, subsequent dates do indeed set the foundation of pre-pottery neolithic Jericho well before 7000 B.C. And as we shall see, this was only the first of several surprises in the neolithic of the Near East. But it did not seriously disrupt the systems of dating described in the last chapter, since it had always been acknowledged that all dates before 3000 B.C. were unreliable anyway. Moreover, since it did not seriously conflict with the Egyptian chronology, dealing as it did with a much earlier period of time, the Jarmo–Jericho dispute did not call into question the radiocarbon method as such.

But in the same year as the Jericho exchange – 1957 – there did come a serious attack on its validity. In the same year that it was announced, Professor Vladimir Milojčić had, by an unlucky quirk of fate, published an important and meticulously documented book on the chronology of neolithic Europe; and when it transpired that many of the radiocarbon dates were at least a thousand years older (earlier) than the datings established in his study, he published a detailed critique of the entire radiocarbon method in the archaeological periodical *Germania*. Milojčić's attack seriously disturbed many archaeologists who had come to accept the method as both valid and accurate – for he was suggesting that it was often giving determinations that were at least a thousand years too old.

In his critique of the method, Milojčić was able to point out that not all the assumptions on which it rests were well established. He also high-lighted discrepancies between individual dates from the same or very closely comparable contexts. His criticisms were answered, both in

Germania and in *Antiquity* by several physicists and archaeologists; but with the benefit of hindsight we can now see that some of his comments were just. Seen in historical perspective, this attack was the first indication that there was something seriously wrong, not just with some of the assumptions of the radiocarbon method, but with the conventional chronology as well. But it was not until the tree-ring calibration of radiocarbon that these defects became fully apparent: and as we shall see, the uncertainties that Milojčić emphasized have effects precisely the opposite of those he anticipated.

In Britain, Professor Stuart Piggott at first found himself in rather the same position as Milojčić. His standard work, *The Neolithic Cultures of the British Isles*, had been published in 1954, before many radiocarbon dates were available. In it, through traditional archaeological arguments, he set the beginning of the British neolithic at 2000 B.C. Soon he was confronted with dates for the early neolithic fully a millennium earlier. His reaction was to make the now famous pronouncement that a date of 2600 B.C. from the late neolithic 'henge' monument of Durrington Walls was 'archaeologically inacceptable'.[26]

The changing fortunes of the controversy between doubters like Milojčić and the enthusiastic protagonists of the radiocarbon method are well reflected in the editorials in *Antiquity*, written by Crawford's successor, Glyn Daniel. His close interest in radiocarbon problems kept *Antiquity* up to date with the situation. At first, before Piggott's rejection in 1959, *Antiquity* tended to dismiss Milojčić's doubts and dissatisfactions:

> When all these are resolved we shall see in the next quarter century the one thing that we are all waiting for – a complete and accurate dating of the main stages in the ancient development of man. We shall at last be able to write a truly historical – in the sense of a properly dated – history of man ... We are now entering a new era of prehistory, and many of us are forgetting the drama of the moment ... Radiocarbon dating is the great revolution in 20th century prehistory.[27]

Piggott's disagreement, however, prompted a more cautious approach, and an editorial in a later issue the same year set the tone for much further comment in archaeological circles:

Let us not pretend that these radiocarbon dates for the Neolithic in the Netherlands (4175 ± 60 B.C.), in Brittany (3210 ± 60 B.C.) and in Britain (2721 ± 150 B.C.) are other than shaking. Professor Piggott's chronological table in his *Neolithic Cultures of the British Isles* gave no Neolithic culture in Britain before 2000 B.C. ... The real question is: how far must we shake ourselves? ... Readers will admire the courage of Professor Piggott's trenchant criticism of the Durrington Walls date of 2630–2620 B.C. 'This date', he writes in words which will long be quoted in Honours Examinations in Archaeology, 'is archaeologically inacceptable'; and gives his reasons – very cogent ones they are too.

They are good reasons because they mean laughing off a yawning millennium. We feel, at the moment, the same unhappiness ... Shake, Laugh Off, Refuse to Accept, Make Consonant: where are we? We are at a moment when some of us at least are uncertain how to answer this question: when is a Carbon 14 reading an archaeological fact?[28]

These heart-searchings belong to history now, but they were absolutely reasonable at the time. A wide gap – 'a yawning millennium' – had appeared between the carbon-14 dates for the European neolithic and those previously accepted. Moreover there were inconsistencies among some of the dates, and a few 'sports' or 'jokers' were hundreds of years removed from the emerging pattern. This indeed was the first point which archaeologists needed to appreciate: that a coherent *pattern* of carbon-14 dates promises to be of real value, while one date on its own means nothing. The problems of counting error, the risk of contamination and the possible re-use of old wood in buildings mean that a single date can be wrong, for a variety of reasons. A pattern of dates, on the other hand, such as was beginning to emerge for early farming in Europe, cannot lightly be dismissed. Moreover a very coherent chronology was being built up by botanists for the sequence of vegetational changes in northern Europe since the ice age, based on pollen analysis and then radiocarbon.

A second point is that hitherto there were absolutely no reliable fixed dates for Britain or northern Europe earlier than 1500 B.C., since no direct contacts with the Mediterranean world had been established by archaeologists before then; and as we have seen, before 3000 B.C. there were no calendrical dates anywhere. Gordon Childe, recognizing this, had likened the entire chronology of Europe to flexible bellows which could be expanded or contracted at will: one end was fixed at 1500 B.C., the other earlier one was free to move, giving a longer or shorter chronology very much according to the wish of the archaeologist. Childe displayed his own great flexibility of approach when he wrote that the early bronze age in central Europe could have begun 'about 2800 B.C.' but probably should begin 'not earlier than 1700 B.C.'. And in the last edition of *The Dawn* (1957), he showed great readiness to accept the new radiocarbon dates.

We may single out 1960 as the decisive year, when radiocarbon dating really came of age. It was then that Waterbolk published in *Antiquity* a persuasive account of the conference on radiocarbon held at Groningen in 1959, which dispelled many doubts. Also, Godwin, in his Croonian Lecture to the Royal Society, showed how well the radiocarbon evidence harmonized with varve dating – which set the beginning of 'Recent' (i.e. post-glacial) times, geologically defined, around 8000 B.C. – and also with the vegetational sequence derived from pollen analysis. In the previous year, 1959, the *American Journal of Science* started an annual Radiocarbon Supplement, which soon developed into the independent periodical *Radiocarbon*, to publish the new dates that were then coming in their hundreds from the world's laboratories. And, above all, a coherent picture for the neolithic of the Old World was emerging, which proved acceptable to most archaeologists. Glyn Daniel could now write in his *Antiquity* editorial:

> There are still some archaeologists who are loth to accept Carbon-14 dates: Professor Milojčić of Heidelberg is perhaps the most vocative of them. Some point to the apparent gap of a thousand years between the archaeological and radiocarbon dates, but often on examination this gap is an illusory one. We could say in Britain that there was a gap of a thousand years between the date of the Neolithic given in Piggott's *Neolithic Cultures* and the radiocarbon dates for the beginning of Windmill Hill (Piggott's Early Neolithic), but this gap was due entirely to the fact that our archaeological dates before 1400 B.C. had no firm basis whatsoever. The same is true of Eastern Europe.[29]

The first radiocarbon revolution had taken place.

The unity of world prehistory

The arguments and disagreements about radiocarbon dating chiefly concerned the Old World, where chronologies had become well established in the days before radiocarbon, and where differences were therefore most likely to occur. Yet in many ways, the most significant achievement of radiocarbon dating has been to bring into a unified chronological framework the archaeology of the whole world, and to extend this dating back to much earlier periods.

It has allowed, for one thing, a much clearer view of the later part of the old stone age, the upper palaeolithic, when Australia and the Americas were first peopled. Several other scientific dating methods are available for the palaeolithic period: for instance, the potassium/argon method – which again depends on radioactive decay – now sets the emergence of man back as early as three million years ago. But this method cannot measure short spans of the order of 10,000 years, and is useful only for the earlier palaeolithic. For the upper palaeolithic, which began around 30,000 years ago, and in which, for instance, all the cave art was produced, radiocarbon is very much more useful: it allowed, for the first time, the determination of absolute dates for the period.

Once again, the results came as a surprise. One of the first dates to emerge from Libby's laboratory in Chicago was for the splendidly painted cave at Lascaux, in the Dordogne region of France: 13500 ± 900 B.C. (although it is just possible that the paintings themselves were finished earlier), a much younger (more recent) date than had been expected. Here, indeed, the effect of the radiocarbon dates was to shorten the earlier 'guess' dating, making dates more recent – the very opposite of what was happening to dates for early farming. The Abbé Breuil's book *Four Hundred Centuries of Cave Art* (published in 1952), with the implication that caves were being painted, or at least the little 'Venus' figurines carved, already 40,000 years ago, is seen as mistitled. 'Three Hundred Centuries' would fit the carbon-14 evidence better, while the most splendid of the painted caves date from the so-called Magdalenian period, less than 20,000 years ago.

It now became possible to arrange all the upper palaeolithic cultures of Europe and beyond in their chronological relationships with a precision previously undreamt of. Already by 1960 the basic outline was

1. Earth's oldest inhabitant, the bristlecone pine. In the White Mountains of California these trees reach an age of 4,000 years.

The first stone monuments. 2. (*above*) Megalithic tomb at Essé,
Brittany. 3. (*below*) Decorated doorway at Mnajdra temple, Malta.

4. (*facing page*) The dawn of civilization: marble flute-player from the
Cycladic Islands, Greece, dated *c.* 2500 B.C. (height 20 cms).

5. Europe's first metallurgy;
copper axe-adzes from the Balkans,
c. 4000 B.C. (length 27 cms).

'Proto-writing' from Bulgaria,
before 4000 B.C. 6. (*left*) Incised
signs from Gradeshnitsa (height
12 cms). 7. (*below*) Clay 'seal'
from Karanovo (diameter 6 cms).

War and wealth in the early bronze age of south Britain. 8. Finds
from the Bush Barrow: (*left*) mace and daggers (length 33 cms);
(*right*) gold ornaments (length 18 cms).

9. The Rillaton gold cup
(height 9 cms).

10. Living prehistory: wooden rotundas—a 'temple' and chief's house —of the Louisiana Indians in the 18th century A.D. (drawn by A. de Batz). Buildings inside the henge monuments of the British chiefdoms before 2000 B.C. must have looked very similar.

11. Monument building in a recent Pacific chiefdom: burial platform
in Tahiti 80 metres in length and built in the 18th century A.D.
(illustrated by W. Wilson in 1799).

12. The great stone rotunda at Stonehenge, built *c.* 2000 B.C. (Stonehenge IIIa).

clear, and in that year Hallam Movius published a definitive article, together with a chronological table: 'Radiocarbon dates and Upper Palaeolithic archaeology in Central and Western Europe'. His basic outline, since revised and refined, laid the foundations for the scientific study of the period; in its essentials, it has not been challenged. And today, dates from Africa, Australia and the Americas allow the direct comparison of their upper palaeolithic cultures with those of Europe.

Prehistoric cultures could now be compared and dated on a world-wide basis. Hitherto there had been absolutely no way of comparing the late stone age hunting sites or the early farming villages in the New World and the Old. No one could say when man first reached America or Australia, nor what stage of cultural development had been reached when he did so. Indeed, until the advent of radiocarbon, the continents of the world had been effectively cut off from one another, from the archaeo-logical point of view. For while Egypt and Europe could be related archaeologically by the typological method, to tie in the cultures of Egypt with those of southern or central Africa had proved a much more difficult task. Nor could prehistoric China be related satisfactorily to the Near East: there were too many gaps in-between. And of course to relate the culture sequences of the Americas or the Pacific with Europe and the Mediterranean was not possible. At least, it was not possible with-out the grandiose notions of the 'hyperdiffusionists' led by Sir Grafton Elliot Smith, who simply assumed that Egyptian civilization was earlier than Mesoamerican, and dated the latter on the basis of supposed con-nections with Egypt.

In the course of its first decade, up to 1960, radiocarbon made all of this tele-connection, the dating of cultures by supposed long-distance links entirely redundant, and indeed slightly absurd. By 1960 it was established that man was hunting game in North America in the tenth millennium B.C. – that is to say, before the end of last glaciation of the ice age. Also, the new dates indicated that Australia might have been occupied by man as early as 4000 B.C.; and today there are radiocarbon determinations to push this date back beyond 17000 B.C. Man's occupation of these continents can be dated with accuracy.

The early development of farming in different regions of the world can now be documented too. We shall see below that agriculture was under way in the Near East by 7000 B.C. It is clear too that maize was gathered systematically in Mexico by 5000 B.C., and that well before 3000 B.C. it was showing clear signs of domestication. The rise of civilization in the New World has also become clearer. The Olmecs of the Mexican Gulf Coast were constructing the ceremonial centre at La Venta, among the earliest on that continent, as early as 800 B.C.

These dates are not of interest solely because they are early. What matters is that they allow the development of farming centres and of civilizations, arising quite independently in different parts of the world, to be studied and dated in their own right, and compared with each other.

The first such synthesis, appropriately entitled *World Prehistory*, was published in 1961. Without radiocarbon, its author Grahame Clark would have found so broad a treatment impossible. The debt to carbon-14 is still clearer in the second, 1969 edition, where nearly every chapter has its own table of radiocarbon dates, establishing the basic framework on which the entire narrative rests.

In each area a real study in time depth has become possible. Australian prehistory, for example, can now be subdivided into various developmental stages. The investigation in Africa of the prehistoric cultural development is one of the most exciting fields of prehistoric research at the moment. The iron-working Nok culture of west Africa, for instance, has recently been set in the later first millennium B.C., far earlier than one would have guessed without radiocarbon.

Our focus in this book is on the Old World – on Europe and the Near East – and it is to these that we must now turn. Yet in the final analysis, one of the greatest contributions of the first radiocarbon revolution has been in making possible the study of world prehistory. Developments all over the world may now be studied on a proper comparative basis, with a sound framework of dates. Radiocarbon has made possible a new and unified view of the development of man.

The neolithic of Europe and the Near East

The main force of the radiocarbon revolution in the Old World was to transform the dating of the early farming cultures. The origins of farming in the Near East, set by many archaeologists around 4500 B.C., had been a matter of guesswork – since there was no historical chronology before

3000 B.C. Now at last there was a way of determining dates before the period of the great civilizations. It set the beginning of the neolithic in the Near East some 3,000 years earlier than before.

A further surprise was the relative backwardness of neolithic Egypt. 'The oldest farmers', as they had been thought to be, were certainly farming by about 5000 B.C. in radiocarbon years, but this was not strikingly early compared with dates before 6500 B.C. for early farming in Palestine and in western Iran. It seems clear now that Anatolia, the Levant and the western Zagros (Iraq and Iran) were the regions where wheat and barley were first intensively exploited. Egyptian agriculture, on the basis of the dates now available, came later.

An interesting additional consequence of radiocarbon dating has been to limit the scope of the term 'mesolithic'. Formerly this was seen as representing a world-wide epoch in man's existence, in which man lived the life of the fisherman and the hunter of small game, after the end of the final glaciation of the last ice age, yet before the inception of farming. We can now see that in the Near East he was already beginning to specialize in the exploitation of some of the plants and animals that were later domesticated *before* the end of the ice age – in palaeolithic times; and by 7000 B.C., when the mesolithic way of life is seen in northern Europe, there were already farmers in several regions of the Near East. Rather than appearing as a universal stage of human evolution, this mesolithic way of life appears as one possible, localized mode of adjustment to the new environmental conditions. An ultimately more significant one, at the same date in the Near East, was the gradual development of a farming economy.

Although this new dating for the period before 3000 B.C. made early farming so much older, it did not really change the relationships between different areas, the relative chronology. The old idea of a spread of farming from the 'hearthlands' in the Near East westwards to Mediterranean Europe and then north to Britain and Scandinavia was not at first seriously challenged. Indeed, while the dates themselves were very different, the emerging pattern convincingly confirmed Gordon Childe's emphasis upon the Danube as a key route for the transmission of farming techniques from the Mediterranean to central Europe. The earliest farms of Europe were, just as he had suggested, in Greece. From there, it still seemed, farming had spread northwards and westwards, up the

Danube valley, on to the Low Countries, where dates back to 4000 B.C. for farming sites were obtained.

The emerging pattern of dates for early farming settlements was elegantly illustrated by Grahame Clark in 1965 (Fig. 11). It shows well how a coherent pattern may be extracted from the radiocarbon dates, even when individually they may be subject to appreciable errors.

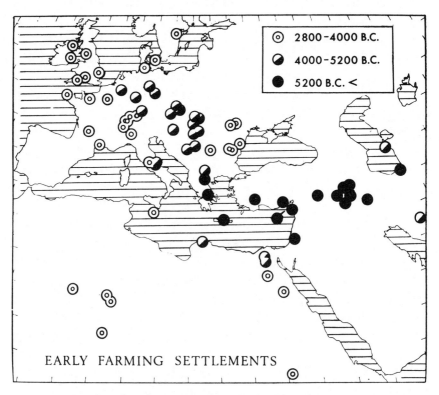

FIG. 11. Radiocarbon dates (not calibrated) for the earliest farming sites in various regions of the Near East and Europe, indicating the spread of agriculture to Europe. (*After J. G. D. Clark*)

In Britain, as we have seen, the early neolithic dates were much older than had been expected. Piggott's original dating had set the beginning of the British neolithic just after 2000 B.C., and its end, at the neolithic/early bronze age transition, around 1500 B.C. In 1962, however, pollen evidence, supported by radiocarbon dating, indicated forest clearance by the first farmers around 3200 B.C., and dates for artifacts – pottery and stone axes –

soon backed this up. Yet the beginning of the early bronze age was still to be set around 1500 B.C. The chronological 'bellows' had been greatly extended.

The succession of cultures which had previously been squeezed into 500 years now occupied more than 1,500. This implies more than the alteration of a few dates: it changes the entire pace and nature of the cultural development. But again it did not greatly affect the relative chronology for the different regions of Europe: the megalithic tombs of Britain, for instance, were still later than those farther south.

The very considerable discrepancy between the old 'historical' dates for Europe and the radiocarbon dates for the spread of farming was illustrated diagrammatically by Clark (Fig. 12). He showed how the radiocarbon dates were at least a millennium earlier than the historical chronology put forward by Milojčić and Piggott.

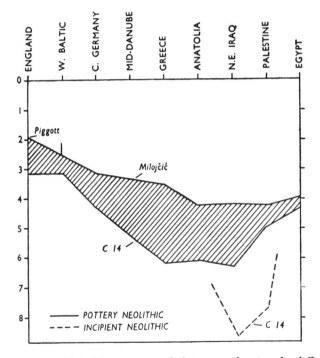

FIG. 12. Graph published by J. G. D. Clark in 1965 showing the difference (shaded) between the traditional chronology and the radiocarbon dates for the beginning of the neolithic in Europe and the Near East.
(Scale in millennia B.C.)

None of the changes so far described challenged in any way the conventional view that the significant advances in the European neolithic and bronze age were brought by influences from the Near East. It simply put these influences much earlier. Admittedly, some of the radiocarbon dates for megalithic tombs in Brittany, setting them well before 3000 B.C., were uncomfortably early – too early to allow the round tombs of Early Minoan Crete, with their collective burials, to be their predecessor. But at this stage, after the first radiocarbon revolution, the Breton dates stood alone. The dates for megalithic tombs in Britain and Denmark did not go back as early as 3000 B.C., and there were no Spanish dates before 2500 B.C. Moreover, there was a suspicion, not perhaps expressed in print but often voiced, that the dates from the French radiocarbon laboratory at Gif sur Yvette might not be quite right. So the conventional dating for the megaliths was not yet directly challenged.

In south-east Europe the situation was rather different. Milojčić was acutely aware that the radiocarbon dates for Vinča, and for the Vinča culture of Jugoslavia, were putting its beginning before 4000 B.C., and this did not tally at all with his view (and Childe's) that the Vinča culture was inspired by the early bronze age of the Aegean, some time after 3000 B.C. As we have seen, Milojčić's reaction was at once to reject the radiocarbon dates, and this remains his position today.

James Mellaart, the excavator of the famous sites of Hacilar and Çatal Hüyük, was the first to try and follow the logic of these dates in the Balkans. In 1960 he wrote an article boldly grasping the nettle and accepting the radiocarbon dates. But he did not deny the connection between the Aegean and the Balkans. Instead he set the Aegean dates earlier, putting the foundation of Troy (for which there were no radio-carbon dates) right back to 3500 B.C., fully 500 years earlier than the excavator, Blegen, had proposed. Thus Mellaart was able to retain the idea of cultural and chronological links between the Balkan neolithic and the Aegean early bronze age, and the cultural priority of the Aegean was not called into question.

Many scholars, however, believed rather, in the words of Robert Ehrich, that 'there may well be some as yet unrecognized factor that affects the radiocarbon dates throughout Temperate Europe before 2000 B.C., making them uniformly too old, but at the same time allowing the emergence of a consistent pattern.'[30] Sinclair Hood has expressed similar views.

The controversy between the proponents of the new, radiocarbon chronology for south-east Europe on the one hand, and the defenders of the traditional chronology there on the other, was heightened, and the traditionalists given great comfort, by the discovery in Romania in 1961 of the now famous Tartaria tablets (Fig. 38). These three pieces of baked clay, reputedly found in levels of the Vinča culture, had signs and symbols incised upon them resembling those of the world's earliest writing in Mesopotamia, in the 'proto-literate' period of Sumer. The Sumerian tablets could not be dated many centuries before 3000 B.C., so that unless one were prepared to argue that writing began in Romania and spread to the Near East from there, the context where the tablets were found could not be much earlier than 3000 B.C. either. Milojčić enlisted the aid of the distinguished Sumerologist Falkenstein, who pronounced that the signs were definitely Sumerian. Yet radiocarbon implied a date for the Vinča culture several centuries earlier.

This gave a significant boost to the case for the traditional chronology. To Milojčić it was the final proof of the fallacy of radiocarbon. But it has subsequently been suggested that the tablets may not actually belong to the Vinča culture levels at Tartaria, but from later, bronze age deposits. This would overcome the chronological problem and reconcile the tablets with the radiocarbon dates. In my own view, however, this is not the right explanation. It seems very possible that the signs on the tablets are a local invention, and that the resemblances with those of proto-literate Sumer are entirely fortuitous. This would, of course, imply that the Tartaria 'writing' developed in Romania well before the world's first script is seen in Mesopotamia. That implication is discussed further in Chapter 9.

Despite this interesting find, all was not well with the conventional chronology, which already, in the Balkans, had come into direct conflict with radiocarbon. It was open to criticism in other regions also. In 1965 I suggested, on purely archaeological rather than strictly chronological grounds, that the traditional picture for Iberia was not convincing. Closer examination of the evidence revealed that the idea of a transmission of metallurgy and of collective burial in monumental tombs from the Aegean to Spain was not well documented. Other than vague 'parallels', there was really no hard evidence to support the theory of Aegean 'colonists' in Iberia at the beginning of the early bronze age. I took the view that 'it would seem wiser to hold in doubt the question of Aegean influence on the Iberian Neolithic or Chalcolithic. Although such influence seems possible and indeed plausible, there is no reason why the Iberians should not have produced themselves most or all of the forms in use in Chalcolithic times.'[31] And if the contacts were questionable, so was the chronology.

It was also possible to question on purely archaeological grounds the supposed links with the Aegean on which Milojčić based his Balkan chronology. A close study of the Aegean 'parallels' showed them to be much less like the Balkan finds than was generally supposed. The sequence of deposits at the great Bulgarian tell at Karanovo also seemed to contradict the theory of Aegean contacts, since finds of the Balkan late neolithic were stratified metres below material which seemed related to the Aegean early bronze age.

These, then, were difficulties which could not easily be reconciled. They suggested that the traditional chronology might be seriously in error in the Balkans, and possibly in Brittany as well. At first, archaeologists thought that these might be just minor inconsistencies which later work would tidy up; but now, since the tree-ring calibration of radiocarbon, they are recognizable as significant faults that undermine the traditional chronology as a whole.

Just when most archaeologists had come to accept that radiocarbon dates give a reliable chronological picture, a sound framework for prehistory, there came a further shock. Its implications were in many ways more revolutionary than those of the first radiocarbon dates. For this time the whole framework of thought about Europe's prehistoric past was jeopardized.

This new development originated in an unexpected quarter, in a remarkably long-lived tree, the bristlecone pine, growing in the White Mountains of California (Pl. 1). Already in the 1950s and early 1960s, tree-ring work had shown these trees to be exceedingly ancient. But it was not until 1966 that the first papers were published which used radiocarbon determinations of wood from the bristlecone pine to cast serious doubt on the existing radiocarbon chronology. Then in 1967 the American chemist Professor Hans E. Suess presented an important paper to a conference in Monaco, where, for the first time, a graph was given which could be used, albeit tentatively, to correct the radiocarbon dates. The amount of the correction required is considerable.

Radiocarbon dates before 1200 B.C. have to be 'calibrated' – revised, using such a curve, and set several centuries earlier. Back at 3000 B.C. the necessary change is as much as 800 years. These changes bring with them a whole series of alarming reversals in chronological relationships. The megalithic tombs of western Europe now become older than the Pyramids or the round tombs of Crete, their supposed predecessors. The early metal-using cultures of the Balkans antedate Troy and the early bronze age Aegean, from which they were supposedly derived. And in Britain, the final structure of Stonehenge, once thought to be the inspiration of Mycenaean architectural expertise, was complete well before the Mycenaean civilization began.

The calibration in outline

The principle for the calibration is very simple. It is made necessary by the failure of one of the four basic assumptions of the radiocarbon method, discussed in Chapter 3. Libby assumed that the concentration of radiocarbon in living things has remained constant through time, so that the original concentration of radiocarbon in the sample when it was alive would be the same as the concentration of radiocarbon in living things today. We now know that this is simply not true. Tree-ring work supported by radiocarbon analyses shows that the concentration of radiocarbon in the atmosphere, and hence in living things, has in fact varied considerably – 6,000 years ago it was much higher than it is today. Consequently, organic samples of that period have much more radiocarbon in them than Libby realized. Using his assumption, we obtain for them a date which is misleadingly young (i.e. recent) – as much as 800 years too young.

Fortunately, since 1966, there has been a way by which radiocarbon dates can be checked, and corrected when they are found wrong. If the check, for instance, shows that a radiocarbon date of 3000 B.C. is too young by 700 years, the remedy is to add 700 years to the age of all radiocarbon dates of 3000 B.C. and thereabouts. *Dendrochronology* offers the means of checking the dates.

Everyone knows that the yearly growth of trees in spring produces a series of annual tree-rings in the wood. By counting these rings on a tree-stump, the age of the tree at the time of felling can be computed. Dendrochronology, the method of tree-ring dating, is based on this principle, and builds on it to reach far back into the past. The crucial point is that the different annual rings vary a good deal in density and thickness, depending on the climatic factors that year in the area in question. Over a number of years a distinctive pattern of thick and thin rings is built up in the tree, and this pattern can be picked out in the wood of different trees in the same region. So if we have counted the rings in a recently felled tree back through a couple of centuries to when the tree was young, we can try and match up these early rings with their counterparts in the wood of a tree long dead. In this way, using distinctive sequences, one can link tree with tree, and build up a continuous sequence of tree-rings extending just as far back as there is wood available from trees long dead. This dendrochronology, of course, gives dates for the wood expressed in solar or *calendar years*, since the rings on the tree are caused by variations in climate linked to the annual rotation of the earth around the sun.

The next step is to exploit this long chronology to help solve the problems of radiocarbon. Samples of wood from rings of known age are taken, and radiocarbon determinations for them are performed in the laboratory in the usual way. In this way straightforward ages, in what we may call *radiocarbon years*, are obtained for wood samples whose true age in calendar years is already known. Of course, if the assumptions of the radiocarbon method were correct, the two ages should be the same (allowing for an acceptable error in measurement), and there would be no difference between radiocarbon date and tree-ring date. It turns out, however, that the assumption of constant atmospheric concentration of radiocarbon through time is not correct, and as we have seen, the radiocarbon ages before around 1200 B.C. are too young, too small. A correction is needed to convert them into true dates in calendar years.

By performing large numbers of radiocarbon determinators upon tree-ring samples of known age from the bristlecone pine, Professor Suess has constructed a graph which may be used to convert radio-carbon dates (in radiocarbon years) to true or tree-ring dates (in calendar years). The calibration curve is seen in Figure 14. To calibrate a radio-carbon date, its position on the horizontal axis (*x* axis) is found. The point on the curve which lies vertically above it is then located. The corrected, calendar date is the date on the vertical axis (*y* axis), reading horizontally along to the left from this point on the curve. For example, a radiocarbon date of 2000 B.C. takes us up vertically to the curve and then left horizontally to the vertical scale where we read the calibrated age as 2500 B.C. The straight line on the graph simply indicates the line along which radiocarbon dates would equal calendar dates: if the original assumptions of the radiocarbon method held, the curve would in fact lie along this straight line. Unfortunately it doesn't.

Sometimes the bends and kinks in the curve complicate the picture, and make it possible for a single radiocarbon date to offer a choice of equivalent calendar dates. This is confusing, and often considerably reduces the accuracy of the calibration in practice. But the large magnitude of the discrepancy between radiocarbon dates and calendar dates is not obscured by these kinks.

The basis for the calibration

While the new changes in chronology came as a shock to archaeologists, to physicists they were far from unexpected. Already in the early days of radiocarbon it had been pointed out that changes in the earth's magnetic field would affect the creation of radiocarbon in the atmosphere by cosmic radiation. Climatic changes too might have affected the proportion of radiocarbon in the atmosphere.

Moreover, by the 1960s it had become clear that the calendrical chronology for early Egypt and the radiocarbon chronology were not in such good agreement as they ought to be. In 1963 Libby wrote an article, 'The accuracy of radiocarbon dates', in which the discrepancy was considered. He found that 'the radiocarbon dates for Egypt for the period 4,000 to 5,000 years ago may be consistently too recent relative to the historical dates, but that the two sets of dates agree back to 4,000 years ago.'[32]

Before about 4000 B.P. (i.e. 2050 B.C.) the radiocarbon content of the samples deviates by some 5 per cent from the predicted level. That is to say that the samples from Egyptian contexts of known calendar date have 5 per cent more radiocarbon in them than they 'ought' to have. This makes them appear younger than they are in reality. It seemed possible that there had been more radiocarbon than usual in the atmosphere at the time. The alternative possibility – that the actual samples were indeed younger (more recent) than they had previously been thought to be – would imply that there was something wrong with the Egyptian historical calendar, as reconstructed by the Egyptologists. They would seem to have got their dates wrong. Otherwise the entire radiocarbon calendar would have to be revised.

Understandably, Libby, the inventor of the radiocarbon method, preferred the second alternative. 'This plot of the data suggests that the Egyptian historical dates beyond 4,000 years ago may be somewhat too old, perhaps five centuries too old at 5,000 years ago, with decrease to 0 to 4,000 years ago. In this connection it is noteworthy that the earliest astronomical fix is at 4,000 years ago, that all older dates have errors, and that these errors are more or less cumulative with time before 4,000 years ago.'[33] That seemed a fair statement at the time, and the Egyptologists admitted that their calendar could be wrong. As H. S. Smith, now Professor of Egyptology in the University of London, wrote in 1964: 'Under these circumstances it is not surprising that most Egyptologists will wish to suspend judgement in this matter ... The historical grounds for the 3rd millennium dates, though not unchallengeable, are strong.'[34] At first, indeed, it looked as if the Egyptologists might have their dates wrong. Now we see that, on the contrary, it was the radiocarbon calendar which needed revision.

The solution came through a third and independent dating method quite unrelated to the other two – dendrochronology. The first direct use of the annual growth of tree-rings to investigate several centuries of radiocarbon dates was published in 1960. Samples from a huge section of a Sequoia tree were taken at fifty-year intervals across the radius, and were

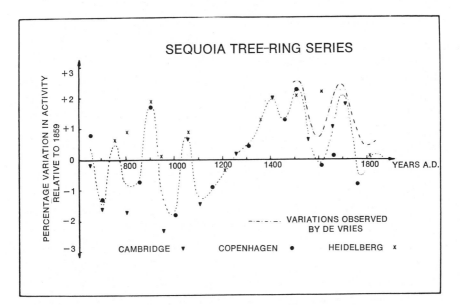

FIG. 13. The first use of tree-ring dating to check radiocarbon dates, in 1960. Each point on the graph indicates the radiocarbon date of a dendrochronologically dated Sequoia sample. The horizontal axis indicates predicted values. Three laboratories took part. Small but significant variations from the predicted level (up to 3 per cent) were observed. (*After E. H. Willis, H. Tauber and K. O. Münnich*)

dated at three different radiocarbon laboratories (Cambridge, Copenhagen and Heidelberg) so as to minimize laboratory errors. The resulting curve is seen in Figure 13.

This curve shows two things. First, as the Dutch radiocarbon specialist De Vries had pointed out two years previously, there had been variations in the quantity of radiocarbon in the atmosphere, causing the observed changes in the activity of the samples (and hence in the radiocarbon ages obtained). There had been several fluctuations over the past 1,200 years.

Secondly these fluctuations, although real, were fairly small: over the past 1,200 years they did not exceed 2 per cent. It was concluded that 'over the past 1,200 years the fundamental assumptions of the radiocarbon dating method are empirically correct to about 1·5 per cent'.[35] These variations would cause errors of only about fifteen years in the radiocarbon ages and clearly were of little significance. So far there was no cause for alarm.

Until 1955, no trees older than about 2,000 years were known. There was no obvious way of extending the continuous tree-ring sequence obtained from the *Sequoia gigantea* back into the pre-Christian era. This meant that tree-ring dating could not be used to check the assumptions of the radiocarbon method before this time. Then Edmund Schulman of the Laboratory of Tree-Ring Research at the University of Arizona realized the great potential of the Californian bristlecone pine, *Pinus aristata*, recently renamed *Pinus longaevia* (Pl. I).

These astonishing trees, high in the White Mountains of California, live to a very ripe old age. The oldest living tree yet discovered has been alive for 4,900 years – the earth's oldest living thing. The rainfall in this area is very low, and the tree-rings are 'sensitive' – varying greatly in thickness from year to year. Sometimes parts of some of the rings are missing, but if several borings are taken at different places in the circumference of the tree, they can usually be detected. Professor Charles Wesley Ferguson, who took over after Schulman's death, has succeeded in building up a continuous tree-ring sequence, which at present extends back nearly 8,200 years, using the wood from many trees both living and long dead.

Computerized handling of the data allows the rings of different trees to be compared effectively to build up a chronology covering the life-spans of several trees, and statistical techniques are used to interpret the results. The use of wood from different trees, and comparison of trees in different areas, helps to detect any missing rings. The other common pitfall of tree-ring dating, the existence of several tree-rings for a single year, is less important: in this species multiple growth-rings are rare.

The Arizona tree-ring laboratory has made wood from dated tree-rings available to three radiocarbon laboratories. These three, at La Jolla in

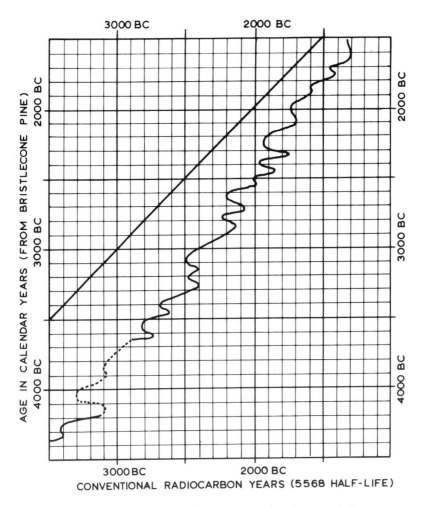

FIG. 14. Calibration chart for radiocarbon dates, based on work by H. E. Suess. It allows approximate values in calendar years to be given for radiocarbon dates (see text). The precise form of the graph is at present being revised: calendar dates obtained from it are approximate only.

California, at the University of Arizona itself, and at Philadelphia, have all produced radiocarbon dates using these rings of known age. The first date lists came out in 1966 and 1967, and all three laboratories agree that before 2000 B.C. the radiocarbon dates are systematically too young.

Perhaps the clearest picture has been given by Professor Suess at La Jolla. In 1967 he was able to publish a preliminary calibration chart, allowing the conversion of radiocarbon dates to calendar years, and vice versa, over the period 4100 to 1500 B.C. This chart has been used as the basis for Figure 14.

In 1970 he published a revised version covering the time range from the present back to 5300 B.C. (Fig. 58). This chart, based on the work of Fergusson and Suess, summarizes in a convenient form the first comprehensive calibration of the radiocarbon calendar. The most effective way of using this chart is discussed below, but first it is useful to consider the reasons for its curious shape, and indeed for its being necessary at all.

The causes of the deviations

In 1956 it was realized that changes in the strength of the earth's magnetic field in the past would have changed the intensity of cosmic radiation reaching the earth, as this magnetic field has the effect of partially deflecting the cosmic rays. Since it is this radiation which produces radiocarbon in the atmosphere, the atmospheric concentration of radiocarbon would have been altered. This idea has been taken up by the Czech geophysicist V. Bucha, who has been able to determine, using samples of baked clay from archaeological sites, what the intensity of the earth's magnetic field was at the time in question. Even before the tree-ring calibration data were available to them, he and the archaeologist Evžen Neustupný were able to suggest how much this would affect the radiocarbon dates.

There is a good correlation between the strength of the earth's magnetic field (as determined by Bucha) and the deviation of the atmospheric radiocarbon concentration from its normal value (as indicated by the tree-ring radiocarbon work). It seems likely, therefore, that the main deviation of the curve away from the straight line originally predicted by Libby, is caused in this way.

The second-order fluctuation in the curve – the kinks – is caused by more rapid, shorter-term changes in the atmospheric concentration of radiocarbon. For recent centuries it has proved possible to correlate some of these with the sunspot activity of the sun. The sun's own 'cosmic' radiation was probably affecting the earth at such times. This may also be the cause of a still shorter disturbance which has been detected by the ingenious, if expensive, method of dating 'vintage' whisky, when the date of distillation and of the harvest of the grain is accurately known.

All of this is uncertain at present, and some workers have pointed out that the kinks on Suess's curve do not agree very well with the results from the Arizona and Philadelphia laboratories. But there is at least fairly general agreement about the major, first-order deviation, and some consensus that, however uncertain its precise details may be just now, there is a second-order deviation imposed upon this. The detailed explanation of these effects will be of considerable interest both to geophysicists and to climatologists.

Calibrating radiocarbon dates

The calibration of single radiocarbon dates using the Suess calibration curve is fairly easy. A radiocarbon date of 2000 b.c., as already described, yields a calendar date of 2500 B.C. (A convenient convention, now increasingly adopted, is to use 'b.c.' when speaking of simple, uncalibrated radiocarbon dates* and 'B.C.' – in capital letters – when the dates are expressed in calendar years after calibration.)

Often, however, the kinks in the curve present a problem. A date of 2100 b.c., for instance, yields, on the Suess curve, alternative calendar dates of 2550 B.C. and 2700 B.C., and the true date could lie anywhere between these alternatives (Fig. 14). When the kinks are very complicated – around 1900 b.c. in radiocarbon years, for instance – the range of choice is even wider.

The really important thing to remember, however, apart from the doubts expressed by some scholars about the accuracy of the kinks in the

---

* In this book, the b.c. dates are calculated using Libby's value for the half-life of radiocarbon (see Appendix), and it is important to establish, in any publication, which half-life is being used. Here, the B.C. dates are obtained using the calibration described. Since at present there are several calibration curves in existence, differing slightly in the results they give, the calibrated date in calendar years B.C. is always accompanied in serious publications by the original radiocarbon date.

curve, is that all radiocarbon dates have associated with them an estimate of probable or standard error – the 'plus' or 'minus' quantity that accompanies them. To use the calibration curve properly, this has to be taken into consideration, together with the errors associated with the curve itself.

As we saw in Chapter 3, the plus or minus one standard deviation of the radiocarbon dates expresses 65 per cent confidence limits. There is a 65 per cent chance that the correct radiocarbon determination lies between the limits given, a 35 per cent chance that it lies outside them. If, for example, we take a date of 2350 b.c. $\pm$ 100, there is a 65 per cent probability that the correct radiocarbon measurement lies between 2450 and 2250 b.c.

Naturally the calibrated dates will also have a standard error associated with them. At first sight, using the calibration curve to calibrate these limits it would appear that the new, calibrated 65 per cent confidence limits should be 3300 B.C. and 2900 B.C., which already differ by 400 years instead of the 200 years which the original $\pm$100 might have led us to expect. But this operation overlooks the statistical errors associated with the curve itself, so that the true 65 per cent confidence limits would be even farther apart, if the shape of the curve were of precisely the form suggested by Suess.

Plus or minus two standard deviations will give us the 95 per cent confidence limits for the radiocarbon dates, as discussed in Chapter 3 and the Appendix. In the example we are discussing, therefore, there is a 95 per cent chance that the correct radiocarbon determination lies between 2550 and 2150 b.c. At first sight this would give us 95 per cent confidence limits in calendar years of 3350 B.C. and 2550 B.C., using the calibration curve. These already differ by fully 800 years instead of the 400 years which $\pm$200 might suggest. But again, this does not take into account the statistical error associated with the calibration, and the true limits would be farther apart.

Recent statistical work by Malcolm Clark of Sheffield University, who has carefully investigated the shape of the calibration curve, suggests that some of the kinks can be smoothed somewhat, so that the confidence limits of calibrated dates will not be so inordinately wide. However, the errors introduced by the use of a curve must not be overlooked – and they cannot be avoided if we wish to use dates expressed in calendar years.

The kinks in the curve imply that single radiocarbon dates are very much less reliable than we had thought. The uncertainties in the kinks themselves make precision even more difficult. It is necessary, therefore, to have a good pattern of carbon-14 dates before setting too much store on them or their calibrated equivalents.

There is, however, one way in which the accuracy can be increased. If we have a series of radiocarbon dates, for samples whose sequence is independently known, some check on these kinks becomes possible. This has been elegantly demonstrated by Ferguson, Huber and Suess, using tree-rings in wood from a prehistoric Swiss lake village. The tree-ring sequence extended over only a couple of centuries, so it could not date anything on its own – it was a 'floating' tree-ring chronology. But by radiocarbon dating wood from it at twenty-year intervals, it was possible to get some check on the atmospheric variation of radiocarbon over this time period, and so to use the kinks in the curve to calibrate the dates more accurately. Rainer Berger of the University of California at Los Angeles has done this with medieval samples from timber buildings with excellent results.

Theoretically, any sound sequence of samples can be used in this way, even when the time interval between them is not precisely known. The 25 radiocarbon samples from the tell at Sitagroi in north Greece, for instance, make much more sense when taken together in their stratigraphic order than when treated in isolation.

At present, however, no great precision is to be expected in the calibration of dates, and the kinks and their interpretation present considerable statistical problems. The main feature of the calibration, which is not in doubt, is the considerable magnitude of the correction that must be applied to dates before 2000 B.C., rising to as much as 1,000 years at times. Whether this correction for a particular date should be 600 or 800 years may not yet be clear. The main thing is that a correction of that order is certainly necessary.

The reliability of the calibration

The archaeological reaction to the calibration has been, in general, one of dismay tempered with a cautious scepticism. No one who accepted the validity of radiocarbon dating in general has come out and said, 'This must be wrong.' Yet the archaeological world, having recently adjusted itself to one new and surprising set of dates – the first radiocarbon revolution – has been understandably cautious about adjusting itself again.

The physicists appear unanimous that the main, first-order deviation exists, and that, whatever the detail of the kinks on the curve, its final appearance should not be too different from its present one. The archaeologist, however, wants to know if there may not be something wrong with the entire calibration. Is it conceivable that it might not all be explained away one day as the result of some special factor? To answer this question it is necessary to look again at the four main links in the logical argument on which the calibration rests.

The argument is as follows. First, we have a tree-ring chronology stretching back to 6000 B.C. (*Query:* Is it reliable?) Second, the wood of the tree-rings is supposed to reflect accurately the level of atmospheric radiocarbon in the atmosphere in the White Mountains of California at the time in question. (*Query:* Is there not something special about these trees, and are we certain that the wood has not been contaminated by more recent carbon?) Third, the radiocarbon determinations given by the laboratory are assumed to be accurate for the wood samples in question. (*Query:* Are the laboratory determinations as accurate as they claim?) Fourth, it is assumed that the atmospheric concentration of radiocarbon at the time in question was the same everywhere in the world as in the White Mountains of California, so that the calibration is of world-wide validity. (*Query:* Are we sure that the level of radiocarbon in California has always, at a given time, been the same as in Europe and elsewhere?)

For the first of these steps in the argument, scholars have to rely on the accuracy of the work of Ferguson and his colleagues in Arizona. If they are wrong, so is the entire calibration. Their work, however, is based on the meticulous compilation of data, using many trees, living and dead, with a full awareness of the statistical problem and of the difficulties caused by missing rings and multiple growth-rings. Where it has been possible to compare their work with other dendrochronological studies, namely in the time range extending back from the present to the beginning of the Christian era, it compares well.

The second query is probably more serious, for it is conceivable that the wood of the early tree-rings has in some way been altered in its isotopic composition, perhaps by the more recent sap in the tree. Of course, the resin is always removed chemically before the wood is dated, but the damage might already have been done. This problem has been investigated, for living trees, with both the bristlecone pine and the European oak in an ingenious way. The very high radiocarbon content of the air since the detonation of nuclear weapons in the atmosphere may be used as a 'tracer'. In theory this high carbon-14 concentration should be seen in the appropriate year rings and in later rings, but not at all in earlier rings, unless they have been contaminated in the way we suspect. Rainer Berger has investigated this, and has concluded that the effect is at most a minor one and cannot amount to more than one or two per cent of the modern level.

The answer to the third query is that the laboratory determinations are probably not, in fact, quite as accurate as they claim. There are sizeable differences in the results obtained by different laboratories for the same piece of wood. This, indeed, is why there is controversy about the precise nature of the kinks in the calibration curve. But although the discrepancies are a nuisance at a detailed level, they are relatively small and do not affect the general validity of the calibration. There is no disagreement between laboratories about that.

Finally there is the question of the world-wide level of radiocarbon in the atmosphere. British archaeologists have been heard to mutter: 'Why should I concern myself about this obscure Californian shrub?' The answer has been given by Libby in these words: 'The principle of simultaneity means that radiocarbon dates are the same at any given epoch over the entire earth, so that a calibration at one location is equivalent to a world-wide calibration ... finding the same concentration of neutral radiocarbon all over the world and in different forms of life nearly guaranteed this result.'[36] Later work has supported this in general. But it has also been suggested that the high altitude of the bristlecone pine trees has exposed them to effects of direct cosmic radiation, or at least to the neutrons from it. They could be responsible for the creation of extra carbon-14 in the tree itself, which would be in addition to the normal proportion taken up during photosynthesis. This ingenious idea, however, is not likely to reveal a serious error, and there is certainly little evidence that it has been operating over the past 2,000 years.

These quite legitimate questions, however, make it important to seek corroboration by independent means for the tree-ring calibration. There are at present three possible ways of checking the calibrated radiocarbon dates.

The first is by thermoluminescence dating, an entirely independent technique used chiefly on pottery and baked clay. It depends on the radioactive minerals present in the clay, and an accuracy within ±10 per cent is at present claimed for the ages obtained. The first comparison of thermoluminescence dates and calibrated radiocarbon dates for this purpose was published by David Zimmerman and Joan Huxtable in *Antiquity* in 1970. Pottery of the Danubian early neolithic (Linear Pottery culture) was tested for the purpose. The dates from three sites were 5350 B.C., 5330 B.C. and 4610 B.C. respectively. Uncalibrated radiocarbon dates for such material cluster between about 4400 b.c. and 3800 b.c. in radiocarbon years, equivalent to a range in calendar years of 5300 B.C. to 4600 B.C. As the authors remark, 'these results provide strong support for a "long" chronology,' and hence for the calibration.

A second, independent chronology is varve dating, briefly discussed in Chapter 2. In Scandinavia and North America long varve sequences allow a count going back to glacial times. There are two problems, however, in using them to check the calibration. The first is to find any organic material actually in the varves, which can be radiocarbon dated; the second is to relate the top end of the varve sequence reliably with the present. There are uncertainties in the existing varve chronologies for these reasons, and they are not yet sufficiently reliable to check the calibration as a whole. The great potential of varve dating, however, is that theoretically it could provide a check on radiocarbon dates stretching right back into ice age times, well before 8000 B.C. It is unlikely that the bristlecone pine dendrochronology will ever extend back so far.

Finally, of course, and most obviously, there is the comparison of radiocarbon dates and historical dates for ancient Egyptian samples of known origin. In the early days the samples were not always from the very best and safest archaeological contexts, and the British Egyptologist Geoffrey Martin has recently been collecting samples for analysis with these problems in mind. The British Museum and U.C.L.A. laboratories are at present collaborating on the careful analysis of these samples. The results so far do support the bristlecone pine calibration, but, as Rainer Berger put it in 1969: 'As a matter of fact, the bristlecone pine correlation appears to exaggerate the magnitude of the deviations slightly, although

not greater than, very roughly speaking, the maximum historical uncertainty.'[37] The results of this investigation will clearly be of great
interest.

At present, then, there is nothing which leads one to doubt the general
validity of the calibration, however problematical some of its details may
be. Only this question of diffusion of recent material across the older rings
of the trees as a possible source of contamination is disquieting. This would
have just the effect of making the radiocarbon dates from the bristlecone
pine appear too young, thereby artificially increasing the deviation. Such
an effect could account for the observation, suggested by Berger for the
Egyptian dates, that the calibration may sometimes over-correct. However, a recent statistical examination by Malcolm Clark has shown that
the Egyptian historical dates and the calibrated radiocarbon dates for
Egypt are not significantly different, and this finding does give independent support to the validity of the calibration. In any case, the broad
magnitude of the calibration has not been seriously questioned in scientific
circles. The Twelfth Nobel Symposium at Uppsala in 1969 was devoted
to the theme 'Radiocarbon Variations and Absolute Chronology', and
the calibration was there accepted by all participants.

The archaeologist has the responsibility, then, of assessing the effect of
the calibration upon European prehistory, while at the same time avoiding
any exaggeration of the accuracy of calibrated radiocarbon dates. The
consequences for European prehistory are of fundamental importance.

5 The Collapse of the Traditional Framework

The tree-ring calibration does much more to the prehistory of Europe and the Near East than simply correct a few dates. A shift in absolute dates is itself of considerable interest, of course, since it indicates that certain periods were of much longer duration than had been thought. This has an obvious bearing on the way things were developing, and on the rate of evolution in the period in question. But simply to shift all the dates back would not change any fundamental relationships.

The effects of the calibration are dramatic precisely because relationships are changed. The key point here is not so much that the radiocarbon dates for Europe, and indeed everywhere else, are set earlier; it is that the accepted dates for Egypt and the Near East remain unchanged. In these areas, archaeologists have always used the historical dating system, based on the historical chronology that exists from 3000 B.C. onwards. It seemed more reliable than the radiocarbon dates, and indeed it was. For, as we have seen, a discrepancy developed between the radiocarbon dates and the historical dates, in which the latter seemed too early. Now we know that the reverse is true: that the radiocarbon dates were too recent. The calibration removes the discrepancy, and the calibrated radiocarbon dates now agree well with the traditional historical dates.

This means that archaeologists can go on using the dates for Egypt and the Near East that they have always used. They can also retain the traditional chronology for the Aegean, where the uncalibrated radiocarbon dates had seemed, in the same way, too recent. They did not agree with the generally accepted datings arrived at by cross-datings with Egypt. But with the calibration, the accepted dates in the Aegean are vindicated too.

Outside the Aegean and the Near East, however, this agreeable harmony no longer prevails. For throughout Europe, a radiocarbon chronology had been accepted by most scholars; and the calibration now sets this chronology for early Europe as a whole several centuries earlier than

84

before. Thus the conventional chronological links are snapped; and the east Mediterranean innovations, which were supposedly carried to Europe by diffusion, are now found earlier in Europe than in the east. The whole diffusionist framework collapses, and with it the assumptions which sustained prehistoric archaeology for nearly a century. These are the consequences of what may justifiably be called the second radiocarbon revolution.

In Chapter 2 the three chief paths were discussed by which formative influences supposedly reached Europe from the east Mediterranean: from the Aegean to Iberia; from the Aegean to the Balkans; and from Mycenaean Greece to central Europe and Britain. The effect of the calibration, in setting the European dates earlier, is to invalidate all three. Since these were the crucial links for the traditional chronology of Europe, they are worth examining in turn.

'Colonists' in Iberia

Iberian prehistory has always seemed of central importance to the prehistory of Europe in general. For here, it was supposed, were the earliest megalithic tombs of Europe. Here it was that the practice of collective burial, originating in the east Mediterranean, first reached European shores. With it, perhaps, came the belief in the great Mother Goddess. And from Spain and Portugal, it was argued, the custom of collective burial in megalithic tombs spread up the Atlantic seaways to Brittany, to Britain and Ireland, and to northern Europe. At first, in the opinion of some at any rate, these were simple tombs, dolmens. Later, perhaps, a new wave of influences from the Aegean initiated the Iberian passage graves, with their corridor and central burial chamber, and sometimes with their handsomely corbelled vault. These are seen in south-east Spain, for instance at Los Millares and near Antequera, in the Seville region, and in Portugal. Very similar tombs, which in the diffusionist scheme of things were derived from Iberia, are seen in Brittany: Île Longue near Carnac (Fig. 5) is a good example. From there, it was held, they spread up to Ireland, leaving us the great tombs of the Boyne cemetery such as Newgrange and Knowth (Fig. 23), and finally to the *ultima Thule* of the passage grave expansion – to the northern isles, where Maeshowe in Orkney is the most splendid example.

The most imposing corbelled tomb in the Aegean is the Treasury of Atreus (Fig. 5), one of the splendid *tholos* (beehive-vaulted) tombs of the Mycenaean princes. These are dated after 1600 B.C. by acceptable cross-datings with Egypt, and it was realized early on that they were too late to be the point of departure for the tombs of Iberia. However, circular tombs are found already in Early Minoan Crete by 2500 B.C. It is not clear whether these were ever surmounted by a vault, as their original excavator Xanthoudides claimed; but in plan at least, they make a plausible proto-type for the Spanish tombs such as those of Los Millares.

The cult of a Mother Goddess was felt to hint at the motivation for the widespread construction of such monuments. As Glyn Daniel expressed it: 'The great megalithic tomb builders of western Europe were imbued by a religious faith, were devotees of a goddess whose face glares out from pot and phalange idol and the dark shadows of the tomb walls, whose image is twisted into the geometry of Portuguese schist plaques and the rich carvings of Gavrinnis and New Grange.'[38]

Only if the Iberian megaliths were the first in Europe could this explanation have any force. And it might be expected that, if the explana-tion was correct, indications of contact with the east Mediterranean would be found in Spain and even Portugal.

Just this conclusion was reached in the late nineteenth century by the first serious excavators in Spain, the brothers Henri and Louis Siret. They discovered in the south-eastern province of Almeria the first traces of the rich late neolithic (or 'copper age') culture which is now named after its principal site at Los Millares. As well as impressive chambered tombs, they found traces of copper metallurgy and a number of seemingly exotic features, such as simple figurines in stone, representing a very schematized human figure, and carved bones incised with a pair of eyes. To them it was exciting and surprising that such things should be found in early Europe, and they came to the conclusion that the finds must be of Phoenician origin. Subsequent authorities changed the date – for the first millennium B.C. was soon seen as too late – but the idea of an east Mediterranean origin was accepted. Montelius used it for his chronology, and as we have seen, it was the central argument in the first edition of Childe's *The Dawn of European Civilisation*. While a number of scholars at first rejected the notion of influence from the east, preferring a local evolution, the dif-fusionist view was soon generally accepted.

The most authoritative statement of this view was given in 1961 by Dr Beatrice Blance, in an article in *Antiquity* entitled 'Early Bronze Age Colonists in Iberia'. Her thesis was that a number of sites in Iberia, including Los Millares, were actual colonies, established by people coming directly from the Aegean. Probably, she felt, the principal parent regions were the Cycladic islands of Greece, and the west coast of Anatolia. The case was set out methodically with a wealth of detail. She found some rather striking similarities in the two areas, for instance in the fortification wall at Los Millares, with its round bastions, and the wall of the early bronze age stronghold at Chalandriani on the Cycladic island of Syros in the Aegean (Fig. 15). Most scholars found her argument a convincing one, explaining, as it did, the appearance in Iberia of fortified settlements, of metallurgy, of collective burial in megalithic tombs, and of a number of minor individual features, which taken together built up an impressive case. The first radiocarbon date from Los Millares, of 2345 ± 85 b.c., for

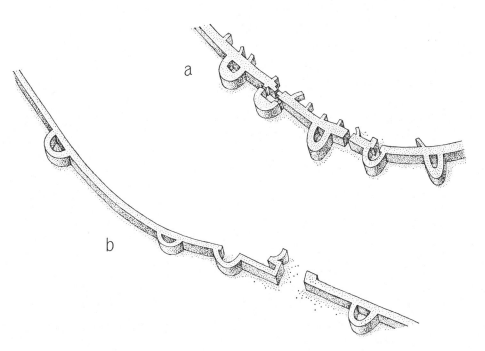

FIG. 15. The bastioned fortification walls at copper age Los Millares in Spain (b); and at Chalandriani on the Aegean island of Syros (a). On the traditional view the copper age innovations in Iberia were the work of Aegean colonists.

a developed phase of the settlement, harmonized very well with her view that the period of colonization was from 2700 to 2400 B.C.

This case, although impressive, was not overwhelming. For one thing, there were no actual imported objects in late neolithic or 'copper age' Iberia that could be shown to have come from the east Mediterranean. As Childe wrote himself in 1953: 'Though much has been learnt about the Peninsula's prehistory and foreign relations in the past six years, reliable evidence for chronology based on an interchange of actual manufactures has not been achieved.'[39] Moreover, a thorough examination of the Aegean evidence showed that the similarities with the finds in Spain and Portugal were not really very striking, and that they occurred all over the place, at very different times. If there were any 'colonists', it was difficult to see where they could have come from.

The procedure often adopted by archaeologists in Iberia was simply to select any features from the whole range of evidence that seemed striking or 'exotic' and classify them as 'imports'. The complete lack of any satisfactory relative chronology for late neolithic Spain or Portugal allowed the lumping together in this way of finds which were most probably very different in date. It turns out, too, that there are no megalithic tombs whatever in the Aegean, so that the whole exercise, whose aim is to find there an origin for the megaliths of western Europe, is a curious one.

Two other important and substantial arguments for Aegean influences remain. First of all, there is the similarity in some of the fortifications, but, as I wrote in 1965, 'to put the matter bluntly, is there any more reason why they should originate in the Aegean than in Iberia?'[40] Secondly, there is the evidence of the practice of copper metallurgy in the late neolithic or 'copper age'. If the notion of Aegean colonists or influences is denied, there are only two possibilities: that metallurgy reached Iberia from elsewhere, or that it was invented locally. The former does merit consideration, since it now appears that metallurgy was practised very early in south-east Europe. But at present, in the absence of any good evidence either way, a local innovation and development seems the preferable conclusion. The case for a local invention of metallurgy in the Balkans is argued in Chapter 9, and the same arguments could be applied in Spain.

These various doubts made it possible, quite irrespective of radiocarbon dating, to reject entirely the idea of 'colonists' arriving *en masse* from the

Aegean and setting up little colonial enclaves in Iberia. This does not mean, of course, that there could have been no contacts between local groups along the shores of the Mediterranean. It is possible that individual innovations might have been transmitted in this way, by the process that John Evans has called 'culture creep'. But the purely archaeological evidence for it is not convincing.

When we turn to the radiocarbon dates, the doubts are fully sustained and the colonist case becomes untenable. Here the radiocarbon dates for the Breton megaliths are a key factor. We have to remember that on the traditional chronology, the Iberian passage graves began after 2700 B.C. – since their supposed prototypes in the Aegean could not be set much earlier than this – and that according to the traditional view, Iberia was the place of origin for the Breton megaliths. As Childe stated in 1957: 'Brittany offers the first land-fall on the northward voyage from the Iberian peninsula to Cornish tin-lodes and Irish goldfields ... Corbelled passage graves are concentrated on the coasts and islands and are obviously inspired by Iberian, immediately by Portuguese, models.'[41] Yet the radiocarbon dates for the Breton megaliths, even before calibration, are far too early for this.

In such a discussion, single dates can be dangerously misleading and a pattern of dates is needed. For this reason it is appropriate to list here the available early dates for the Breton passage graves, some of which of course continued in use until much later. Dates for the Irish passage grave at Newgrange and the two in Denmark are added. (See page 90.)

Very approximately calibrated dates are given on the right: it should be remembered that the standard error may be much larger for them than for the uncalibrated dates, because of the kinks in the calibration curve (Fig. 14). Laboratory numbers are given for the dates: Gif-sur-Yvette and Saclay are French laboratories; the dates from the laboratories in Groningen and Copenhagen give useful confirmation.

It is again important to stress that individual dates should not be given too much weight, and that the calibration is at present approximate only. For instance, the early date from Kercado has a 16 per cent chance of lying as late as 3580 b.c., and a 3 per cent chance of being as late as 3280 b.c. in radiocarbon years. But the implications are altogether clear: passage graves, some with corbelled vaults, were already being built in these regions before 2500 b.c. in radiocarbon years, and thus by 3300 B.C. in

EARLY PASSAGE GRAVE DATES IN NORTH EUROPE

(Dates are quoted on the 5,568 half-life.)

Passage grave	C-14 date b.c. (radiocarbon years)	Lab. no.	Approx. mean Calibrated date B.C. (calendar years)
Sept Îles (Brittany)	3055 ± 150	GsY 64	c. 3800
Sept Îles (Brittany)	3215 ± 130	GsY 64	c. 4200–4000
Sept Îles (Brittany)	3430 ± 135	GsY 64	c. 4300
Barnenez A	3500 ± 150	GsY 1310	c. 4350
* Barnenez F (Brittany)	3600 ± 140	GsY 1556	c. 4400
* Barnenez F (Brittany)	3150 ± 140	GsY 1116	c. 4200–3950
* Barnenez G (Brittany)	3800 ± 150	GsY 1309	c. 4600
Île Gaignog (Brittany)	2550 ± 120	GsY 813	c. 3350
* Île Carn (Brittany)	3270 ± 75	GrN 1968	c. 4200–4000
Kercado (Brittany)	3880 ± 300	Sa 3880	c. 4800
Mané Karnaplaye (Brittany)	2470 ± 120	GsY 88	c. 3300–3000
Mané Karnaplaye	2785 ± 120	GsY 88	c. 3500
* Newgrange (Ireland)	2550 ± 45	GrN 5462	c. 3350
* Newgrange (Ireland)	2465 ± 40	GrN 5463	c. 3300–3000
Jordhøj (Denmark)	2540 ± 120	K 978	c. 3350
Tustrup (Denmark)	2470 ± 110	K 718	c. 3300–3000

* Corbelled vault

calendar years. Quite obviously, if they have their ultimate origin in the Aegean, this must have been a long time before 3000 B.C. Yet there are no collective built tombs in the Aegean until after this date. The Breton dates, even without calibration, make nonsense of the diffusionist case. If there are earlier passage graves in Brittany, why derive the Iberian ones from the east Mediterranean?

Fortunately we now have just enough radiocarbon dates from Iberia to make this same point. They do not yet build a coherent picture, but they are sufficient to disrupt the old one. (See table on facing page.)

At present, the calibration is to be regarded as approximate only, but already we may be confident that Los Millares and its passage graves began comfortably before the supposed prototypes were flourishing in the Aegean. Evidently the simpler forms of megalithic tomb began considerably earlier.

With these early dates the diffusionist case for Iberian origins collapses completely. The archaeological doubts expressed earlier are sustained. It is clear that the Iberian custom of burial in megalithic tombs, and the fortified strongholds, owe nothing to Aegean influence. The origin of Iberian metallurgy is still in doubt, since it might be rather later than the dates given here. But in the absence of any convincing contact of any kind between the Aegean and Iberia during the late neolithic or 'copper age', it seems at present preferable to seek another explanation for metallurgy also.

The first of the traditional links is definitely sundered. Archaeologists have now to think again about the origins of the European megalithic tombs, and the beginning of metallurgy.

An 'Aegean civilization' on the middle Danube

The neolithic and 'copper age' periods of the Balkans were virtually unknown when Montelius was building up his chronological systems for Europe. One of the pioneer excavators was Miloje Vassits, who published

EARLY DATES FOR IBERIAN MEGALITHS
(Dates are quoted on the 5,568 half-life.)

Site	C-14 date b.c. (radiocarbon years)	Lab. no.*	Approx. mean Calibrated date B.C. (calendar years)
Carapito I (Portugal, dolmen)	2900 ± 40	GrN	c. 3700
Carapito I (Portugal, dolmen)	2640 ± 65	GrN	c. 3400
Orca dos Castenairos (Portugal, megalithic tomb)	3110	—	c. 3800
Orca dos Castenairos (Portugal, megalithic tomb)	2660	—	c. 3400
Praia das Macas W. (Portugal, passage grave)	2300 ± 60	—	c. 3700
Los Millares (Spain, collapse of fortification wall)	2345 ± 85	H 204	c. 2950
Los Millares (Spain, passage grave 19)	2430 ± 120	KN–72	c. 3300–3000

* Where no laboratory numbers are given, the dates have been published in the periodical *Madrider Mitteilungen*, 6, 13, and 9, 61-2.
'H' indicates the Heidelberg radiocarbon laboratory.

in 1908 his first conclusion about Vinča, the great settlement mound which he was excavating near Belgrade. Overlooking the Danube in the Balkan state of Serbia – the heart of modern Yugoslavia – Vinča was destined to become one of the key sites in European prehistory. Like the Siret brothers in Spain, Vassits was impressed and indeed baffled with the sophisticated nature of the finds unearthed. There were simple objects in copper, handsome human figurines in stone and baked clay, and a series of rather enigmatic 'cult objects'. Vassits also found pottery with incised

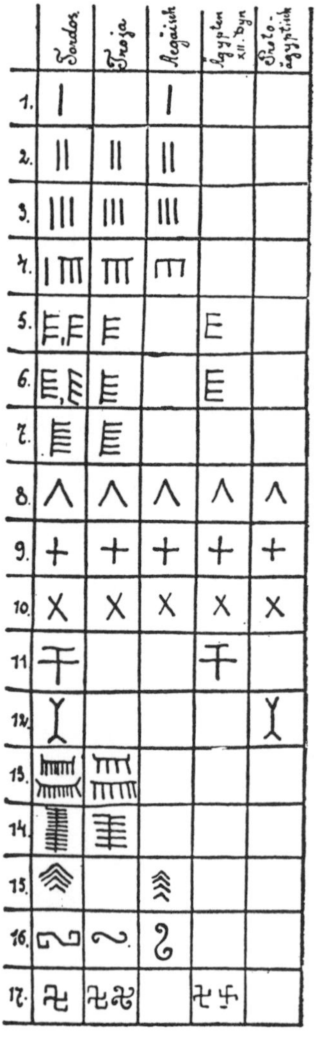

FIG. 16. Comparison, published by Hubert Schmidt in 1903, between the incised signs found on pottery at copper age Tordos in the Balkans (*first column*), and signs from early bronze age Troy (*second column*), from the Aegean (*third column*) and from Egypt.

signs in what seemed to be a primitive script. Already, five years earlier, Hubert Schmidt had published an article on the signs found incised on pottery at the similar site of Tordos, and had compared them with the early scripts of the Mediterranean (Fig. 16). Vassits's article was entitled 'South-eastern elements in the prehistoric civilisation of Serbia', and with it he initiated a line of research that was to occupy two generations of scholars and still preoccupies many Balkan specialists. Later he actually decided that the early settlers at Vinča were Greeks, in the first millennium B.C. But like the Sirets' theory of Phoenicians in Spain, this view did not do justice to the antiquity of the site.

The acute mind of Gordon Childe soon recognized the fundamental importance of Vinča for European prehistory as a whole. It became, for him, the key connecting link between the prehistory of the Aegean and that of central Europe. In 1924 he was already writing on this theme, and in 1929, with the publication of his book *The Danube in Prehistory*, it was authoritatively expressed. Where previously Childe had emphasized the significance of diffusion to the west Mediterranean, now the Danubian farmers took pride of place, displacing the Iberian colonists. As he put it: 'The sea-voyagers who diffused culture to Britain and Denmark in the first chapters of the first *Dawn* (1925) ... were relegated to a secondary position in the second edition of *The Dawn* (1927).'[42] The evident cultural links between Vinča and the Aegean, especially early Troy, were the first steps in building up a chronology for the whole of prehistoric Europe.

As Childe saw it, almost everything in Vinča reflected Aegean influences.

The whole of the civilisation ... is bound up intimately with the culture of the East Mediterranean and Anatolia. The commonest pottery is really a poor variant of 'black Mediterranean ware' ... The anthropomorphic lids (Fig. 17) call to mind the well-known lids from Troy II, though the parallelism is by no means exact ... Figurines belong to the very essence of the Aegean and Anatolian cultures ... Finally, many of the curious signs scratched on the cases from Vinča and Tordos agree with the marks on Egyptian vases of pre-dynastic and protodynastic times. Others recur in Crete and the Cyclades, and the correspondence between the marks from Tordos and figures incised on clay whorls from Troy is particularly close.[43]

The presence of copper metallurgy was another persuasive argument.

Some scholars used the same comparisons to give the opposite conclusion, arguing that these features originated in the Balkans and spread
from there to the Aegean. Childe's arguments were, however, widely
accepted. And in any case, to reverse the arrows on the diffusionist map,
as these prehistorians wished to do, 'in no sense destroys the validity of
the parallels cited above as proofs of an "aboriginal" community of culture
between the oldest Danubians and the oldest inhabitants of both sides of
the Aegean basin'.[44] Until the advent of radiocarbon dating hardly anyone doubted that there was some connection between the Balkan 'copper
age' and the Aegean early bronze age, or that the two were broadly
contemporary. In 1949 Professor Vladimir Milojčić published his detailed
study on this theme, and his views are still followed by the majority of
Jugoslav and Romanian archaeologists. The radiocarbon dates have been
rejected by them, and the calibration, in their eyes, is a highly suspect
attempt to bolster up an already discredited attack upon their comparative stratigraphic method.

Recent excavations in southern Jugoslavia, in the Priština district, have
produced some wonderful terracotta sculptures (endpapers) in contexts of
the Vinča culture, increasing our respect for the artistic accomplishments of

FIG. 17. Faces on pot-lids from copper age Vinča (*left*) and from the second city levels
at Troy (*right*). The comparison was traditionally used to date Vinča to *c.* 2700 B.C.

these very creative people. This has given encouragement to the diffusionist case, since nothing so splendid is seen in the Aegean until the time
of the beautiful marble sculptures of the Cycladic islands in the early
bronze age (Pl. 4). And the discovery of the Tartaria tablets, discussed in
Chapter 9, has brought to the fore again the whole question of the Vinča
script, which Childe in his later years had rather avoided. As we have seen
already, the signs on these tablets (Fig. 38) have been compared with those
of proto-literate Sumer, and the similarity used to give support to the
diffusionist case. In 1965, the Jugoslav archaeologist Vladimir Popović
published a well-illustrated article, 'Une civilisation égéo-orientale sur le
moyen Danube', in which these arguments were reiterated. The Balkan
finds, including some baked clay 'seals' – clay discs with incised signs –
were compared with those of the early bronze age Aegean and the
Orient.

> The recent discoveries from the Vinča–Tordos culture have once
> more set before us the old saying: *Ex Oriente Lux*. We know the
> interminable arguments to which it has often given rise. The middle
> Danube was illumined, it seems by this light from the Orient, coming
> almost directly from its source. It seems that the Tartaria tablets can
> now put an end to the controversies and arguments which, until now,
> have sought to give a different interpretation or to construct a
> different historical evolution in the Balkans.[45]

The battle rages: Milojčić has dismissed attempts to build a chronology
using the radiocarbon dates as 'vollständig indiskutabel'. And a careful
demonstration by the Czech scholar Evžen Neustupný indicating the logic
of the dates is dismissed as a 'temperamentvolle Apologie' and 'methodisch
kaum möglich Verfahren' (a procedure hardly tenable methodologically).
As he remarks darkly of the calibration: 'It is always an unfortunate
situation for a method when the clear findings require "corrections".'[46]

Yet despite these fulminations, the logic of the radiocarbon dates
cannot be escaped unless the radiocarbon method is dismissed in its
entirety. The situation is quite simple, and the two positions are totally
irreconcilable. They are contrasted below. The argument is one not only
of dating, but of the entire relationship between the prehistoric Aegean
and the Balkans. 'A' indicates the traditional short chronology of Childe
and Milojčić. The key equation is between the Vinča culture and its

contemporary in Romania and Bulgaria on the one hand, and the Aegean early bronze age, with early Troy, on the other. The alternative, 'B', is the long chronology suggested by the radiocarbon dates. Vinča and Gumelnitsa are now over long before the Aegean early bronze age, being set instead as contemporaries of the Aegean later neolithic. The contemporary in the Balkans of Troy and the Aegean early bronze age cultures is now the early bronze age Baden culture and its successors.

The absolute dates for Vinča proposed by Milojčić are 2700 B.C. to 2000 B.C., which does indeed – on both chronologies – cover all the later part of the Aegean early bronze age. The uncalibrated radiocarbon dates for the Vinča culture (on the 5,568 half-title) range from 4400 b.c. to 3600 b.c., and for the Gumelnitsa culture between about 4000 b.c. and 3300 b.c. In calendar years, using the tree-ring calibration, this gives a time

Table A

BALKANS	AEGEAN	CALENDAR DATE B.C. (approx.)
		─1600─
Early Bronze Age	Middle Bronze Age	
		─1900─
Gumelnitsa and Vinča (Late Neolithic)	Troy I–II (Early Bronze Age)	
		─2700─
Starčevo (Early Neolithic)	Dhimini (Later Neolithic)	
		─3000─
	Sesklo (Early Neolithic)	
		─3500─

FIG. 18. The traditional chronology for the Balkans (*Table A*) and the new calibrated radiocarbon chronology (*Table B*).

range for the Vinča and Gumelnitsa cultures of approximately 5300 to 4000 B.C. It is likely, I think, that the Gumelnitsa culture persisted later than this in some areas. But the dates show clearly that the material in the Balkans which Milojčić thinks contemporary with the Aegean early bronze age was going out of use fully a millennium before the Aegean early bronze age began. A gap of a 'yawning millennium' separates the two chronological systems.

Fortunately the new, 'long' chronology does not rest on radiocarbon alone. Most of the resemblances between the Balkan 'copper age' finds and those of the Aegean are extremely vague ones – generalized pot-forms and so on – and some of them, like the 'stamp seals', have their origin in the early neolithic of both areas, so that it is not necessary to assert that all were independent. The stratigraphic excavations at the

Table B

BALKANS	AEGEAN	CALENDAR DATE B.C. (approx.)
		—————2000—————
Early Bronze Age	Early Bronze Age (and Troy)	
		—————3000—————
Gumelnitsa and Late Vinča (Late Neolithic)	Dhimini (Late Neolithic)	
		—————4500—————
Early Vinča (Middle Neolithic)	Late Sesklo and Middle Neolithic	
		—————5200—————
Starčevo (Early Neolithic)	Early Sesklo (Early Neolithic 2)	
		—————6000—————
	Proto-Sesklo (Early Neolithic 1)	
		—————6500—————

great Bulgarian tell of Karanovo have already been mentioned. Material of the Gumelnitsa culture was stratified there well below finds which the excavator, Dr G. I. Georgiev, rightly equated with the Aegean early bronze age, specifically with early Troy.

To test this hypothesis, I set out in 1966 to choose a settlement site in the north Aegean where stratigraphic excavation might reveal decisive evidence for the relationship between the two areas. In 1968 and 1969, in an excavation organized jointly with Professor Marija Gimbutas, the settlement mound of Sitagroi in the Plain of Drama was investigated in this way. Over ten metres of stratified deposits were revealed. At the bottom, material was found resembling that of early Vinča and its contemporary in Bulgaria. Further up, in stratum III, there were abundant finds, with attractive graphite-painted ware, which were almost identical with those of the Gumelnitsa culture complex in Bulgaria. Above these were three further strata with unpainted pottery belonging to the Macedonian early bronze age. This had a number of similarities with early bronze age Troy, and there was no doubt in our minds that this material belonged with the Aegean early bronze age. The site itself, of course, is in the Aegean basin.

Here at Sitagroi, therefore, we have Aegean early bronze age levels stratified far above those of the Balkan 'copper age': stratigraphic documentation for the radiocarbon-based scheme 'B'. Twenty-five radiocarbon dates are now available for Sitagroi, and they harmonize entirely with this system. It is no longer possible to suggest, as some have done, that there is some geographical factor affecting the Balkan radiocarbon dates and making them too young, while leaving the Aegean ones unaffected. At Sitagroi, both are found in the same ten-metre stratigraphy. There are no inconsistencies. The radiocarbon picture is entirely vindicated, and another diffusionist link collapses.

The Mycenaean inspiration of the European early bronze age

The two chief links for European chronology operated, as we have seen, between the late neolithic of Europe and the Aegean early bronze age, at a date around 2500 B.C. The third and final connection between the Aegean and the rest of Europe occurred very much later, around 1600 B.C. In the intervening millennium the rich early bronze age cultures of the

Aegean had changed very considerably. In Crete, at the outset of what is termed the middle bronze age, the first palaces are seen, with their well-organized storerooms kept in order with the aid of written records. This is generally regarded as the beginning of full civilization in the Aegean, at around 2100 B.C.

On the Greek mainland, civilization in this sense did not begin so early. The late bronze age, or Mycenaean period, begins in Greece with the very rich finds discovered inside the citadel wall at Mycenae in the famous Shaft Graves. With their impressive weapons, and their great treasure of gold and silver drinking vessels, these are often taken as indicating the starting point of the Mycenaean civilization around 1650 B.C. Amongst the other finds, the discovery of beads of amber was particularly significant for northern Europe. The chief source of amber in Europe is the Baltic, and recent analyses have confirmed that most of the Mycenaean amber came from there. A trading link of some kind between Denmark or north Germany and the Mycenaean world must therefore already have been in existence.

Childe built on this piece of evidence to form a theory for the beginnings of the central European bronze age which was, in most respects, the exact counterpart of his theory for the origins of Aegean civilization. In this case, however, the Aegean was now the wealthy and civilized land in search of raw materials, and it was to central Europe that her traders and smiths were supposed to have turned, just as a millennium earlier the metal prospectors from the civilizations of the Near East were thought to have brought with them the elements of civilization to the barbarian Aegean early bronze age. As Childe put it:

> The Aegean surplus ... served as the foundation for a bronze industry in Temperate Europe in which Aegean traditions of craftsmanship could operate freely ... The commercial system this disclosed had been called into being to supply the Aegean market: it was the accumulated resources of the Minoan–Mycenaean civilisation that guaranteed to the distributors a livelihood, indeed an adequate recompense, for the hazards and hardships of their travels ... In the Early Bronze Age peninsular Italy, Central Europe, the West Baltic coastlands, and the British Isles were united by a single system for the distribution of metalware, rooted in the Aegean market.[47]

One or two parallels in central Europe seemed a little earlier, finding their closest equivalent in Syria not long after 2000 B.C., so that the Mycenaean theory was not entirely satisfying. 'Were the prospectors who had first located the ores of Central Europe and initiated their exploitation, immigrants from Syria? That seems highly probable, even if we admit that they could not profit from their discoveries till Minoan Crete and Mycenaean Greece offered a market for their winnings that was both reliable and accessible.'[48]

The hard evidence for this theory was not very abundant. The chief early bronze age culture of Czechoslovakia and Germany, the Únětice culture, displayed a number of forms resembling Aegean ones, and some of the bone metal types in the Hungarian bronze age were decorated with spirals and other motifs similar to some on the goldwork of the Mycenaean Shaft Graves. That was the chief evidence in central Europe.

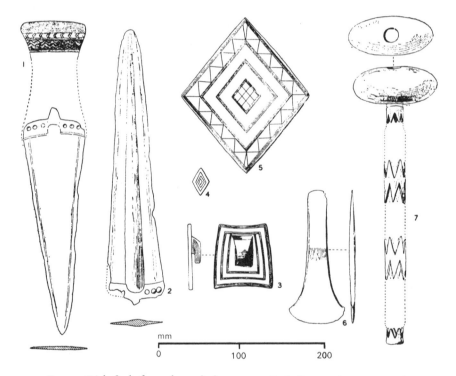

FIG. 19. Rich finds from the early bronze age Bush Barrow in Wessex. The dagger (1) has a gold-studded hilt, the objects in the centre (3–5) are of gold, the axe (6) of bronze. The sceptre (7) has a stone head and bone mounts.

The strongest arguments for contact, however, were put forward for south Britain, for the early bronze age 'Wessex culture'. In Wiltshire and Dorset, the ancient Wessex, a good number of burials had been found, beneath circular burial mounds, with very rich grave goods (Fig. 19). Most of these graves contained bronze daggers, the hilts occasionally decorated with little gold studs. There was other goldwork too, and at Rillaton in Cornwall a burial had been found accompanied by a very beautiful little cup of gold (Pl. 9), often compared with Mycenaean examples. These graves and their contents were the subject of a special study in 1938 by Stuart Piggott. He suggested the possibility of direct contacts between Britain and the Mycenaean world:

> The existence of such trade contacts between Mycenae and the north in the years around 1600 B.C. renders less startling the fact that the gold *pointillé* technique of the Breton and English dagger-hafts occurs not infrequently on the hilts of daggers both at Mycenae and else-where in Greece, that the Rillaton cup ... finds its best parallel in the two gold cups from Shaft-Grave IV, that gold-plated cones form a constant feature of Mycenaean grave furniture ... while the practice of capping a stone bead with gold is essentially Mycenaean. Such resemblances may be individually fortuitous, but in their cumulative effect are too remarkable to dismiss.[49]

Other specific resemblances corroborated this link, and it soon became the chief support for the dating of the European early bronze age as a whole. A final and very strong argument was offered by the little blue beads of glazed sand or 'faience', which were found in the Wessex culture and also in Czechoslovakia. The British ones, chiefly little ribbed cylinders, resemble closely those of the east Mediterranean world. In view of the sophistication of the technique, it was concluded that these were direct imports from the Mediterranean to Britain.

The different lines of evidence seemed to fit together pretty well. In this way, the beginning of the British early bronze age was set by most scholars after 1600 B.C. The great sarsen structure at Stonehenge (Pl. 12), which was thought to have been built during the span of the Wessex culture, was similarly dated.

The radiocarbon evidence now suggests that even this plausible picture may be without foundation. There are now three rather early radiocarbon dates for the Únětice culture: 1895 ± 80 b.c. for Prasklice in Czecho-slovakia, 1655 ± 40 b.c. for Leki Male in Poland, and 1775 ± 80 b.c. for Helmsdorf in north Germany (all on the 5,568 half-life). The last two were associated with material from a developed phase of Únětice, not from the beginning of the culture. Calibration sets all these dates between 2400 and 1900 B.C., and it seems likely that the Únětice culture had begun well before 2000 B.C.

These dates fit very well into the emerging pattern for the chronology of central Europe, but of course there are too few of them to give a reliable picture at present. They do suggest, however, that the Wessex culture, which has many evident links with late Únětice, may also be much earlier than had been thought. In 1968 I wrote an article suggesting a duration for the Wessex culture between 2100 and 1700 B.C.[50] This was supported by the radiocarbon dates for Stonehenge, which suggested that the sarsen structure with its trilithons was constructed before 1800 B.C. and probably before 2000 B.C.

The faience beads of the Wessex culture are no longer of much value for dating. In the first place, statistical analysis of a chemical examination of their composition suggests that they may be significantly different from the majority of beads in the east Mediterranean. This is even more clear-cut for the Czechoslovak beads, and an Aegean source seems very unlikely for them. And in any case, it is now clear that similar beads were worn in the east Mediterranean around 2500 B.C. Even if the faience beads were imports, they would be of little use for dating, since the manufacture of such beads occurred over such a long period of time in the east Mediterranean. As we shall see in Chapter 11, it is now very possible that they were made locally.

Nearly all the other pieces of evidence for Mycenaean influence in the Wessex or Únětice cultures are, when taken in isolation, rather unconvincing. There is no reason why the Rillaton cup and other goldwork should not be entirely local, and most of the other parallels can also be dismissed as fortuitous resemblances. No undisputed Mycenaean imports have been found in secure early bronze age contexts in Britain or central Europe. European amber was certainly reaching Mycenae from the period of the Shaft Graves onwards, but its use in the Wessex culture could be very much earlier. Actual Mycenaean exports in Europe are very rare, except in Sicily and south Italy. None has been found farther west, and all that has been found on the European continent is one or two weapons from Albania and Bulgaria. This is very inadequate support for Childe's notion of a 'commercial system ... called into being to supply the Aegean market'.

Although the Wessex culture is likely to have begun well before the beginning of the Mycenaean civilization about 1600 B.C., there is some evidence now that burials in rich dagger graves of the same kind were still taking place after this date. Uncalibrated radiocarbon dates of 1219 ± 51 and 1264 ± 64 b.c. for the dagger grave at Earls Barton in Northamptonshire, and of 1239 ± 46 b.c. for the dagger grave at Hove near Brighton, in which a splendid amber cup was found, suggest a calibrated date of about 1500 B.C. in calendar years. So it looks now as if the time spans of the Mycenaean civilization and of the Wessex culture did overlap. Nonetheless the origins of the Wessex cultures are likely to have been considerably earlier.

In this case the new chronology is not yet firmly established, and it will differ by at most four or five centuries from the old one – there will be no yawning millennium. So we cannot claim that the third link is decisively snapped by the calibration. For instance, Christopher Hawkes has suggested that Stonehenge might have been completed before the time of the Wessex culture, so that the Stonehenge radiocarbon dates would no longer be relevant to early bronze age chronology. It will be some time before we have a coherent pattern of radiocarbon dates for the full span of the Wessex culture itself.

But already, I think, it is clear that Childe's view underestimates the originality of the European bronze age, although he was himself at pains to stress some aspects of its individuality. No one today could hope to build a reliable chronology for the early bronze age of central Europe on the basis of direct links with the Mycenaean world.

The chronological 'fault line'

The two chief props of the diffusionist chronology have thus been knocked away. The late neolithic cultures, both of Iberia and the Balkans, are far earlier than had been thought, very much earlier than their supposed ancestors in the east Mediterranean. The third link, relating the European early bronze age with Mycenaean Greece, is in an unsafe condition. More carbon-14 dates are needed yet to establish a really sound chronology for it. But this third link is now too weak a support to sustain a diffusionist chronology or a diffusionist explanation for the cultures of prehistoric Europe. The whole carefully constructed edifice comes crashing down, and the story-line of the standard textbooks must be discarded.

In Figure 7 the logical structure of the traditional argument was illustrated graphically. And in Figure 20 the effect of snapping the three key links is indicated. In Figure 21 the effect is shown in relation to the map of Europe. In effect, there is a line running round the Aegean and east Mediterranean. Inside this arc, the dates in the third millennium B.C. are not much altered by the radiocarbon chronology and its calibration. But outside this line, where the uncalibrated radiocarbon dates had been used until now for the chronology (in general without contradicting the earlier diffusionist datings too seriously), everything is shifted several centuries earlier.

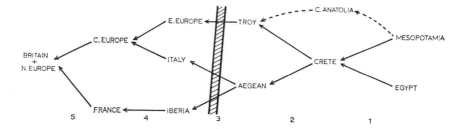

FIG. 20. The chronological 'fault line' produced by the calibration. To the right of the fault, the conventional and calibrated ages are not significantly different. But to the left, the calibration sets all traditional dates several centuries earlier.

The whole thing is rather like the formation of a fault in geology. Inside and outside the line there is a sequence of levels – the geological strata, or in this case the well-established sequence of cultures in each region. Now suddenly along this fault line, the whole outside area slips down together, leaving the area inside unmoved. Strata or cultures which used to be on a level with each other are now displaced, those of western, central and northern Europe slipping down and becoming earlier. Where the late neolithic cultures of Iberia or the Balkans were formerly on a level with the Aegean early bronze age, they slip down, coming to rest instead at a much lower level, alongside the Aegean neolithic.

The important thing, however, is that the European cultures move earlier *en bloc*. Their relations, one with another, are unaltered, since they move back together. And inside the fault line there are no changes whatever. It is only *across the fault line* that the relationships are changed so fundamentally.

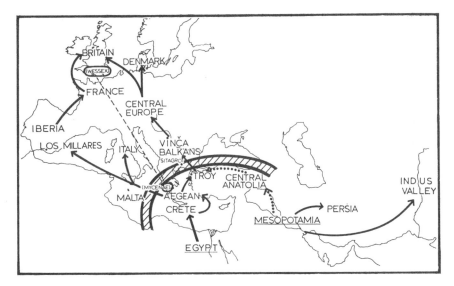

FIG. 21. The fault line in prehistoric Europe: the basic links of the traditional chronology are snapped and Europe is no longer directly linked, either chronologically or culturally, with the early civilizations of the Near East.

So all is not chaos, and it is possible to salvage a great deal that is of value from the ruins of the traditional structure. For western and northern Europe the pioneering work of Montelius and Childe and their successors is not too seriously disrupted. When they were studying the cultures of these areas in their own right—and this was indeed one of the strong points of Childe's approach—much of what they wrote remains perfectly acceptable today. To reject one major, central element of their work is not to undermine the real value of their achievement. Here, indeed, it is relevant to quote from the final paragraph of Childe's 'Retrospect'. The following were the very last lines which he wrote for publication, before leaving for Australia on his last voyage:

Now I confess that my whole account may prove to be erroneous; my formulae may prove to be inadequate; my interpretations are perhaps ill-founded; my chronological framework – and without such one cannot speak of conjectures – is frankly shaky. Yet I submit the result was worth publishing ... Incidentally it emphasizes once more the urgency of establishing a reliable chronology; a great deal of the argument depends on a precise date for the beginning of Únětice what is at best very slightly the most probable guess out of perfectly possible guesses ranging over five centuries.[51]

Childe and his contemporaries made the best and most coherent picture possible out of the evidence which was available to them. Today, radiocarbon dating has made it possible to construct a better one – as Childe would have been the first to realize. The very essence of a scientific procedure is that its conclusions are open to modification in the light of further evidence. Prehistoric archaeology is particularly fortunate that radiocarbon dating has made such evidence available.

Towards a new chronology

It is too early yet to construct a reliable and detailed chronology for Europe, using the tree-ring calibration. The details of the calibration curve have yet to be corroborated or modified through further radiocarbon analysis of independently dated samples. And also there are not yet enough radiocarbon dates from secure archaeological contexts for each region and period to build up a sound radiocarbon pattern.

What we can do now, however, is to sketch out the outlines. The sequence of cultures for each specific area – the relative chronology – is usually clear enough without radiocarbon. It can be established from the stratigraphies of excavated sites within a limited geographical area, and from typological studies. When these are restricted to individual regions, and the underlying assumptions are clearly brought out, they continue to provide valid information. The radiocarbon dates can then be used to test the relationships between these different areas, and cross-dating by means of undoubted exports and imports remains a legitimate procedure. Long-distance synchronisms, on the basis of general resemblances, are no longer acceptable, however. That is one of the lessons of the second radiocarbon revolution.

Basic elements of the new chronology table:

DATE B.C. (calendar years)	EGYPT	SUMER	AEGEAN	BALKANS	IBERIA	MALTA	N. FRANCE	BRITAIN
1500								
2000	MIDDLE KINGDOM	HAMMURABI OF BABYLON	Mycenae Shaft Graves MIDDLE BRONZE AGE	MIDDLE BRONZE AGE	EARLY BRONZE AGE — Bronze	EARLY BRONZE AGE — Copper	EARLY BRONZE AGE — Bronze	WESSEX — Bronze ——Stonehenge——
2500	PYRAMIDS — EARLY	SARGON OF AGADE — EARLY	Phylakopi I Lerna (House of the Tiles) EARLY BRONZE AGE	EARLY BRONZE AGE — Bronze	LATE NEOLITHIC	TEMPLES	BEAKER — Copper	BEAKER — Copper — Silbury Hill
3000	DYNASTIC — Bronze — Hieroglyphs →	DYNASTIC — Bronze →	Bronze — Troy I — Copper		Los Millares	EARLY TEMPLES	LATE NEOLITHIC	HENGES
3500	Copper — PREDYNASTIC	PROTO-LITERATE — LATE	FINAL	FINAL	PASSAGE GRAVES — Copper	PROTO-TEMPLES	LATER — MEGALITHS	Newgrange MEGALITHS CAUSEWAYED CAMPS and
4000		URUK — EARLY URUK — Early writing	NEOLITHIC — Occasional Copper	NEOLITHIC	EARLY MEGALITHS – DOLMENS		MEGALITHS	LONG BARROWS
4500		Copper — LATE UBAID	Dhimini — MIDDLE	GUMELNITSA	EARLY NEOLITHIC		PASSAGE GRAVES — FIRST FARMERS	FIRST FARMERS
5000		EARLY UBAID — Occasional copper	NEOLITHIC	LATE VINČA — Copper and Proto-writing				

FIG. 22. Basic elements of the new chronology. (Contrast Fig. 8)

In Figure 8 a table was presented giving Childe's 1957 chronology for selected regions of Europe. The way such a table will look on the calibrated radiocarbon chronology is seen in Figure 22. The construction of such a table at present involves the recognition of a pattern among the dates, and the rejection of some of them as too young or too old. Admittedly, then, such a table still contains some subjective elements. But I believe that the outline is now a sound one, its validity depending only on that of the radiocarbon method as a whole.

A larger and more complicated table, which is inevitably unreliable in its details, was built up in 1969 using the dates then available. At that time the calibration only extended back to 3500 b.c. in radiocarbon years. Calibration has now become possible back to 4200 b.c. in radiocarbon years, and the table can be extended accordingly. Before this time, around 5000 B.C. in calendar years, the absolute dates remain a matter of guesswork. Several very exciting points emerge from such a table. For instance, megalithic tombs are seen throughout Atlantic Europe by around 3500 B.C. And metallurgy is seen in the Balkans before 4500 B.C. The temple cultures of Malta were under way by 3000 B.C., and had ended by around 2000 B.C. As we shall see in Chapter 8, they can have owed nothing to the Aegean late bronze age or the immediately preceding period which was supposed to have inspired them. Nor can the architect for Stonehenge have had any contact of any kind with the Mycenaean civilization. Even the wealth of Wessex and the technical skill of the European early bronze age must have been essentially independent of Aegean inspiration.

These are some of the products of the calibration. But they create more problems than they solve. It is much easier to dismiss the traditional explanations than to set up others in their place. If the 'barbarians' of prehistoric Europe did not learn of these things from the civilized Orient, how did they accomplish them? The new relationships and dates at first seem the end-products of a sophisticated process of reasoning, based both on stratigraphic archaeology and on geophysics. And so indeed they are. But in another sense they are starting points, setting out an entirely new pattern of the prehistoric past, which it is now the prehistorian's task to explain.

Radiocarbon dating has now replaced the traditional methods of dating with their very questionable assumptions. But a good objective chronology does not say *what* happened in the prehistoric past, only *when* it happened: it offers no explanations. We are left with an alarming void – with a mass of well-dated artifacts, monuments and cultures, yet with no connecting interpretation of how these things came about, and of how culture change took place.

That is the great challenge which the new situation presents: it forces us to go beyond the diffusionist notions of cultural contact, and to look at cultures and peoples in their own right, seeing the 'events' of European prehistory as the result of purely local processes, in essentially European terms.

This is exactly what the traditional diffusionist explanations refused to do. And today we can see how the traditional view did not merely get its dates wrong: the explanations it purported to give were to a large extent illusory as well. For the chess game of migrations, which pre-historians used to play with such enthusiasm, moving 'cultures' and 'peoples' from place to place, very rarely led to any very satisfying conclusion. The culture in the suggested 'homeland' of the migrating people often bears very little resemblance, in terms of the actual finds, to that of the people in the area under study whose origin the migration was supposed to explain.

This point applies with greater force when the explanation suggested is not an actual movement of a group of people but a diffusion of culture achieved through peaceful contact. As Childe himself justly remarked: 'Gratuitously to invoke migrations or "influences" from outside may be a mere cloak for laziness and has the effect of relegating to the wings all the action of prehistoric times.'[52]

Here is the crux of the matter. A statement of diffusion gives no insight into the actual processes of culture change which are involved. Neither the mechanism of contact nor the way this contact resulted in change of some kind are revealed by it. Perfectly cogent explanations can, of course, be justly based on the effects of contact between different societies, but they require elaboration and documentation. A mere statement of contact is not enough.

Seen in this way, the old argument between diffusion and independent invention appears a very sterile one, entirely missing the real issues. For a statement of diffusion asserts little more than that significant contact was taking place between two areas. Likewise an assertion of independent invention is a total non-explanation: of itself it states nothing more than that significant contact was *not* taking place. The old controversy need-lessly set into opposition two processes that really are in no way exclusive. In doing so, it often avoided a real explanation of either in persuasive human terms.

All this is not to say that diffusion – the transmission of innovation from one group to another – does not take place. For the ability to pass on ideas, and innovations and inventions, from one individual to another is what distinguishes human culture and differentiates human existence from that of all other animals. There are, indeed, numerous cases where the transmission of ideas and discoveries can be documented in detail, with altogether convincing proofs of contact. And some inventions, like that of the alphabet, really do seem unique. Joseph Needham, in the first volume of his *Science and Civilisation in China* (1961), where one of the principal fields of study is the extent of transmission of ideas between East and West, has stressed the importance of what the American anthropologist A. L. Kroeber called 'stimulus diffusion'. In stimulus diffusion, it is not the details or the full complexity and elaboration of a new product or new process which is transmitted, but rather the idea, the realization that such a process is possible, and some understanding of how to bring it about. In our own time, the explosion of the atomic bomb at Hiroshima by the Western allies made abundantly clear to all that such a device was workable. It was then only a matter of time before other nations such as Russia and China were able to develop the bomb – and this would have been so even if they had not benefited by 'secret' information, another kind of diffusion. Needham cites the case of a syllabic 'alphabet' invented for the north American Cherokee language in 1821 by a man who knew no English but was impressed by the advantages of writing. It was the idea which spread, and not the details of the writing system itself. Stimulus diffusion may be defined as a new growth pattern initiated by precedent in a foreign culture: the crux, in Kroeber's words, is the receipt of 'a stimulus towards an original but *induced* local invention'.[53]

Diffusion of this kind is not easy to recognize, since the innovation takes on new forms in its adopted culture which are very different from those in the parent or donor. The recipient culture may adopt some innovations readily because they fit into the culture system, performing a useful function without arousing the hostility with which many new-fangled ideas are received. Yet others may be rejected, seeming pointless or even harmful to the recipient system. In this way new ideas can 'suffer a sea change', ending up, indeed, as something very 'rich and strange' when compared with their original form.

It may seem desirable, therefore, to find some way of deciding, in individual cases documented in the archaeological record, whether the diffusion argument or the evolution argument is right, since both can be argued on theoretical grounds. The problem was very clearly posed by Francis Galton in 1889 in a critique of an important paper by the great anthropologist Edward Tylor. Tylor had introduced the idea of 'cross-cultural survey', where a study of different cultures all over the world showed that certain customs and practices regularly occur together. To the evolutionist this correlation is an exciting demonstration that different and independent cultures do indeed hit on the same inventions and similar customs wherever human society exists. But Galton pointed out that the correlations and associations revealed by Tylor's cross-cultural method might not, after all, be revealing similar workings of the human mind in different places, but simply the spread of ideas and complexes of ideas. Since then, the argument has raged in many areas between those preferring a 'historical' (i.e. diffusionist) explanation and those preferring an evolutionist (i.e. independent invention) explanation for specific inventions.

Two basic points have to be made. In the first place, it is sometimes possible to find incontrovertible proof of contact when it did occur. The discovery of Roman pottery and coins in India, for instance, brought with it some obvious and inescapable conclusions; certainly contacts of some kind had existed during the first century A.D. between India and Rome. Yet, even when contact between two regions did not in fact occur, it is logically impossible to prove the point. No conceivable find can ever show that contact did *not* take place. All that can be said is that the absence of evidence to the contrary makes the assumption tenable – which is not a very strong or conclusive statement. This being so, the onus of proof must always be on those arguing contact as a significant factor in initiating culture change.

However, the argument may not be particularly important. What matters is not to know whether some ingenious idea reached the society in question from outside, but rather to understand how it came to be accepted by that society, and what features of the economic and social organization there made the innovation so significant. To do this, we have to penetrate beyond simplistic and ultimately not very illuminating assertions of 'diffusion' and 'independent invention', and investigate the processes at work within the society itself. The old controversy between the diffusionists and the evolutionists has become irrelevant, and is not worth pursuing further. As we shall see, new approaches can offer a far more satisfactory solution.

Understanding culture change

For twenty years now, the sciences have been presenting archaeology with ingenious and powerful methods for investigating aspects of the prehistoric past. Already in the last century geology suggested the use of the stratigraphic method – the careful interpretation of the layers of deposit on a site – which still forms the essential basis of careful excavation. Botanists and zoologists worked on the identification of the plant and animal remains recovered, and petrologists on the stones and the definition of their natural sources. The analysis and metallographic examination of metal objects has for more than fifty years been revealing the details of prehistoric technology. Chemical analyses have offered great new possibilities in the study of early trade. In the past decade, statistics and computer technology have taught us to handle data more competently, and geographical techniques of locational analysis to understand and investigate the patterns revealed in the distribution of finds and of settlements.

Each advance of this kind rightly provokes a burst of enthusiasm, but sometimes excitement about the details of the method itself tends to obscure its actual usefulness. The strategy of research, the essential objective, is sometimes lost from sight amidst the distractions of tactics. The recent excitement in archaeology over the use of computers and numerical methods has in this way rather obscured some of the new opportunities now open to us. Naturally the new methods have first been used to tackle old problems, to construct new models for migrations and diffusion processes, and only then to work on the new problems now becoming apparent.

The chief new fields, I believe, are population studies, economic organization (including trade) and social organization. Their investigation becomes possible because of the successes in recent decades in two other fields: technology and subsistence. Prehistoric archaeology's first focus of interest was technology, for the old Three Age system, of stone, bronze and iron, was expressed in technological terms. Prehistorians like Gordon Childe worked hard to show that these divisions were related to economic stages. 'Neolithic' was seen to mean farming, 'bronze age' to imply the development of craft specialization, and 'iron age' that of more complex societies. Methods are now available which allow us to say a great deal about early technology, and there is little doubt that we understand the work of the prehistoric smiths, for example, somewhat better than they did themselves.

After the Second World War the interest shifted to the food supply and the way the food quest conditioned man's culture – the ecological approach. Grahame Clark's *Prehistoric Europe, the Economic Basis* (1952) offered a new dimension to our understanding of the life of hunting and early farming communities in central and northern Europe, and the work of Robert Braidwood and his successors in the Near East has given us a much fuller appreciation of one of man's greatest achievements, the invention of farming. It is now a matter of routine to use flotation techniques upon excavated soil to recover carbonized plant remains, and sieving or careful hand-collection to recover bones for specialist study. The reconstruction of prehistoric diet by these means is today a well-established, specialist task, and the relationship between a site and its environment a natural focus of study.

Increasingly, however, the interest of archaeologists is in more complex societies, for whom the food quest was only one of a number of pressing concerns. These societies had, so to speak, developed beyond the simple subsistence economy, and other economic interests occupied an increasing proportion of the time of a growing number of their members. Craft specialization became widespread, and there was a movement from part-time to full-time specialization. These developments depended only to a very limited extent on new subsistence techniques, and the new technologies were not the sole important new factors. The economic and social organization and their interrelations were at least as important. The whole question of trade and exchange, and their role in society — social as well as economic — becomes especially interesting.

Population. As we are now beginning to realize, many of these factors are related to the size and density of population. This has recently become of crucial relevance for the prehistorian. Previously, because of the very real difficulties involved in their estimation from the prehistoric material, they had been overlooked, or regarded as an ultimate level of speculation, the last details to be filled in rather hesitantly in the reconstruction of pre-historic societies.

The change has come about for several reasons. Firstly, the increasing interest in settlement studies has led archaeologists to pay more attention to the size and the concentration of individual settlements, so that estimates of the population of single villages are more common. The increase in archaeological site survey, often helped by aerial photography and the application of more sophisticated geographical methods for analysing the data, has made it possible to give rough estimates, albeit highly approximate, for the population of a given region at different points in time (cf. Fig. 45).

Secondly the whole trend of work on primitive agriculture has been to indicate that population is not merely something determined by the environment and the way it is exploited. On the contrary, it is often population pressure which leads to agricultural change, as Esther Boserup showed in her book *The Conditions of Agricultural Growth* (1965). In most areas it is possible to develop more intensive methods of agriculture, which allow more food to be extracted from a given area of land. But it turns out that this is only possible with more intensive work for the individual: to get more food from the same land means more work for each daily ration of food which that land produces. Without the pressure of population, of more mouths to feed, there would be no incentive to work harder just to produce a little extra food. It is often the increased population density which is ultimately responsible for the changing agricultural pattern, or so Boserup argues.

The idea that population growth itself is a major causal factor in many prehistoric changes is of great interest to the archaeologist. For, given a tendency for population to increase in many societies unless held in check by limited food or by social factors, we can begin to see how the whole sequence of agricultural changes in the past may have come about.

As the population density increases, food production has obviously to become more efficient in terms of produce per unit area. This implies more intensive agriculture, generally with a greater input of work per head, and sometimes the development of specialization -- some areas are more suited to one crop, some to another. Any regional ecological diversity will make exchange desirable, hence favouring social systems which promote efficient exchange, sometimes through a redistributive system. We can see, therefore, how a consideration of population is relevant to the whole question of economic organization.

Moreover, increasing population, and larger residence groups, imply also some purely social problems. The anthropologist Anthony Forge has suggested that the upper size limit for a neolithic egalitarian society may generally be of the order of 400 to 500 persons. If the population increases beyond this figure, the problem can sometimes be solved by the budding off of some members to form a new society, otherwise new forms of social classification in the society may become necessary. These can include both classification by occupation, and classification by ascription of status in some hierarchical scheme. Such developments are likely to occur, it is suggested, since 'Homo sapiens can only handle a certain maximum number of intense face-to-face relationships, successfully distinguishing between each.'[54] Here, then, we gain a first insight as to why an increasing population in a restricted region may favour further social differentiation, and a society where men may be classed in terms of role, occupation and status.

In other words, when the social or settlement unit develops beyond a certain size, new forms of social organization become necessary to hold it together and keep it functioning. Different societies find different solutions, but often they include the development of a hierarchical structure and the increased importance of the head man or chief. The consideration of population thus becomes of fundamental importance to the study of early societies, even if the estimation of actual population figures is still, to an infuriating extent, as much a matter of guesswork as of satisfying argument.

Economic organization and exchange. We are beginning to see also that what distinguishes the simplest farming villages of the neolithic from the more complex societies which followed them was not so much their food-production technique, nor indeed the population density alone, as the economic and social organization which came with them. It is only recently that archaeologists have moved beyond specific and often rather superficial ethnographic parallels to consider economic organization in more general terms. In the idealized, simple neolithic village each family may be entirely self-sufficient, producing for itself all the food it needs, making and firing its own pottery, weaving its own textiles, grinding and chipping its own stone tools. One of the key features of larger and more complex societies is that these activities are carried out by specialists. A crucial point in their organization is therefore the manner in which goods are exchanged, for without exchange of some kind, craft specialization is impossible.

Many primitive societies manage entirely without a market, or exchange rates or commercial trade at all. The exchange of gifts among friends, on a *reciprocal* basis, although primarily a means of reinforcing friendship and hence largely a social transaction, does have the effect of allowing the circulation of special goods from hand to hand. Stone axes were exchanged in this way among the aborigines of northern Australia, and perhaps in Europe in prehistoric times. The prehistoric 'trade' in shell bracelets from the Aegean into the Balkans may have been some sort of reciprocal exchange. The distribution of finds suggests that it may to some extent have resembled the ceremonial gift exchanges such as that of the Trobriand Islanders of the western Pacific, observed in recent times.

In some societies, as the chief or head man becomes more important, he acts as a centre for a further kind of circulation termed *redistribution*, in which as chief he receives a tithe of produce from all groups in the community, and redistributes some of this within the community. This has the important function of making possible craft specialization without the existence of markets or even sometimes of any commercial transaction at all. The economist Karl Polanyi has shown how important this system was in a number of early societies, and as we shall see in Chapter 10, it formed the economic basis for the first civilization of Europe.

Armed with this theoretical approach, relating economic and social organization, we begin to see much of prehistory in a new light, and a good deal that has been written about it now seems implausible – for instance, in its assumption of a market economy. Only eight years ago, one archaeologist was able to write about the great early neolithic site of Jericho: 'It is, however, most unlikely that agriculture should have flourished more at Jericho, 200 metres below sea level, than elsewhere in Palestine. Some other source of revenue must have existed, and this was probably trade. Jericho was well situated for commercial enterprise: It commanded the resources of the Dead Sea, salt, bitumen and sulphur, all useful products in early societies ... Had the workshops or warehouses been discovered, many other materials might have been added.'[55] This is, it seems, simply a projection of a modern mercantile society, with its commerce and its warehouses, on an early prehistoric community with a very different economic basis. Of course, our verdict must come from the evidence, not from *a priori* concepts of reciprocity or redistribution, but the fact is that we have no evidence for *commercial* trade anywhere until much later – no hoards of manufactured goods, no large specialist workshops or evidence of accounting. An altogether different economic organization has to be suggested.

We must hope to trace, in successive prehistoric societies, the development of exchange systems which gradually made possible an increasing degree of interdependence and of specialization. This we can indeed do in the Aegean, although commercial trade did not develop until the second millennium B.C. and markets a thousand years later. In central and northern Europe, too, we shall have to examine the evidence afresh in order to learn to what extent the developing metal industry of the bronze age depended on a system of redistribution, and just when a purely commercial trade, without complicated social ties, got under way.

Social organization. It is, above all, in the field of social organization that we should be seeking explanations for the changes and developments observed. For quite clearly, some of the communities producing impressive monuments, such as some of the megalithic tombs or even the temples of

Malta, did not have any very elaborate economic organization. There may have been redistribution, although there is little evidence of it yet, but craft specialization was not yet highly developed. Since the old idea of contacts with the advanced societies of the Near East (which *did*, of course, have a developed redistributive system and social hierarchy) must be discarded in the light of the new dating, we have to consider what kind of social organization could have led to the building of such monuments in rather small communities with a relatively undifferentiated economy. This leads us to consider the extent to which these early societies embodied a social hierarchy, and the degree to which the leaders were able to mobilize manpower and resources. Much of what can be written today is speculative, but it is also plausible, and more evidence, when it is available, will put its validity to the test.

These, then, are some of the approaches which must be used to build a new and worthwhile picture of European prehistory from the rubble of the conventional, diffusionist structure. This task cannot be achieved overnight, but the prospects look good, and the ultimate picture should be a persuasive and convincing one. All the different features of a culture – population, subsistence, technology, economy, social organization and so forth – are inextricably linked, and to attempt an explanation in terms of one need not imply a rejection of the others. We can see, for instance, how an increasing population may ultimately make necessary the greater efficiency of craft specialization, coupled with an effective redistribution system. Such redistribution can most effectively be conducted – although other mechanisms are possible – if there is a strong and powerful central organization, which generally implies a definite social hierarchy. The patronage of top men, and their competition for prestige, can, in the right conditions, favour technological innovation and advance. We can begin to see how, at suitable places and times, the entire cultural system may grow and develop, in all its different fields or sub-systems.

The succeeding chapters are a first attempt to account for some of the more impressive achievements of prehistoric Europe by thinking about the society and the economy, and deliberately assuming a minimum of outside influence. They take in turn the major episodes very much as formerly they were outlined in the diffusionist prehistory: the 'coming' of farming, the 'arrival' of the megalith builders, Aegean 'influences' on the west Mediterranean during the later neolithic period, the 'arrival' of metallurgy in south-east Europe and the beginnings of Vinča, the 'transmission' of civilization in the Aegean, and the 'spread' of Mycenaean influence to Britain and Europe. Each of these 'events' (with the exception of the first), supposedly brought about by contacts with 'higher' cultures in the Orient, may be seen instead as the result of essentially local processes. And while farming in Europe depended largely on Near Eastern plants and animals, the manner of its adoption and the new way of life were themselves characteristically European.

These explanations have yet to be formulated in full and convincing detail: indeed, it will be decades before we have a really persuasive prehistory of Europe that carries the same conviction, with a comparable analysis at a detailed level, as the old diffusionist picture once did. This, however, is the programme of research for the immediate future, upon which prehistorians are now embarking. It is exciting to speculate, just now, when the past is changing so fast, exactly what form their explanations will take.

Some of the suggestions and conclusions of the succeeding chapters may be modified by further work; a few could turn out to be plain wrong. But at last 'barbarian' Europe emerges as a society or group of societies where striking developments and changes were taking place all the time, where ingenious technological discoveries were accompanied by, and perhaps related to, fundamental social changes. And I have no doubt that it is in terms of social and economic processes that the new prehistory of Europe must be written.

7 The Enigma of the Megaliths

Suddenly and decisively the impressive megalithic tombs of western Europe are set earlier than any comparable monuments in the world. There are no stone-built monuments anywhere approaching them in antiquity. Perhaps even more remarkable, some of these underground burial chambers, with their roofs of stone, are preserved entire, so that we can enter them and stand inside a stone chamber which looks today just as it did more than 5,000 years ago. Some of them, like the great chamber of Maeshowe in Orkney, or the Cueva del Romeral at Antequera in Spain, with its long entrance passage, seize the imagination by the force of their design and the skill in its execution. This is not merely building: it is architecture, however that term be defined – even though it is architecture 3,000 years before the introduction of writing to western Europe.

No wonder, then, that these monuments have, for generations, been a source of amazement. For a while the diffusionist explanation succeeded in making them more intelligible: the skill reflected in their construction, and the impetus to invest so much effort in stone monuments, was seen to have come from the east, from more civilized lands. The comparative poverty of the material culture of their builders was thus made to seem less extraordinary when contrasted with the monuments themselves. Now the paradox is with us again: that such impressive monuments were created many centuries before the Pyramids by barbarians who lacked even the use of metal. The urgent task confronting us is to explain just how these monuments did come to be built, if it was not by colonists from the early civilizations of the Near East.

The megalithic tombs are found predominantly in the lands bordering the Atlantic and the North Sea – in Spain, Portugal, France, Britain, Ireland, Holland, Germany, Denmark and Sweden (Fig. 25). They do not occur in central, east or south-east Europe, or – apart from a few in

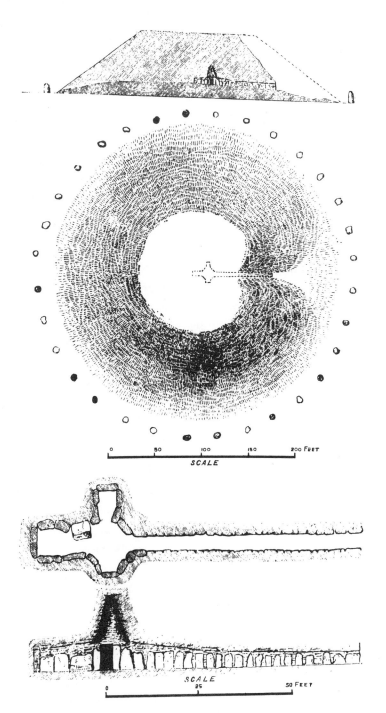

FIG. 23. Newgrange, one of the most notable of the Irish passage graves, as illustrated by Fergusson in 1872.

Palestine – in the east Mediterranean. In the west Mediterranean, except for Spain and France, they are not widely found, and those in south Italy and the Balearic islands are of later date.

All the tombs have certain things in common, despite great variations in their plan and construction, and in the mounds of earth or stone with which they are covered. They are stone-built, often of very large stones, as the term 'megalithic' itself implies (Greek: *megas* – big; *lithos* – stone). They were used for collective burial, for a considerable number of internments on successive occasions. And the grave goods accompanying the burials were generally unimpressive – a few pots, a stone axe, a flint blade or two. In almost every area of Europe where they are found, the tombs were built long before metallurgy was practised, although later burials sometimes contain copper daggers or ornaments. In general, then, the megalithic tombs of western Europe are neolithic.

At this point it is useful to distinguish between these tombs and the other monuments which are of 'megalithic' construction, like the temples of Malta, the great stone alignments of Brittany and indeed the stone circles of Britain (including Stonehenge). The size of the stones used does make these monuments similar in some ways to the tombs, but their function and indeed their appearance are quite different, so that the two groups should be discussed quite separately.

This is not the place to describe the tombs in detail, but two of the most typical forms distinguished by Glyn Daniel can be mentioned: the passage grave and the gallery grave. Passage graves (Fig. 23) have a central stone-built chamber, generally set in the middle of a circular mound or tumulus. It is entered by a narrow stone-built passage which is sometimes very long – in Spain there are tombs with passages up to thirty metres long. The classic megalithic passage grave is built of great slabs of stone, the upright slabs of the passage (the orthostats) being covered by horizontal slabs to make the roof. The burial chamber itself, of larger slabs, is wider and higher.

Quite often the walls of the passage are built up of smaller stones lying flat, in drystone-walling technique. And in a number of regions, from the Orkney Isles, off the north coast of Scotland, right down to south Spain, passage graves are found with corbelled roofs. In such tombs, drystone technique is used to roof the central burial chamber, each stone being laid flat to overhang the one beneath it so that as the false vault gets higher

the walls approach each other until they are close enough to be surmounted by a single capstone. This is not the same technique as the arch
or true vault, since all the stones are laid horizontally. These corbelled
passage graves are among the most impressive of all the collective
chambered tombs, although speaking strictly they are not 'megalithic'
at all if they do not employ large stones. But of course they belong
together with the megaliths proper.

Gallery graves do not show a differentiation between the narrow
entrance passage and the wider burial chamber. The single rectangular
space is entered directly at its full width, and often the surmounting
mound is rectangular rather than round (Fig. 24). The finest examples are
found in Denmark and France (Pl. 2).

Of course, not all megalithic tombs are imposing structures of the two
types just described. There is a whole range of forms, and many are just
simple 'dolmens' – three or four large stones supporting a heavy capstone
(Fig. 2). Indeed the very variety of forms has always made the systematic
classification of the tombs difficult, so that although a broadly diffusionist
explanation was accepted until recently, there has never been a single
agreed explanation for the full range of the monuments.

The earliest dates for the tombs so far come from Brittany: a coherent
picture emerges of chamber tombs being built before 4000 B.C. in calendar
years. Britain and Denmark both had tombs of stone before 3000 B.C.
Yet the early stone Pyramids of Egypt still lie around 2700 B.C. It is true
that recent work shows them to have had predecessors in mud brick, and
we know as yet all too little about Predynastic architecture in Egypt.
But so far we have nothing of stone in Egypt before 3000 B.C. that is
remotely comparable with the early megaliths of the west. Childe's
diffusionist explanation, which as we have seen brought the tombs
west to Spain and then up the Atlantic coast, made the attractive proposal
that they were the work of 'megalithic missionaries'. He wrote:

> The course of prehistory in the British Isles was profoundly modified
> by a religious movement which affected all the coasts of the Mediter-
> ranean, the Atlantic and even the Baltic ... Strict agreements in
> arbitrary details of funerary architecture over large tracts of Mediter-
> ranean and Atlantic Europe are as good evidence for a megalithic
> religion as are mosques for Mohammedanism. The distribution

of tombs, predominantly along the coasts and radiating from coastal ports, indicates the channels of the religion's propagation and the area of its domain.[56]

But we are no longer obliged to see the tombs as the result of a single movement, whether it originated in Iberia or in Brittany (as one could now argue, on the basis of the new dates). Instead our task is to create some social model, some simple picture of how it all came about. We have to ask how the tombs in a specific area could have been built, and what sort of society was responsible. Perhaps the tombs did develop in one place, and then spread by some mechanism yet to be understood; but

FIG. 24. Plan of a large gallery grave: Essé in Brittany. (*After Daniel*)

O   5
METRES

it is just as likely that there were separate and essentially independent developments in several different areas.

Local developments

The first step in building up a new picture is to look again at the distribution and dating of the tombs. Simple typological and chronological arguments at least offer us some clear regional divisions.

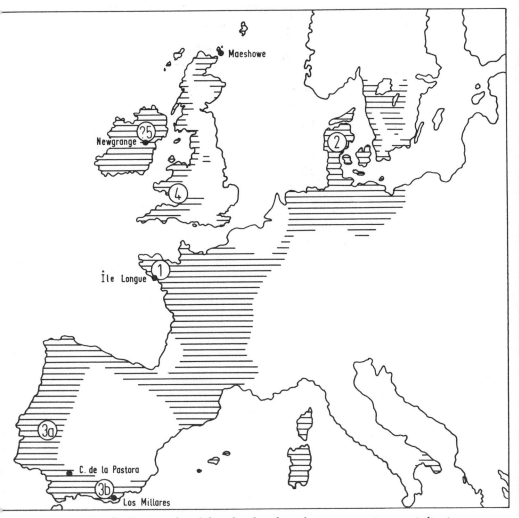

FIG. 25. The distribution of neolithic chambered tombs in western Europe, indicating the four or five regions where such monuments may have developed independently.

At first sight the tombs do suggest an almost continuous distribution along the Atlantic coasts from Denmark to south Spain (Fig. 25). This does not extend down into central Europe, the territory of the early Danubian farmers and their descendants; but it does occupy all France and Spain. Yet if we imply that there is or was a 'megalithic province' we fall into a simple diffusionist trap. For there is no unity whatever in the prehistoric cultures of these different lands. Even setting aside the Mediterranean islands – as the diffusionists themselves were content to do, since the monuments there are so different – the finds in the remaining lands where megalithic tombs occur have very little in common. They are all neolithic, of course, since the first megaliths in each region were built before copper was worked there; they thus contain only pottery, stone and bone. But that is an entirely superficial resemblance, since there is nothing else they could have contained before the use of metal. To define a 'megalithic province' risks removing the tombs from their parent cultures and the communities which built them and used them. It involves a circularity inherent in many diffusionist arguments, where features in different cultures, often widely distributed in space and time, are selected for comparison because they do show similarities. It is then held to be significant that the features thus selected are indeed so similar. In reality, however, much of the force of this argument comes from the exclusion of the other evidence which could suggest very different conclusions.

With the aid of radiocarbon dates and of typological study within different areas, we are beginning to see instead a number of separate regions where the custom of collective burial in built stone tombs seems to have developed individually in its own unique way, and where it may have originated independently.

In Denmark it has long been realized that the earliest stone graves were long dolmens (*langdysser*), often just open rectangular settings of stones containing one or more enclosed chambers of large stones (Fig. 26) which could not be entered once the mound was erected. Montelius himself thought them an idea originating locally, although others have sought to derive them from the south and east. Later, by 3000 B.C. in calendar years, the prehistoric Danes developed this simple form into a rectangular chamber beneath a mound, naturally entered through a short passage. Montelius believed this advance to have been inspired ultimately from the east Mediterranean. But today an entirely local development appears possible, and a passage seems the inevitable functional component of a tomb whose central chamber lies beneath a mound. The new dating does, however, leave open the possibility that the innovation reached Scandinavia from Brittany.

In south Britain it has become clear that the early farmers did not at first build stone tombs at all. Indeed, the Oxford prehistorian Humphrey Case has rightly pointed out that the farming settlers, coming across the channel in their animal-skin boats, might not at first have built monumental tombs even if this were part of their parent culture. Soon, though, we see earthen long barrows without any chamber of stone. A whole series of elegant excavations has, however, shown that many of these were not originally 'unchambered': they often contained a wooden mortuary chamber, now completely destroyed, located at one end of the mound.

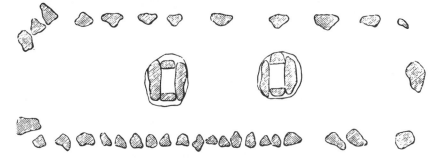

FIG. 26. View and plan of a long dolmen at Valdbygaards, Denmark, as illustrated by Fergusson in 1872.

The first stone-built tombs in south Britain, such as West Kennet or Nympsfield, follow this plan in a very striking way. They too are in long mounds, with a single chamber at one end. They are not 'gallery graves', but the realization in stone of the wooden mortuary chamber of the earthen long barrow. They may thus be regarded, not as the reflection of some partly digested idea from the south, but as an entirely local adaptation – though the earthen long barrow itself was perhaps a local version of what may have been a widespread idea in north Europe.

A third region with its own local evolution of collective burial in built tombs is Brittany. The details of the development are far from clear, but the very early radiocarbon dates set its independence beyond reasonable doubt. Already by 4000 B.C. in calendar years, we see splendid tombs with corbelled chambers in drystone technique, such as the one at Île Longue (Figs. 5 and 28). The uprights of the passage with their lintels, as well as some in the main chamber, are large stones in the megalithic manner. And here in Brittany, for the first time in Europe, or indeed in the world, we meet the corbelled vault, or *tholos* as it is known in Greece, where the same technique was later used for the great Mycenaean tombs around 1500 B.C. (Fig. 5).

The range of grave forms in Brittany is very striking. Among these are 'allées couvertes' (i.e. gallery graves) of truly monumental proportions – the example at Essé is twenty metres long, five metres wide and two metres high (Pl. 2 and Fig. 24); there are also many curious variant forms. It is clear now that the evolution was largely local, although this would not exclude contacts and the exchange of ideas with nearby areas, such as northern Iberia or Ireland.

In Iberia, just as in Britain and Denmark, there seem to be simple early forms which evolve gradually into more complex structures. In the south-east, in the Almeria region, simple stone-built round tombs are found which seem to precede the more impressive passage graves at sites, such as Los Millares, in the same area. And in the west, in Portugal, there are many simple dolmens, with just a few upright boulders surmounted by a capstone, which may be the predecessors of the megalithic passage graves of Atlantic Spain and Portugal.

We have very few radiocarbon dates yet for Iberia, and it is not yet possible to disprove the old view that the simple tombs are merely degenerate and late copies of the large sophisticated ones. Yet we do have enough dates to show that the latter were in use before 3000 B.C., which seems to rule out the idea of an origin in the east. The possibility that they were inspired from Brittany to the north cannot yet be excluded, but the evidence of early and simple local prototypes, provided by the Portuguese dolmens and the Almerian round graves, already provides a sufficient basis for a theory of local evolution.

All this suggests that we have in western Europe at least four potentially independent developments of collective burial in stone tombs: in Denmark, in south Britain, in Brittany and in Iberia. Moreover such developments may have proceeded in other areas also, and quite independently. One such possibility is Ireland, where a different tomb type is seen. This is the 'court cairn', with a central unroofed court from which a burial chamber opens, which is subdivided into segments by upright slabs. It is not yet clear whether the earliest neolithic settlers in Ireland began almost at once to bury their dead in stone tombs – in which case the idea at least may have been brought from Brittany – or if this was a local development taking several centuries.

In all these separate regions, more impressive constructions with passages leading to burial chambers set in a mound developed out of simple prototypes. In just a few cases, in south Britain for instance, wood was used as a building material, but generally the permanence of stone made it more suitable.

In each area craftsmen were faced with similar technological problems, if they wished to construct a chamber set beneath a mound which could be entered on successive occasions for the burial of the dead. In regions where the stone was naturally massive, and difficult to split or trim without metal tools, the result was true megalithic construction. This was the natural response to a specific problem, and it is difficult to see how else the task could have been accomplished.

Given enough labour and some tough ropes of hide, the erection of these giant stones was not as difficult as it might at first seem. Modern experiments by Professor Richard Atkinson, who was particularly interested in the construction of Stonehenge, suggests that 600 or 700 men were needed, all tugging on hide ropes, to shift a stone of 35 tons. About eighty men would be required for a five-ton stone. As he points out, the upright stones would be set in position using a crib of timbers or of smaller stones. A hole was first dug to take the lower part of the stone, and the end of the latter positioned over it in readiness. The crib would gradually be built up beneath the outer (top) end of the stone to provide support for the levels by which it was gradually raised (Fig. 27).

In considering the roofing of the megalithic chamber tombs with huge lintel slabs, one cannot do better than quote Atkinson directly:

> The raising of the capstones of chambered tombs presents few difficulties if it is assumed that the mound surrounding the chamber was first built up to the level of the tops of its walls, to provide a sloping ramp up which the capstones could be hauled and levered, resting on rollers. The main necessity would be the very careful strutting of the chamber walls to resist lateral pressure; and indeed it seems probable that the interior of the chamber was packed solid,

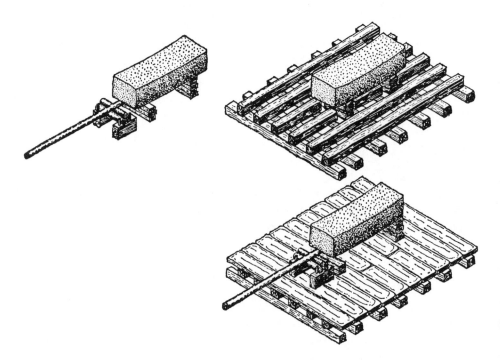

FIG. 27. Three stages in the raising of a megalithic lintel by means of a crib (*after R. J. C. Atkinson*). The lintel is raised by lever while wooden packing is wedged beneath. A platform of alternate layers of parallel timbers is then built beneath and around it, and the lintel again raised and the process repeated.

either with rammed earth or with lengths of timber wedged in place, the packing being removed, not perhaps without some trepidation, only after the capstones were all in place.[57]

Atkinson has calculated that the impressive capstone of the burial chamber at Tinkinswood in Glamorgan weighs approximately fifty tons, and that at least 200 people were needed to get it into position. Feats such as these are impressive both for the skill and for the manpower required, but there is no reason to think they were beyond the competence of neolithic communities. Indeed we now know that the prehistoric inhabitants of western Europe were the first in the world to solve the problems of shifting and erecting large stones in this way.

In other areas, where the stone splits easily into conveniently small flat slabs, the tombs are of drystone construction rather than truly megalithic, and they have a corbelled drystone vault. In such areas, a cairn of the readily available stones is often seen in place of a surrounding

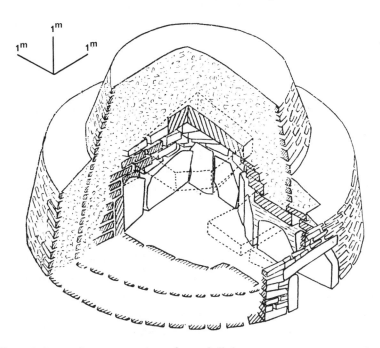

FIG. 28. Isometric reconstruction of a corbelled passage grave at Er-Mané, Carnac in Brittany, showing details of construction (*after L'Helgouach*). Note the corbelled vault.

earth mound. So it is that when we look at Île Longue in Brittany, or the Cueva de la Pastora in Spain, or Newgrange in Ireland (Fig. 23), or Maeshowe in Orkney, we see monuments that are to us closely similar (Fig. 28).

In fact, the builders of these corbelled tombs in different areas were using the only technique available to them in the absence of large stones. And in each area, one can distinguish local peculiarities that suggest local origins for the tombs: in Spain, the corbelling tends to be neatly circular, since the stones are small; while in Orkney, with its large flagstones that break so neatly in straight lines, the tombs tend to have rectangular vaults, with corners and straight edges.

In purely constructional terms, therefore, the neolithic chambered tombs of each region – whether true megaliths or of drystone con-struction – are best seen as purely local developments, local adaptations, in response to similar social demands. But we still have to ask how these early communities were able to mobilize the manpower needed for such impressive monuments.

The social context

Is it really possible that tombs like these were the unaided work of simple neolithic societies at so early a date? In most cases we have regret-tably little evidence for the settlements of the farmers who built them. Indeed it is conceivable that in some regions there was no single permanent settlement at all, and that swidden agriculture was practised: that is, the village would remain in one place for a dozen or so years and then, as the land nearby became exhausted, move on to fresh fields in the same region. The tombs might be the only element of permanence in the shifting existence.

The only way open to us of reconstructing something of the societies of the tomb builders is to take one or two specific cases, where the loca-tions of the tombs and the relationships between them are particularly revealing. In some cases we can learn much of the size and nature of the communities by thinking about these factors in relation to land use. Two regions of particular interest are Arran and Rousay, since they possess a fairly dense concentration of tombs, and it is likely that few if any have been destroyed. In studying them, we may get as close an

FIG. 29. Map of Arran, Scotland, showing the distribution of megalithic tombs in relation to modern farming land (stippled). Hypothetical territories are demarcated by straight lines. (Contours at approximately 100-metre intervals)

approximation to the original settlement pattern as we are likely to find anywhere.

The island of Arran in west Scotland preserves eighteen tombs, of rather modest construction, set in mounds up to forty metres long. Being an island, Arran makes a convenient geographical unit for study, and because the farming there has never been very intensive, most, if not all of the original tombs have been preserved. Figure 29 shows their distribution superimposed on the land recently used for agriculture, which may represent the effective arable land of neolithic times also. Gordon Childe observed long ago that the megalithic tombs of Scotland lie near such land, and in fact seventeen of the eighteen tombs in Arran are within 500 metres of land probably suitable for agriculture in the neolithic period.

The tombs are fairly regularly spaced, with the exception of one adjacent pair, and this encourages us to think in terms of about sixteen or seventeen roughly equal *territories* based upon this arable land, each territory being served by one tomb. This is a crucial point – although it looks deceptively simple – for we are moving at this stage from a purely geographical observation – the distribution of the tombs – to a social one, about the territories occupied by communities. Yet if the tombs do show some indications of regular or even spacing, this implies that the existence of one tomb inhibited the construction of others very close to it. The easiest explanation, although perhaps not the only possible one, is that the nearby land was occupied by a single farming community. In the absence of actual settlement finds, we do not know whether this would have been based on a permanent village or if the village would change location in the process of shifting agriculture.

The latter indeed seems the most likely, in view of our knowledge of the first farmers of the Danube area. In such a case, if the village was shifting every ten or fifteen years, always within its own territory, the tomb would represent one of the few permanent elements in the community's existence. This argument already begins to set the monuments in a new light: it suggests that they had a very special significance. For each community, the monument was not just the ancestral tomb but an enduring symbol of the continuity of its occupation of the land.

It is essential at this point to think in terms of population density. The population of Arran in A.D. 1755, well before modern farming techniques were introduced, is recorded as 3,650 persons. This, no doubt, is greater than the neolithic population, especially if shifting cultivation were then practised, perhaps without the use of the plough.

To obtain a rough estimate, we can use modern ethnographic parallels in Africa, collected by W. Allan, to suggest that each person could be fed from the produce of one acre of land in favourable conditions. Allowing a fallow period of between two and twenty years, we must therefore think in terms of two to twenty acres of effective arable land per head. Using this figure for the arable land in Arran sixty years ago, we can expect a prehistoric population of between 600 and 1,200 persons (if very low densities are excluded in view of the good potential for grazing animals on other land nearby).

For the sake of simplicity we can divide this population up equally between the seventeen territories, each served by one tomb, giving between 35 and 70 people living in each territory. On the basis of the argument set out above, this would appear to be close to a maximum estimate, and if the arable land were not exploited to its full potential we could reduce these estimates by a factor of five or ten. Then we would have each territory, served by one tomb, occupied by a single farming family of up to about ten persons. The territories would then be the equivalent of the crofts of recent times.

These quite small figures for the prehistoric population of the territories, however approximate, do inject an element of realism into the discussion, and make us very cautious of thinking in terms of a 'megalithic civilization'.

Rousay, one of the Orkney islands, with thirteen tombs constructed in drystone-walling technique, offers, like Arran, a suitable area for study. Thirty years ago, Gordon Childe published a map of the tombs, commenting upon their distribution in relation to modern farms. The correlation between the two is made clearer if one takes into account the geology of Rousay, since the modern arable land is in every case on glacial deposits. The map shows the relation of the tombs to these deposits (Fig. 30). Once again we may regard each tomb as defining a prominent point of a territory, and it is indeed striking that these territories, on the arable land, show an analogous distribution to the crofts and farming settlements of the last century.

Using similar arguments as for Arran, we obtain a population in neolithic times between 300 and 650 persons – not very much smaller than the eighteenth-century figure of 770. Again the prehistoric population could have been much less; it is unlikely to have been more.

In this case, the tombs are of very varied size and clearly some of the communities which they served were bigger than others. However, division of the population (300 to 650) by the number of territories established (13) may give an average population of between 25 and 50 persons per territory. This figure is of the same order as that reached for Arran, and, although approximate, may serve as a good basis for discussion.

Once again, it is assumed that the tombs were in use at the same time – and again the spacing supports this assumption. A difficulty is that in

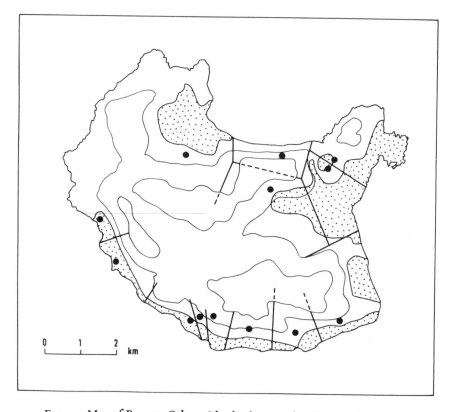

FIG. 30. Map of Rousay, Orkney Islands, showing distribution of chambered tombs in relation to modern arable land (stippled), with hypothetical territorial boundaries. (Contours at approximately 100-metre intervals)

most cases only a few skeletons were found in these tombs when they were excavated, but in all probability the disarticulated bones of long-forgotten ancestors were cleared out when fresh burials took place.

These estimates of population are useful in setting some limits on the kind of social organization involved. If the population of individual territories was as low as 25 or 50 persons, we cannot possibly think in terms of groups with a very large number of different ranks or statuses, or of territorial chiefs. Each territory must surely have been occupied by an extended family or lineage, all its inhabitants tracing their descent, or that of their spouse, back to a common ancestor. Modern ethnographic parallels suggest a tribal organization, and it is possible that each Orcadian island supported a single tribe or a segment of a tribe.

There is no evidence in the Orkneys, or indeed in Arran, that any one territorial area was of paramount importance—unless one wishes to single out the great tomb Maeshowe on the Mainland of Orkney, with its two adjacent henge monuments, the Ring of Brodgar and the Stones of Stenness. We are led to think, then, in terms of a straightforward and fairly egalitarian tribal organization; and the extreme paucity of the finds in these tombs certainly does not contradict this view. We are not, of course, entitled to apply this notion at once to the megaliths of western Europe in general, but in a number of regions—in Britain, Scandinavia and France especially—the suggestion does seem appropriate.

We are now beginning, without having to exercise our imaginations unduly, to obtain a fresh and revealing idea of the scale of things. Each of these tombs evidently needed considerable labour, even if some were built in several stages. Midhowe, the biggest of the Rousay cairns, is over thirty metres long. This is rather shorter than the earthen long barrow at Fussell's Lodge in Wiltshire, which its excavator Paul Ashbee has estimated to represent 5,000 man hours of work. Midhowe may represent more work than this, and indeed some estimates would put the figure much higher, but we might use this figure as an order of magnitude. It does not follow, of course, that these monuments were completed during one single project, even if that lasted several years. Increasingly, evidence is being found for several phases of construction in collective tombs, and the final monument may represent the accretion of the work of several generations.

If the twenty or so able-bodied inhabitants of a territory set about building such a monument, it would take this task force over thirty man days. Such an investment of labour could probably be made over the course of a year or two, at times when there was little farming activity.

At this point it is illuminating to look at some modern, non-industrial communities in other parts of the world: these suggest some further possibilities. What is particularly suggestive in the present context is the picture these communities give of the potential availability of neighbouring groups – whether lineages or whole tribes – to join in the construction work. All of them imply some social framework where such co-operation is possible. And often the motivation for the construction is less religious than social, the desire for an impressive monument which will reflect credit on the community as a whole and not simply on the dead man. In this sense, impressive funerary monuments are often designed for the living rather than the dead.

Indeed, if there is suitable incentive, co-operative effort can work to build impressive monuments even for single individuals. The Kelabits of north Borneo have a living 'megalithic' tradition, where imposing monuments of large stone are erected as memorials or tombs, generally to a single man. One of these, erected in 1959, was built by an old, heirless man by the usual expedient of inviting his neighbours to a great feast, in return for which they willingly lent their services. Tom Harrisson records the graphic statement of the old man in question:

> The whole of the perishable rest (of my belongings), salt, rice, pigs, buffalo as well as many other things to purchase, like tobacco, betel nut, eels, and labour, I will expend with due notice at a mighty feast after the next rice harvest. I am in a position to give a very big feast. Hundreds of people will come, including my relatives over in the Kerayan and Bawang to the east and as far as Pa Tik beyond Kubaan to the west. It will be a splendid amusement, splendid exchange.
>
> On the last day I will declare my monument. All my imperishable property is to be collected in a heap on the ground over there, a dart's flight from the long-house ladder. Every man present will come out when it has stopped raining and form a line from the fine old dragon jar in the centre of the slope down to the single bank of the stream bed. Along this living chain, from hand to

hand, should pass first the small surface stones and gradually as the work goes down, larger stones and then boulders. All this will travel from the river bed up to bank on to the little knoll above flood level, slowly shaping a pile of stone. Presently this will grow into a mound higher than the long-house is off the ground, and twice the width anyone can leap. All mine.

Thus will my belongings be secured forever. Thus my own memory will stand to eternity. It will be larger than any ordinary man's can be, because so many come to my feast and are so well entertained – since I have nothing to keep and pass on, I will spend the lot in one great final display; and in consequence make a mighty effort to do well by me, piling rock upon boulder upon pebble upon stone.[58]

This splendid description cannot, of course, be compared in its details with the collective burial monuments of Europe, yet it does reflect two general points which may well be applicable. In the first place there is the importance of the social occasion, the feast, at which the actual construction of the tomb is only one among a number of memorable events. And secondly there is this passionate concern for status – whether personal, or of the family or group – which can be enhanced by the display and the conspicuous consumption of wealth. Families and tribes will invest considerable labour in accumulating the food resources and the other 'capital' needed to hold such a feast and impress neighbouring groups.

Another example, from a different tribe in Borneo, is reported by Tom Harrisson and Stanley O'Connor; this time it concerns the erection of impressive standing stones or 'menhirs'. These were brought from far away and erected as a proof of rich and powerful status, as a memorial to bravery, or to mark the grave of a person:

As the stones were collected from a distant place, those bringing the stones were likely to meet with all sorts of enemies. Head-hunting at that time was frequent. To erect a stone would therefore need a strong force. A great gang of people was needed to meet these dangers and to transport the stone to the erecting spot. Only big stones were used by powerful families. It involved three to four days to get a stone to its destination. The ceremonies were almost the same whatever the reason for erecting the stone. One buffalo a day was killed for bravery; and one buffalo and one pig a day were killed for status—and the same number was necessary for childlessness. The total number of animals depended on the number of days involved in the operation of erecting the stone.

Repeat ceremonies took place yearly following the erection of the stone.[59]

Often in Borneo the occasion for feasting and the erection of monuments is entirely funerary. And in general there is no great difficulty in gathering together a band of willing helpers, if the occasion is primarily a great feast, at which it would be churlish to refuse one's co-operation.

Indeed, in some societies the whole process of feast-giving, with the accompanying exchange of gifts, takes place on a regular basis and is the very core of the social life of the area. An example is afforded by the Kyaka people of the western highlands of New Guinea. Here the exchange and the feasting are certainly not *ad hoc*, on-off affairs like the rather informal examples already described. Groups or clans occupying adjoining territories entertain each other in a regular manner, which is prescribed by a definite cycle. Much effort goes into the accumulation of foodstuffs for the feast, and into the preparations. The success and magnificence of the occasion is of crucial significance to the whole community, governing as it does its esteem or standing in the eyes of its neighbours.

Settlement here, as in Arran or Rousay, is dispersed, in homesteads or homestead clusters, and each clan, numbering between 20 and 160 adult men, has its own continuous territory. These groups are identified or referred to by the name of their best-known ceremonial ground. Children of clan members marry outside the clan, and the clan generally acts together in the event of hostilities, as well as in the ceremonial exchange festivals.

These festivals do not involve the erection of permanent monuments, and indeed I do not know of an ethnographic instance where the erection of such monuments takes place as part of a regular annual festivity of this kind. Yet it is easy to see how such a social cycle could be turned to advantage if a cairn or other monument had to be built.

The three instances discussed here, all from south-east Asia, certainly offer a plausible range of social circumstances that could have facilitated the building of the tombs in Arran or Orkney. Indeed, I believe that we should regard these Scottish tombs as the chief monuments of basically egalitarian tribal societies of this kind. In most cases, they must surely have been the principal feature of the territory in question, which may itself have been known by the name of the monument, just as the Kyaka clan territories are often known by their chief ceremonial ground.

In this perspective we can see the megalithic monuments – 'tombs' now becomes too restrictive a term – as permanent social centres for the group within whose territory they lay and whose dead they received. We can visualize too that, as in New Guinea, when the population of one territorial group rose above an acceptable figure, some of the younger members would break away, and set up a comparable group with its own territory. The construction of a megalithic tomb would be one of the steps such a group would have to take in order to establish its identity, just as among the Kyaka it would be necessary to be the host community at one of the ceremonial feasts and exchanges in the annual cycle.

I suggest that we should view the tombs of Arran or of Rousay as an indication of societies where co-operation between neighbouring lineages or clans was effected by exchanges of the kind we have been describing, and sometimes by participation in the construction of chambered tombs. Moreover, this social and ceremonial activity involved some elements of competition. In Rousay, for instance, the stone cairn of Midhowe must have been a source of great pride to the group which it served, and of admiration or even envy to adjacent communities. It is, in its way, a magnificent monument, and very probably its grandeur was dearly bought through the extravagant use of cattle and sheep in feasting, offered in exchange for labour.

There is, indeed, evidence for ritual or feasting activity outside some of the chamber tombs of Britain, where animal bones have been found in excavation; and a number of the tombs have impressive exterior features, such as the 'courts' in northern Ireland, or the façades, of massive upright stones, of the Cotswold tombs. Moreover, the abundant evidence for a traffic in stone axes over long distances in neolithic Britain has already been interpreted by Grahame Clark as an indication of ceremonial gift exchange. Since we have this independent evidence for formal exchanges, as well as indications of feasting, it seems appropriate to place the mega-liths in this wider social context.

Ethnographic comparisons can be misleading if too much is made of similarities and differences in point of detail; and indeed, to make too close an equation between prehistoric Orkney or Arran and modern communities in Borneo or New Guinea would be rather foolish. Yet the comparison helps us to see how small farming communities, living not far above the level of minimum subsistence, and with very limited technologies, can co-operate in impressive enterprises. In the same way small neolithic communities could well, in the right social framework, create monuments which at first sight seem more appropriate to a great civilized state, such as Egypt.

Why megaliths?

One problem remains to be solved before we can explain the phenomenon of the megaliths convincingly. Why, in a specific area – western Europe – do we find such a concentration of megalithic tombs, while in other regions of Europe and the Near East there are hardly any comparable monuments? Even accepting the arguments set out above about the social context in which they were built, might this localized distribution not suggest a spread, from a single centre, of the idea of collective burial in built tombs?

At first sight it does seem an altogether remarkable coincidence that in these neighbouring parts of Europe, and in these parts alone, such similar developments should come about within a few centuries of each other. Yet this is very much the circumstance which we face when discussing the origins of farming in the Near East (as well as in Central America), where similar developments are observed at about the same time in adjacent areas. Archaeologists are now coming to believe that the 'neolithic revolution' was a process occurring over a wide area and a long period of time. To make the coincidence understandable, all we have to do is show that the development of monumental building in this way was, in the special circumstances of each individual area, the natural result of intelligible processes operating more generally. If similar conditions held in other areas, there is no cause for surprise that in some of them similar developments are observed. Lewis Binford, the leading proponent of the New Archaeology in the United States, has outlined such a general explanation for the emergence of farming in the Near East, and indeed around the world, at the end of the ice age. I am confident that some such explanation will develop for the megaliths also, and although it cannot yet be formulated clearly and persuasively, some of the relevant factors are now emerging.

The most promising approach seems to be in terms of population. The main concentrations of the chamber tombs of western Europe are along what P. R. Giot and T. G. E. Powell have called the 'Atlantic façade' – 'a phenomenon against which westward moving cultures were halted and accordingly modified'.[60] Current thought about the spread of the farming economy from the Near East, bringing the neolithic way of life to Europe (and there is no doubt that the basic cereal plants were brought from there), suggests that a 'wave of advance', an increase in population density across a wide front, travelled westwards and northwards across Europe. This population wave must ultimately have come to a halt against the 'Atlantic façade'. And here we are led to consider the role played by the local population of Atlantic Europe, the 'epi-palaeolithic' or 'mesolithic' people who were living in these areas before cereals were cultivated. For there is no doubt that there were hunter-gatherers and fishermen occupying the coastal areas of north and west Europe when the first farming techniques arrived. As Gordon Childe wrote in 1925: 'The great centres of megalithic architecture in Europe are precisely those regions where the palaeolithic survivals are the most numerous and best attested.'[61]

The point has recently been stated more explicitly by Humphrey Case, who has written: 'The passage-grave may indeed be an invention of Atlantic Mesolithic communities.' The argument is based not only on the existence of mesolithic communities in Brittany and coastal Iberia, as well as Scotland and north Ireland, but upon the mesolithic burials which have been found in Brittany. Téviec is a rocky islet on the west coast of the Quiberon peninsula of Brittany, where an extensive pre-farming midden deposit, chiefly of shellfish, has been found, with several hearths. Here ten graves were unearthed, containing 23 bodies, up to six in each. This, then, was family burial, and on a modest scale much the same practice as is later seen in the smaller chamber tombs of the early farmers. In some cases these graves were surmounted by simple cairns of stone. There is a radio-carbon date for Hoëdic, a similar and nearby site, which also has graves, of 4625 ± 350 b.c., and a date of 4020 ± 80 b.c. for the mesolithic site at Beg an Dorchenn, Finistère, lying in the range of 5500 to 5000 B.C. in calendar years. The earliest dates for passage graves in Brittany lie about 3800 b.c. in radiocarbon years (*c.* 4600 B.C. in calendar years).

These, then, were areas of Europe which were already settled before farming practices reached the region, whether such practices were brought by immigrant farmers or adopted by the local population. In the Danube region it seems that the first farmers were exploiting different local areas which were not much frequented by the original mesolithic population, who may have continued their hunting-gathering existence for some time. But in the Atlantic west, it seems possible that the mesolithic communities rapidly adopted the new economy.

In this case they enjoyed an environment which had been viable even without farming, and no doubt became much more productive when agriculture and stock-rearing were added to the marine and other resources exploited. A much greater density of population must have become possible, and it is likely that the population increased very rapidly, both through the growth of local communities and through the arrival of immigrants. This must have had a number of social consequences, one of which must have been a developing scarcity of land, accompanied by a greater concern for establishing and defining for community territories and boundaries.

Beyond this point, the argument is as yet purely hypothetical, but we can see that those communities which were close-knit, at peace with themselves and able to resist pressures from neighbours would be at a considerable advantage. Now it is precisely this common participation in social events and religious observances, which the megaliths symbolize, that often serves to strengthen a community, especially a dispersed community where the homesteads may be several kilometres from each other. The mesolithic people of Téviec and Hoëdic with their well-organized family burials, already marked and given significance by a stone cairn, may have found such solidarity of real value when dealing with their new neighbours. In such circumstances, with an increasing population and an increasing pressure on the land, the features favouring solidarity in the community would be reinforced, so that the social significance given to proper burial and the importance of the actual physical memorial would be enhanced. These factors, together with the usually peaceful competition of neighbouring groups, expressed in social terms by generous gift exchange or the erection of still finer monuments, would favour the rapid evolution of unifying and prestige-bestowing monuments and hence of megalithic architecture.

This scenario is at the moment very general and remains untested against the detailed archaeological evidence. But some explanation of this kind, applicable in several regions at once, could make clear for us how it was that chamber tombs were built all along the Atlantic seaboard, and yet not in other regions, at the very beginning of the neolithic period. Humphrey Case has hinted at a similar development for the first megalithic tombs in Ireland. It is interesting that the first dated monument there, the round cairn at Knockiveagh, with a radiocarbon date of 3060 ± 170 b.c., does not conform well with local diffusionist typologies for the spread of megalith building, yet it would fit into a picture of a local evolution, like that of Brittany.

It seems likely that further evidence for a purely local evolution will soon come to light in the four or five primary areas which we have identified. And here the evidence for wooden mortuary houses in the British 'unchambered' long barrows, already mentioned, may be claimed as an indication of an indigenous evolution, even though the idea of burial in an unchambered long barrow may have been brought to Britain by the first neolithic inhabitants.

This, then, is the outline of an explanation to take the place of the now discredited view of Near Eastern colonists or 'megalithic missionaries'. We have seen that in four or five areas of western Europe there is good evidence of local evolution in megalithic architecture, and that the local forms arose largely according to the local availability of building materials. The manpower resources were sufficient, and a study of tomb distribution suggests the kind of society in which the megaliths were built. And finally we can begin to see some of the special local factors which led to the great flowering of megalithic construction specifically in western Europe.

The interactions between the immigrant neolithic farmers and the existing local mesolithic population, as the latter adopted farming practices, created the special interest in demarcating territories, in demonstrating group solidarity and in tribal competition, which the megalithic tombs reflect. Some parts of this picture are admittedly hypothetical at present. But we can now begin to talk about these monuments in human terms, as a product of living communities, and to give full credit to their builders, the world's first architects in stone, without any longer appealing by way of explanation to the convenient arrival of wise men from the east.

The World's 8
First Stone Temples

The great temples of Malta lay claim to be the world's most impressive prehistoric monuments. Like the still older megalithic tombs of Atlantic Europe, they stand out as the single great achievement of the society which created them – a society without cities or written records or any attributes of a civilization other than the monuments themselves.

At first sight it seems inconceivable that such monuments could be built without the organization and the advanced technology of a truly urban civilization, and this is why their inception and construction has in the past been explained in terms of contact with the east Mediterranean. Yet according to the radiocarbon chronology, the temples are the earliest free-standing monuments of stone in the world. In the Near East at about this time, around 3000 B.C. and perhaps even earlier, the mud-brick temples of the 'proto-literate period' of Sumerian civilization were evolving: impressive monuments in themselves but something very different from the Maltese structures. In Egypt we know all too little of the buildings of the Predynastic period, many of which no doubt lie buried beneath the alluvium of the Nile; but so far, stone buildings of this size are not known until the Pyramids of the early dynasties, which are certainly no earlier.

There are still too few radiocarbon determinations to give an entirely secure chronology for these structures and their accompanying cultures, but it seems clear that they were replaced, by 2200 B.C., by what at present seems a rather different culture, paying little respect to them or their sophisticated art. Clearly the 'temples' were being built before 3000 B.C., perhaps several centuries earlier, and this in itself makes outside inspiration unlikely.

The temples

The most impressive of the temples is the Ġgantija on Gozo, the second and more northerly island of the Maltese archipelago. Like Mnajdra, one of the other three very large temples (Pl. 3), the building really consists of two separate systems of courtyards, which do not interconnect. At Taxien and Ḥaġar Qim the temples are more complicated interconnecting structures. In front of the Ġgantija is a spacious terrace, some forty metres wide, supported by a great retaining wall (Fig. 31). The façade, perhaps the earliest architecturally conceived exterior in the world, is memorably imposing. Large slabs of coralline limestone, set alternatively end-on and sideways-on, rise to a height of eight metres; these slabs are up to four metres high for the first course, and above this six courses of megalithic blocks still survive. A small temple model of the period suggests that originally the façade may have been as high as sixteen metres. It forms two concave curves, with doorways to the temples in the centre of each curve.

On entering, one finds oneself in a broad courtyard with curved ends, so that there is an apse to left and right. The courtyards are open to the air now, but the successive courses draw in, in the manner of corbelling,

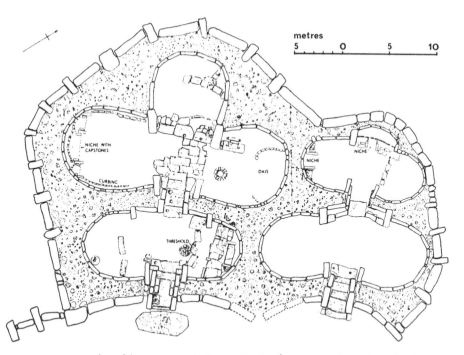

FIG. 31. Plan of the two stone-built temples, the Ġgantija, on the Maltese island of Gozo. (*After J. D. Evans*)

so that the aperture at the top might originally have been roofed with wood or hides. It must have been too large at the Ġgantija to have been roofed with stones.

A doorway similar to the main entrance leads on to a second great court. This time there is an apse in front, as well as to the left and right, so that the court is trefoil-shaped. This great court measures 23 metres from apse to apse, and the wall is preserved to a height of eight metres. It seems altogether appropriate that the medieval Maltese called this place 'the tower of the Giants'.

The second, adjacent temple is similar, but a little smaller. The space between the inner and outer walls is filled with stones and earth, and it is this which has given the Ġgantija the stability to withstand the depredations of nearly 5,000 years.

Among the dozen or so temples on the main island of Malta itself, those of Ħaġar Qim are the most striking. The stones forming the façade are of much softer limestone, which could be carefully dressed, so that the impression is one of imposing regularity. Again, this would seem to be the earliest use of dressed stone in the world – the tools used all being of stone. The plan is less regular than at the Ġgantija, but it contains such interesting architectural details as stone 'porthole' slabs, pillar niches and altar tables.

An idea of how such temples must have looked when complete is afforded by a remarkable underground series of rooms, the hypogeum at Hal Saflieni, all hewn from the living rock. Hal Saflieni was a great charnel house – the bones of some 7,000 people are said to have been cleared from it – and the main chamber has an imitation façade which almost certainly mimics the temples above the ground.

The most splendidly decorated of all the temples are at Tarxien, where several very handsome relief carvings of spirals (Fig. 32) have been found, as well as friezes of animals. The most surprising find of all was a large fragment of a colossal statue of a seated woman. Originally she must have attained a height of two metres in the seated position. This must be the earliest colossal statue in the world.

Fortunately several smaller stone statues have been found in the temples, and these give us a clear idea of the art of prehistoric Malta. Most of them are 'fat ladies', like the colossal statue, splendidly plump personages in stone. They are perhaps too well nourished for modern taste, but artistically some of them form a very pleasing composition of echoing complex curves.

These, then, are some of the principal monuments, and they are indeed so impressive as to make a diffusionist explanation at first the obvious one. Their very singularity, however, makes comparisons difficult. Even Childe, in the first edition of *The Dawn* (1925), found the task beyond him. He wrote:

FIG. 32. Relief spirals at the Maltese temple of Tarxien (*lower*) compared with spirals on a stele from one of the Shaft Graves at Mycenae, *c.* 1650 B.C. The Maltese temples were traditionally dated by means of this comparison.

No significant parallels are at present known to the temples, the carving, the statuettes, or the pottery. Motives adorning the 'neolithic' buildings and ossuaries have been derived by Sir Arthur Evans from the Middle Minoan II decorative repertoire; Professor Schuchardt has found in the same ornaments the prototypes of the Cretan. It is still quite impossible to say whether Malta played the role of master or disciple among her neighbours, and fruitless speculations on this topic had best be omitted.[62]

In the 1957 edition he was a little more constructive, seeing the ideology as east Mediterranean, but the architecture as west Mediterranean, with the suspicion of fresh inspiration from the east in the final temple period.

Professor J. D. Evans, who has studied the temple cultures in great detail, was already in 1959 arguing for a local development. 'It is abundantly clear ... that the Maltese temples and tombs were something indigenous, rooted in the beliefs and customs of the people whose religion they express, and they evolved step by step with these. There seems no question of their having been introduced as a result of influence from other cultures.'[63] His position, as outlined then, seems entirely acceptable today. The one new ingredient is the chronology. For until the application of radiocarbon, Malta had to be dated by reference to the east Mediterranean.

There are indeed some very close similarities between the spiral motifs seen at the Tarxien temples or at Hal Saflieni and those of Crete and Mycenae in the period between 1800 and 1500 B.C., and they were used, until recently, to date the temples to that time. Although Dr David Trump, the excavator of the temple at Skorba, at once accepted the new pattern of the radiocarbon dates (then uncalibrated) that he obtained from his excavations, Evans feels that the Aegean parallels still have a certain force. He wrote in 1967:

Trump, on the basis of these two (radiocarbon) dates would now see the Tarxien phase as ending about 2000 B.C. The present author, however, finds himself unable to share this view, feeling that the evidence for contacts with Crete in the later Middle Minoan period, and perhaps with the beginning of the Mycenaean culture, is too strong to be denied ... it seems difficult to place the beginning of the Tarxien phase before the beginning of the second millennium without denying the validity of most of the evidence set out above. Taking it all into account, the most likely date for the beginning of the Tarxien phase seems to me to be some time after 2000 B.C., and its end not before 1600 B.C. [64]

Yet applying the tree-ring calibration to the Maltese dates, it now seems likely that the Tarxien phase must have come to an end before 2200 B.C. This would seem to rule out the derivation of any of the decorative motifs in the temples from the middle or late bronze age Aegean. And naturally the new chronology at the same time makes untenable the view, asserted by some, that the temples themselves have a similar origin.

The temple builders

The temples are so large, and involved so much labour, that they cannot have been the work of small local groups of only fifty or so people, as we have argued for the megalithic tombs of Atlantic Europe. Some new thinking is needed here, about the society of the temple builders.

The material culture of these people is now well documented, through the work of Evans, who first related the temples securely to the other archaeological finds, and subsequently of Trump. It is now possible to trace the development of the culture from the first settlement in Malta around 5000 B.C. in calendar years. The first farmers had a simple agricultural economy, no doubt like that elsewhere in the west Mediterranean, with wheat and barley, sheep, goats and cattle. Their tools were of stone and bone.

The surprising thing is that the material equipment of the temple builders was not so very different from that of the first settlers. Their pottery was well fired and decorated with incisions. They obtained hard greenstone from Sicily for their handsome little axes and chisels. (Already the first farmers had travelled as far to obtain obsidian, a volcanic glass not locally available, and easily worked by chipping in the same manner as flint.) They made personal ornaments and pendants of stone and shell, and figurines of clay and statuettes of stone.

Almost nothing is known of their settlements. Dr David Trump found some huts while excavating the small temple at Skorba, and it seems that private building was often of clay rather than stone, and has not been well preserved. We can, nonetheless, be fairly confident that the 'megalithic' temples of Malta are quite unconnected with the tombs of western Europe. Beyond the use of large stones, already available in convenient rectangular blocks, they have nothing in common. And the material culture of their builders betrays no contact.

None of this gives us any clue as to how or why the temples came to be built. Their concentration in so small an island—for there are at least sixteen of them—is as remarkable as ever. Trump's excavations did hint, however, at a long evolution. For in levels dating back almost to 4000 B.C. he found clay figurines very possibly ancestral to those dated 1,500 years later. And in the same levels, a room which he called a 'shrine' suggests that functions later served by the temples were already emerging.

In such a quandary, we must turn again to the distribution of the monuments to see if the temples are spaced in such a way, in relation to arable land, as to be assignable to territories, as we have suggested for the tombs of Arran and Rousay. Here the really big temples, with courts measuring more than fifteen metres from apse to apse, must be distinguished from the several smaller ones. There are a dozen of these, generally of simple trefoil shape, as well as several other uncertain sites with large stones, some of which were possibly also small temples.

When the temples are plotted on the map, in relation to modern arable land, we see at once that they fall into clusters or pairs, each lying between 500 metres and two kilometres from other members of the cluster, yet on average some six kilometres from the nearest member of the next group. We can define six of these pairs or clusters, each of which can be seen to command a major area of arable land in the archipelago, which may be termed a territory: these are seen in Figure 33. Why each territory should contain two temples (in two instances, they contain four) is not at first clear, but this pairing in the spatial distribution of the temples must surely reflect some aspect of prehistoric Maltese social organization.

It is desirable at this point to reach some very approximate estimate of the population of Malta. The modern figure of 300,000 is entirely a function of its importance as a commercial port, and population figures from historic times are also of little help. The area of the archipelago is 122 square miles (316 square kilometres), and 60 per cent of this is today classified as arable land. Soil erosion has taken place, and perhaps a higher proportion was originally suitable for agriculture—say 70 per cent— since the light soils of the islands would not have presented the difficulties

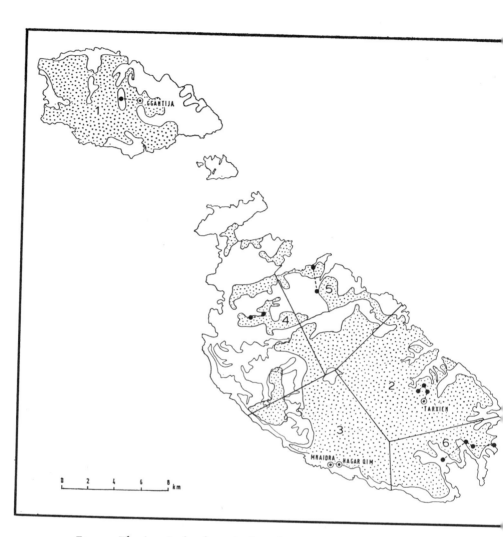

FIG. 33. The six pairs (or clusters) of temples on the Maltese islands in relation to modern arable land (stippled). Hypothetical chiefdom territories are suggested by the straight lines. (Contours at 100-metre intervals)

of the heavy clays of early Britain. Rainfall is only 22 inches per year, and there are no important rivers; so irrigation can hardly have been practised on any scale, though it was perhaps useful in localized areas.

What may well be a minimum estimate can be reached by using the estimated population density for semi-arid south Iran in the early farming period, as put forward by the American workers Hole and Flannery.

They suggested 2·3 persons per square kilometre, giving a population of about 500 for Malta if we consider only arable land – a figure which seems unreasonably small in view of the number of temples. For what may be a maximum estimate, we shall allow as little as two hectares* (five acres) of arable land per head (i.e. fifty persons per square kilometre of arable land), giving a total population of 11,000.

On the basis of this estimate, each territory with its pair of temples had on the average a population of up to 2,000 people. The smaller temples and smaller territories probably served much less than this, while the great monuments, like the Ġgantija (together with its neighbour) on Gozo, or the Ħaġar Qim and Mnajdra temples together, served rather more. Even if these maximum population estimates should be reduced by a factor of two, which is perfectly possible, these territories supported well over ten times the population estimated for one of the Rousay tombs.

We thus have an island of some 300 square kilometres, of little ecological diversity, supporting a population of up to 11,000 persons divided into six territories, each with about 2,000 people. Their staple foodstuffs were wheat and barley, with goats, sheep, cattle and pigs, supplemented no doubt by fish and shellfish. Their technology was of the simplest, with only the temples and sculptures testifying to something more than the simplest, egalitarian farming life. Overseas trade was apparently limited to occasional contacts with Sicily and other islands, which yielded obsidian and stone for small axes. Our task is to explain how such an unremarkable environmental situation could give rise to such impressive monuments. Again, we must seek some social system or organization which could have ensured the efficient mobilization of the labour obviously needed to erect these great edifices, and which is appropriate to a social group numbering between 500 and 2,000 people.

The idea of chiefdoms

Archaeologists have in mind two extremes of social organization when discussing the prehistoric past: neolithic 'egalitarian' society, and the state, with its hierarchical social structure, its bureaucracy and its armies. Yet

---

* A hectare (2·47 acres) is an area of 10,000 square metres, there being 100 hectares in a square kilometre.

between these two extremes lie some of the 'barbarian' societies of prehistoric Europe. The temples of Malta, for instance, are too big to have been the product of single small and independent farming villages.

Anthropologists have recently been thinking very carefully about such societies as Malta must have been: more highly organized and more complex than simple 'neolithic' farming villages existing at the tribal level, yet not civilizations or states like Egypt or Sumer. They have identified what may be called *chiefdom* societies. These share a good many features in common, beyond the obvious one of boasting a chief as leader. In particular, along with the social structure there is often a distinctive economic structure, different from the simple tribal one, with its gift exchanges, and different again from that of the state, with its written records and sometimes its commercial market economy.

The essential feature of chiefdom society is the marked social hierarchy, in which status is governed to a large extent by birth: those most closely related to the chief, and hence closest to direct descent in the male line, often have a particularly high status. Generally the chiefdom is divided into groups, each with its sub-chief, and sometimes (in the case of a 'conical clan') each group will trace its descent from one of the sons of the ancestral founder (Fig. 34). The chief, who enjoys enormous prestige, naturally officiates or takes pride of place at ceremonies, when the whole tribal group may meet together, and he will often command and lead in time of war. A whole series of villages, each with its petty chieftain, can be linked together in a social unit, all owing allegiance to one chief.

The chief has an economic role as well as a social one: he receives, in the form of dues or gifts, a significant part of the produce of each group and area. Most of this he distributes among his people, perhaps at a feast, in the form of gifts. And this redistribution, although perhaps at first sight purely a social courtesy, does have a real economic significance: it makes possible some measure of specialization. Fishermen, to take one example, can specialize in an activity that their coastal situation makes particularly convenient, catching more fish than would be needed simply for themselves and their families. The surplus can then be passed on as a 'gift' to their local chief, who may pass some on to the paramount chief, keep some himself and give the rest to other members of the community. The fishermen know, in making their gift, that they will receive comparable goods, perhaps produce of the land, by the same method.

This redistribution thus allows the ecological diversity of the chiefdom to be exploited much more efficiently, making locally concentrated resources available far more widely. And it encourages craft specialization by potters or metallurgists, or canoe builders, or any others whose craft is so complex that it demands resources of labour and skill beyond those of a single family.

Both socially and economically, then, the chiefdom draws together the various repetitive elements of an unstratified tribal society, where each community is much like its neighbour, and forms out of them a larger, if rather loosely articulated unit where different people have very different social and economic roles. This is the beginning of the shift towards what the sociologist Durkheim called 'organic solidarity' and away from the 'mechanical solidarity' of the egalitarian tribe. The greater efficiency and productivity of this more integrated society makes possible a greater

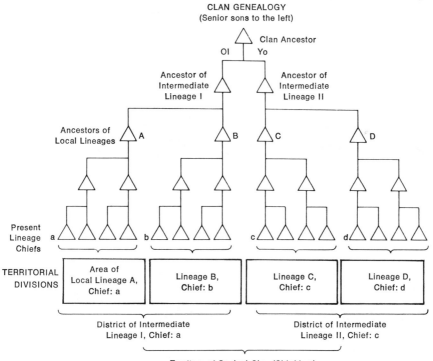

FIG. 34. Scheme of chiefdom descent and territorial division (after M. D. Sahlins). The conical clan is organized by descent in strict terms of seniority.

population density, and often results in larger individual village or settlement groups.

What interests us particularly when we are talking about Malta, however, is that the frequent ceremonies and rituals often seen in a chiefdom, and which serve to express and enhance its unity, are sometimes matched by the emergence of a priesthood – of specialists in ceremony and ritual – who, like the other specialists, participate in the centralized redistribution. Also highly relevant to Malta is the great capacity of chiefdom society for mobilization, for organizing considerable bodies of men who can devote much labour to the fulfilment of some task essential to the well-being of the community. Three features of the chiefdom make this possible. The first is their larger population – so that there are actually hundreds or thousands of people in the group who might be available. The second is the solidarity of the group: it can work together, and people will participate willingly in a common task which has the approval of the groups as a whole and has been organized by the chief. And finally, the system of redistribution gives the economic means – the capital, so to speak – for such enterprises: the chief can arrange for his subjects to contribute foodstuffs which can be used to feed such a task force. In this way, the chiefdom population can undertake impressive public works – irrigation schemes, for example, or monuments – which would be right outside the scope of a single village.

This is the social model which I suggest is appropriate to the temple cultures of Malta, and indeed to the later neolithic of Britain, discussed in Chapter 11. The larger social unit – and in Malta we have arrived at an estimate of about 1,000, or at most 2,000, for each of the six or so regions – is capable of undertaking work on a scale beyond the powers of the isolated and unrelated megalith-building communities of Arran or Rousay, or the long-barrow building groups of south Britain. We must postulate a centralized organization of this kind. And some measure of craft specialization is certainly reflected in the impressive art seen in the temples and their sculptures, as well as, presumably, in the specialist 'priests' who may have officiated in them. This one feature of prehistoric Malta – the temples – is every bit as impressive as the great products of mobilization in the early civilizations – the ziggurats of Sumer or the Pyramids of Egypt – although it was the work of a less complex society.

Comparison with recent non-civilized societies in other parts of the world can help to make this model more vivid and real for us. Above all, it documents in practice how relatively simple societies of chiefdom type can in fact achieve feats of construction that we would more readily expect in a developed civilization. In Africa there are many well-developed chiefdom societies, and indeed states, with elaborate systems of government. Indeed, the great stone buildings at Zimbabwe may well have been built within a comparable social framework.

The most striking similarities of all, however, are found among the isolated societies in Polynesia, some of which were organized as chiefdoms. Here again, generally without any permanent central bureaucratic machinery, ceremonial platforms and burial monuments were constructed that at first sight we might expect to find in a sophisticated urban civilization. Malta is not alone in the creation of massive monuments by a chiefdom society.

Malta and the 'mystery' of Easter Island

Many scholars have found the occurrence of impressive stone monuments in Polynesia altogether mysterious: serious books written around the turn of the century had titles like 'The Riddle of the Pacific' and 'The Mystery of Easter Island'. Quite a number of writers have found it impossible to conceive of their construction without the agency of more 'advanced' and 'civilized' people, from one or other side of the Pacific — generally from China or Peru. Indeed, in 1947 the anthropologist and traveller Thor Heyerdahl sailed on a raft, the *Kon Tiki*, from Peru across to Polynesia, a distance of nearly 4,000 miles, to demonstrate the possibilities of such contacts in early times. Thus the solution often proposed is, as it has been for Malta, an explicitly diffusionist one: the transmission of influences across the seas from the civilized lands to the east.

Despite impressive fieldwork on Easter Island by Heyerdahl himself, now handsomely published, the weight of anthropological opinion is now against this idea. Robert Suggs wrote in 1960 of 'the Kon-Tiki myth':

... the Kon Tiki theory is seen as a remnant from the past, clothed in a more attractive shroud. Its basis is mainly the success of a modern raft voyage that could not even hope to prove anything concerning ancient Peruvian navigation. The meagre scientific evidence for the theory is weak, even in the cases where it is completely acceptable.

Otherwise the similarities which are purported to show Polynesian-Peruvian relationships are completely equivocal. The *Kon-Tiki* theory is about as plausible as the tales of Atlantis, Mu and 'Children of the Sun'.[65]

Most anthropologists now believe that Polynesia was settled from the west, over a long period of time. The markedly hierarchical social structure, and the major monuments seen on some of the Polynesian islands, are not evident to the west, in Melanesia or Micronesia, and have to be viewed as the result of local developments. This does not, of course, mean that they necessarily developed independently in each island or island group, but it does imply that a source outside of Polynesia is discounted.

Tahiti, one of the larger islands, had a markedly stratified social organization. Its ceremonial stepped platforms, or *maraes*, were most conspicuous structures. The great stepped pyramid of stone which so impressed Captain Cook on his visit was the marae of Mahiatea (Plate 11). This platform had ten steps and was 267 feet long, 87 feet wide and 50 feet high. The court adjoining the west face was 290 feet long, and the walls of platform and court were faced with a first course of squared stones. It is recorded that the monument was erected between 1766 and 1767 by the high priestess Purea of Papara for her son Teru-rere. Ceremonial enclosures are found widely in Polynesia, and monumental platform tombs are seen again, for instance, in Tonga.

The structures of Easter Island are, however, the most relevant here: together with the celebrated statues, they constitute a complex of monuments quite as surprising as the temples of Malta, although some four millennia more recent. In fact, Easter Island offers a splendid analogy to Malta: both islands are remote – Easter Island, far in the Pacific, incomparably more so – and both bear enigmatic signs of activities on a gargantuan scale by a vanished population.

The funerary platform, or *ahu*, of Easter Island was a long wall, running parallel to the sea, up to five metres high and in exceptional cases a hundred metres long. It was buttressed on the landward side by a slope of masonry, below which was a gently sloping stone terrace containing burial vaults. The wall had one or more oval pedestals for the colossal statues, which faced inland towards the terrace Fig. 35). Some of the Easter Island statues are more than ten metres high.

Easter Island has a hundred of these image *ahu*, chiefly along the coast, and a further 160 *ahu* of different types. A few, like the Ahu Vinapu, have carefully dressed masonry as impressive as that of Haġar Qim or Mnajdra in Malta. The seaward wall of some of these monuments, with a first course of great upright slabs, has an undeniable if superficial resemblance to the Malta temple façades.

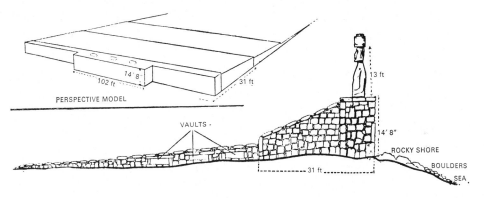

FIG. 35. View and section of an image *ahu*: one of the impressive stone burial platforms of Easter Island, surmounted by the famous colossal statues. (*After Mrs E. Scoresby Routledge*)

The population of Easter Island at the time of its 'discovery' by Europeans in 1722 was probably between 3,000 and 4,000. Its area is 62 square miles, just half that of the Maltese islands, so that the population density may have been comparable. Fortunately, despite the collapse of Easter Island culture after the disastrous Peruvian slave raid of 1862, enough is known to set these various impressive monuments and products in some sort of social context. We know that about half the total area of the island was cultivatable, and that the population lived on sweet potatoes, bananas, yams, taos, arrowroot and sugar-cane. The only edible land fauna (apart from women and children) were chickens and rats. The island was peopled by ten tribes, whose territories are shown in Figure 36.

Each of these tribes traced their descent back to a common ancestor, often a son or grandson of the original settler of the island. The Miru tribe claimed direct descent in the senior line from the original settler, and from it came the sacred paramount chief for the whole island. The anthropologist Marshall Sahlins points out that the principle of seniority pervaded the entire society, and the hierarchical social organization was in many ways like that of other Polynesian chiefdoms.

The ethnologist Albert Metraux was able to record a number of details of the traditional life of the island in the early years of this century, from people who had heard about them from their parents and grandparents. He describes various feasts which involved the redistribution of food by high-ranking men. The most important was the annual feast attended by people from all over the island, for which the food was supplied by the paramount chief. Here we have an evident indication of a redistribution system in operation, and it is clear that some measure of craft specialization was made possible by this.

At the annual feast the famous *rongo rongo* tablets were read. These were flat wooden boards on which ideographic signs were incised (Fig. 40) using a shark's tooth. On notable festival occasions, specialist chanters used these tablets in singing their songs, and there is considerable controversy today as to whether or not the *rongo rongo* signs really represent 'writing'. So far there is no agreed reading of them, and they are indeed exceedingly rare, so that there is hardly enough material to encourage progress in decipherment. Yet these ideographic signs do seem to indicate an object or an idea, so that we could reasonably term them hieroglyphs. Since they undoubtedly conveyed some meaning, we may regard them as a script.

The fascinating picture of Easter Island society as it functioned until its tragic and barbaric disruption in 1862 offers a living background to the monuments. Each *ahu* was the burial place of a lineage occupying the neighbouring territory. The smaller of these *ahu* were thus the Polynesian equivalent of the megalithic tombs of Rousay or Arran. Indeed, Mrs Scoresby Routledge, in her colourful book *The Mystery of Easter Island*, quotes a report of one burial ceremony which may embody several of the features of megalith burial in Orkney or Arran discussed in the last chapter. The process of burying the dead took several years, for first the body was exposed on the *ahu* platform, wrapped in a blanket, until the flesh decomposed.

While the corpse remained on the *ahu*, the district was marked off as *pera*, or taboo, for the dead. No fishing was allowed near, and fires and cooking were forbidden within certain marks – the smoke,

at any rate must be hidden or smothered with grass. Watch was kept
by four relatives, and anyone breaking the regulations was liable to
be brained. The mourning might last one, two or three years, by
which time the whole thing had, of course, fallen to pieces. The bones
were left either on the *ahu* or collected and put into vaults of oblong
shape, which were kept for the family, or they might be buried elsewhere. The end of the mourning was celebrated by a great feast, after
which ceremony, as one recorder cheerfully concluded, 'Papa was
finished'.[66]

This burial was only a family affair, and made no special demands on
the organization of the chiefdom. Yet the bigger platforms, some of them
built no doubt to mark the death of a chief, demanded more labour than
could be supplied by a local residence group. It was here, as in the construction of the ceremonial mounds of Tahiti, that manpower had to be
mobilized, and this was made easy by the chiefdom organization. The
impressive and monumental stone carvings, the work of specialist craftsmen, were likewise dependent on the redistribution system.

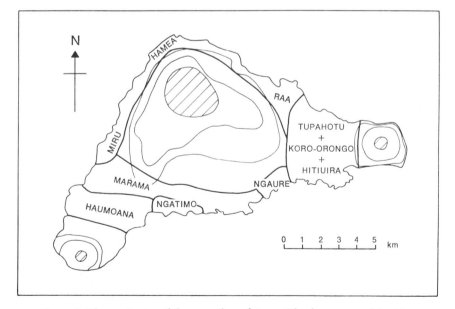

FIG. 36. The territories of the ten tribes of Easter Island, as reported by Mrs
Routledge. Compare with the suggested temple territories of Malta (Fig. 33).
(Contours at 100- and 200-metre intervals; land above 300 metres shaded)

These splendid statues were often, one suspects, not so much a memorial to the deceased as a visible sign of the proper celebration of the solemn festivities. As Metraux wrote: 'The desire for display was certainly a predominant motive for the carving of these giant statues, but it is questionable whether this was sufficient to provoke as much energy as that required for the transportation of enormous statues. On the other hand, to assume that the motive for making the images was entirely religious is to underestimate the tribal pride and competitive instinct of Polynesians.'[67] They were regarded by the Easter Islanders as 'vessels which the spirits entered when invited by priests', and with some of them were associated the 'names of famous chiefs or priests, whose spirits had entered the ranks of the tribe's tutelary deities'.

The picture of a stratified chiefdom society which the social anthropologists have built up in Polynesia helps us to understand the great monuments. There is no longer any 'mystery' in their erection by a society lacking pottery, or metal or any of the essentials of urban living. The Polynesians had a social organization which allowed them to mobilize their manpower and the limited natural resources available. This system served to integrate the island community both socially and economically. In Easter Island the cult of the gods and the ancestors began increasingly to absorb the energies of the inhabitants, stimulated, no doubt, by competition between the tribes. The erection of great mausolea belonging to the various lineages, and of statues to surmount them, was encouraged in the 'hothouse society' of this small island isolated from outside contact, where a fairly high population density may have intensified social pressure.

We have, too, a hint of the adaptive role played by this demanding system. By channelling the energies of the ten tribes into non-destructive competition, it must have worked to reduce hostility and warfare, themselves perhaps encouraged by territorial disputes and population pressures. We know that when Captain Cook visited the island in 1774, many of the statues were still standing on their *ahu*. A century later they had all been thrown down in disastrous and destructive inter-tribal warfare. This was a failure of the system, since competition was now leading to warfare and direct hostilities, but it does underline the value in earlier years of the peaceful competition involved in the erection of the images.

Turning again to Malta, we can begin to see how similar circumstances may have worked in the west Mediterranean. The first farmers of Malta arrived around 5000 B.C. in calendar years, bringing with them the rudiments of mixed farming. In ideal circumstances, the population of a newly occupied island can double every generation, until the limited land available demands more intensive agricultural practices. In the course of a few centuries, the increasing population may have necessitated the adoption of a shorter fallow period, and more intensive cultivation techniques. After 1,500 years or so, increasing population may have put pressure on the land, and in this situation, communities with a social organization capable of meeting, suppressing or turning away hostilities will have had a greater survival potential than others actively engaged in serious skirmishing and warfare. Just as in Easter Island – which is half the size and may have had half the population – peaceful competition between communities may have had a positive adaptive value.

My proposal is that some social organization arose in Malta, just as in Easter Island, resulting in what was effectively a chiefdom society, where the chiefs could mobilize their tribesmen to construct great monuments. We know Easter Island was sub-divided into ten tribal regions, and have tentatively suggested that the Maltese islands may have harboured six. And in Malta, as in Easter Island, these chiefs were not personally very wealthy, lacking large or permanent houses or great stores of goods. Indeed, the chiefs, like the priests and the artists carving the reliefs and statues in Malta, and the images in Easter Island, were themselves part-time specialists. They did not have the bureaucracy or the palace organization of the kings and princes of the great early civilizations.

The analogy between the two islands could easily be pushed too far. Burial monuments in Malta are unknown from the temple period, apart from the great underground burial vaults at Hal Saflieni. Temples or great ceremonial meeting places, apart from the *ahu* themselves, are not preserved on Easter Island. And there is no guarantee that any particular element of the social system was closely similar in both. We do not even have any direct evidence in the archaeological record for the existence of chiefs. The similarities between the two cases spring from a single feature, however, which can hardly be gainsaid in face of the monuments: a social organization which in favourable circumstances could lead to the mobilization of considerable manpower resources to accomplish communal tasks, and which allowed the development of a considerable measure of craft specialization, these things being possible at a fairly low level of technology, and specifically without the use of metal.

David Kaplan, writing of Mexico, yet another area of great and early monumental achievement, has put the general point rather well:

> I think that we have greatly underestimated the ability of many stateless societies, particularly chiefdoms, to engage in communal production on a fairly large scale, the notion apparently being that such production requires the direction of a powerful, centralized, coercive state. We have also underestimated the ability of such societies to engage in specialised production, the idea being that this kind of production requires large numbers of full-time specialists. By doing so we have often overestimated the socio-political complexity of the pre-Hispanic cultures of Mesoamerica to the point where they have become difficult to understand and explain without calling into play such hard-to-find features as large-scale irrigation systems or monopolies over ceremonial trade.[68]

We can apply all of this directly to prehistoric Malta.

We now have an alternative framework, where the local emergence of the temple cultures is seen as both possible and natural. Further work in Malta will improve and no doubt modify this outline, but I believe that the kernel of the explanation will remain the changes in population density and in social organization, and the developments occurring in Malta, rather than the supposed effects of hypothetical contacts with the east Mediterranean.

The Beginning
of European Metallurgy 9

The first known indications of metallurgy are certainly in the Near East.
Native copper was already used there for beads and small objects before
6000 B.C., and there is some evidence that the metal was being extracted
from its ores not long after that time. It has usually been assumed that
metallurgy came to Europe from the Near East, reaching first the Aegean
and then the Balkan peninsula. This was certainly Gordon Childe's view,
and it tied in well with his belief, discussed in Chapter 5, that the Vinča
culture in Jugoslavia, one of the principal groups of the Balkan copper
age, was initiated by colonists from Troy, the important early bronze age
site in the north-east Aegean.

Certainly full copper metallurgy is a complicated process, involving
several techniques. And it appears at first sight unlikely that it should
have developed independently in south-east Europe without any influences
or culture transmissions from the earlier metallurgical centres of the Near
East. As Theodore Wertime, an expert on the origins of metallurgy, has
written: 'One must doubt that the tangled web of discovery, comprehend-
ing the art of reducing oxide and the sulfide ores, the recognition of silver,
lead, iron, tin and possibly arsenic and antimony as distinctive new
metallic substances, and the technique of alloying tin with bronze, could
have been spun twice in human history.'[69]

Yet it is clear now that copper metallurgy was flourishing in the
Balkans, namely in what are now Bulgaria, Romania and southern
Jugoslavia (Fig. 37), several centuries before it reached a comparable stage
of development in the Aegean. The possibility has thus to be faced that
some strands at least of this complex web were in fact spun in Europe quite
independently. (The discussion here does not involve the alloying of
copper with tin to produce bronze, nor the use of iron, but simply the
smelting of ores to yield copper and the casting of the metal in moulds
to give useful artifacts like the shaft-hole tools of the Balkans.)

We must be careful, too, not to oversimplify the diffusionist case, or to imply that scholars working in a broadly diffusionist framework hold any longer the simple notion that metallurgy originated in a single place and diffused outward from there in all directions. Much good work has been done recently to reveal the several logical stages in the development of metallurgy in the Near East. And just as archaeologists working on the origins of food production think in terms of quite a wide area where similar, and perhaps not unrelated, developments were taking place, so it has been suggested that the discoveries involved in metallurgy may have been made at different places in the Near East and learnt elsewhere through contacts. The centre of diffusion would thus not be a single small region but a very large zone embracing much of the Near East. In the light of the

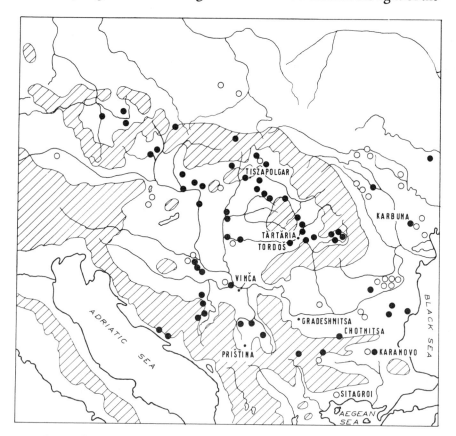

FIG. 37. Important copper age sites of the Balkans, showing findspots of shaft-hole tools (dots) and other sites with early copper objects (open circles).

early dates now available for south-east Europe, some scholars would now extend this zone as far as the Balkans, so that the cultures there, while they may have learnt much from the south and east, could also have contributed to the technological developments.

This is a perfectly possible model, and one that is not easy to reject. But it seems equally possible that the development of metallurgy was not a single and unique process, however wide the area of contact in which it was taking place, but a sequence of inventions and discoveries that may have taken place quite independently at a number of different places and times. The Balkan cultures of the copper age would then be one of these separate instances.

Indeed, it may well be that archaeologists, wrapped up in the old, conventional classification of 'ages' of stone, bronze and iron, have seriously overrated the importance of what were at first rather minor technological advances. For although copper was used first in the Near East before 6000 B.C., it was almost 3,000 years before it was put to any really useful service, and only with the use of the alloy bronze did really effective tools and weapons come into general use.

The diffusionist case in south-east Europe does not, of course, rest upon metallurgy alone. Quite apart from the several specific points of comparison between copper age Vinča and early bronze age Troy already discussed, there is the remarkable development in the plastic arts of the time which has to be accounted for. And further evidence has recently come forward, in the contemporary copper age cultures of Romania and Bulgaria, to support the view that signs, sometimes interpreted as proto-writing, were in use in the Balkans at this time.

It is possible today to contest the view that these were directly due to Near Eastern and Aegean influences, and this is of crucial importance to European prehistory as a whole. For we have seen, in the last two chapters, how the notion of east Mediterranean influences, diffusing westward to Malta and Iberia, can be replaced by more acceptable explanations. If the same can be shown for south-east Europe, we are left with a neolithic development for Europe which was effectively free of Near Eastern influences once the basic farming economy had become firmly established on the European mainland. The development of Europe has then to be seen in essentially European terms, at least until the inception of the bronze age in the third millennium B.C. which we shall discuss in the next two chapters.

The first element in the argument is, of course, the new chronology. And Childe himself realized that a shift in dating might lead us to regard early copper metallurgy as an independent European invention. In the final edition of *The Dawn* (1957) he discussed the possibility that the axe-adzes of the copper age of Hungary (the 'Bodrogkeresztur culture') might have a local origin. (In Childe's terminology, the copper age is 'Danubian III', the preceding later neolithic, including Lengyel, is 'Danubian II'.)

> Obviously the Bodrogkeresztur population was descended from the Lengyel group. But had mining and metallurgy been initiated by prospectors from the Aegean or the Caucasus? No doubt axe-adzes of different shapes were used by Early Aegean peoples and were actually manufactured – by casting in clay moulds – at Tepe Hissar in Northern Iran. Prospectors should have introduced the techniques of casting and smelting, but the Transylvanian products seem made of native copper. The forms could be regarded as translations into this 'superior stone' of Danubian II adzes, hammer-axes and battle-axes of ordinary stone or antler. Native copper-working could perfectly well have originated in such a metalliferous region. Indeed, the Aegean axe-adzes could theoretically be derived from Transylvania, while Heine-Geldern has invoked axe-adzes ... to mark the Aryans' route to India. In other words, the Aegean and Asiatic parallels to Bodrogkeresztur metal types might just as well give *termini ante* as *termini post, quos*. Still, independent invention of casting is hard to admit.[70]

Childe, then, had already foreseen many of the arguments which, in the light of the new chronology, may lead us to admit independent invention of casting. For the first Hungarian and many other Balkan axe-adzes are now dated fully a thousand years earlier than the Aegean ones to which Childe refers. And, if the types are related at all, which is uncertain, the parallels work now, as Childe realized they could, to set the Balkan copper age developments earlier, not later than those of the Aegean bronze age.

Our task now is to outline an alternative to the Aegean or Near Eastern origin for the metallurgy, the proto-writing and the great range of cult objects and 'figurines' in the Balkan copper age. For even if the chronology

THE BEGINNING OF EUROPEAN METALLURGY

now sets copper age Vinča far earlier than Troy, might not the still earlier development of metallurgy in the Near East, prior to that of the Balkans, make a transmission of the specialist techniques, perhaps by metal prospectors, the obvious explanation? The evidence does not support this view.

The development of metallurgical techniques

Metallurgy, in the copper age of the Balkans, implies the casting of tools and decorative objects in copper, some of this copper being smelted from local ores. The products were pins, awls, fish-hooks and other small objects, as well as flat axes and ultimately heavy axe-adzes – tools with a vertical shaft-hole for mounting with a vertical axe edge at one end, and a horizontal adze edge at the other (Pl. 5). Small gold ornaments were also made.

To show that these achievements were essentially local in origin, we have to be able to demonstrate first that metallurgical techniques in the Balkans underwent a gradual and logical evolution.

In the first place, copper ores are widely found in the Carpathian Mountains, where native copper – a very pure form of copper found naturally in nuggets – also occurred. There is no doubt that the actual copper used was of local origin. Much of it may have been native copper, which did not need smelting. But trace-element analysis of copper objects found shows that many of them contain small quantities of other elements as impurities. Such impurities are not generally found in native copper, only in copper smelted from its ores. So smelting was also taking place.

Several finds of copper slag were made in Sitagroi in north Greece, in levels of the copper age Gumelnitsa culture, the contemporary there, as in Bulgaria and Romania, of the Vinča culture of Jugoslavia. Crucible fragments with copper adhering to them were also found. In Bulgaria, analogous finds have been made, and hollow clay cylinders, thought to be the nozzles of bellows, have also been found there. From the point of view of its natural resources, therefore, south-east Europe was well equipped for the development of metallurgy.

This development in general tends to follow a series of steps. These have been well documented in the Near East by Theodore Wertime, and can be listed as follows:

1. *Simple use of native copper.* Native copper—almost pure copper as found in nature—occurs fairly widely in many regions where there are copper ores. In most areas copper may first have been valued simply as another attractive mineral or stone—just as meteoric iron was used in the Near East to make cylinder seals, along with a whole range of attractive stones—long before its metallic properties were exploited.

2. *Cold hammering of native copper.* It would soon be realized that this new mineral did not fracture on hammering so easily as other stones. Shaping by hammering was an obvious way of working.

3. *Annealing of native copper.* Repeated cold hammering makes the copper brittle so that the object fractures. By heating it in an open fire, and hammering while hot, this brittleness can be avoided. Cold hammering can then be used to finish the object, and to give harder cutting edges if desired.

4. *Smelting of copper from its ores.* This represents a notable advance. The ores themselves are often brightly coloured, like azurite (blue) and malachite (green). The oxide and carbonate ores are more easily reduced than the sulphide ones, and a temperature of about 700°C is needed, which can be attained without the construction of a complicated oven. Only fairly small and irregular pieces can be obtained in this way, however, unless the copper is allowed to run off at a higher temperature.

5. *Casting the copper in an open mould.* Casting requires heating to the melting point of copper, 1,083°C, and allows the production of good thick blanks in roughly the required shape. These can then be further worked by annealing and cold hammering.

6. *Casting-in, and the use of the two-piece mould.* More complicated shapes can be obtained by these methods. Shaft-holes, for instance, can be produced during casting by inserting a charcoal core in the mould. A two-piece mould allows a more elaborate shape than in a one-piece mould where the upper surface of the casting is always flat.

7. *Alloying with arsenic or tin.* Arsenic bronze and tin bronze are much

stronger than pure copper, so that the objects are less likely to snap in use. Alloying can also improve the hardness, and also the process of casting, avoiding the formation of blow-holes made by gases dissolved in the melt as they come out of solution on cooling.

8. *Lost wax casting.* A wax model is made in the shape of the desired bronze casting, and coated with clay which forms the mould. The wax melts as the molten bronze is poured in to replace it in the mould. The mould itself is broken and removed when the bronze cools. In this way castings of much more elaborate shape can be produced.

Further developments are possible of course, and the story does not stop there. It is important to note that each step is to some extent dependent on the preceding one, and indeed the sequence can really be regarded as one of increasing competence in pyrotechnology, in the handling of materials at high temperatures. Increasingly specialized skills are involved at each stage, and efficient casting of bronze usually requires some sort of oven where the flow of air can be controlled.

In the Near East, stages 1 and 2, and probably 3 as well, were reached very early over a wide area. Many of the earliest neolithic settlements known, including Ali Kosh in Iran, and Çatal Hüyük and Çayönü in Turkey (the last perhaps not even a farming community), have yielded finds of native copper. Stage 4 is reportedly documented at Çatal Hüyük around 6000 b.c. in radiocarbon years. Stages 5 and 6 come later – the earliest reported instance, not yet documented by metallurgical analysis, is a macehead from Can Hasan in Turkey dated around 5000 b.c. in radiocarbon years.

Alloying with tin, stage 7 in this sequence, was a much later development and is seen around 3000 B.C. (*c.* 2400 b.c. in radiocarbon years) in the Near East, the Aegean and the Balkans. It is about this time also that lost wax casting, stage 8, is first seen.

A similar sequence of development can be demonstrated also in the Balkans. Stage 1 is documented by the find of beads at the cemetery of Cernica in Romania, described as of 'copper mineral', which in this case implies ore rather than pure native copper, worked in the same manner as beads of stone or shell. Cernica is a contemporary of the earlier Vinča culture, and must be dated back almost to 5000 B.C. in calendar years. A little after this time, but still before 4700 B.C., awls and small objects of native copper are found in the Vinča culture and its Balkan contemporaries.

The earliest scientifically documented indication of stage 3, hot working, comes from a site in the western U.S.S.R., dated before 4000 B.C. It is a copper fish-hook which had been heated to 300°C and worked to shape. Tools made from smelted copper, which can be recognized by their greater content of minor impurities, occur at about the same time.

The most striking advances, illustrating stages 5 and 6, are seen in the Gumelnitsa culture. There, certainly before 4000 B.C. in calendar years, impressive axes were cast, with the shaft-hole already in position. Examination by J. A. Charles shows that these were indeed cast in open moulds, with the shaft-hole cast-in rather than being drilled out subsequently. Several have been found stratified at sites in Bulgaria including Chotnitsa, and one was included in a hoard of flat axes or chisels at a Vinča culture tell in Jugoslavia.

From this form developed the axe-adze, with its working edge at each end (Pl. 5). Some of these are magnificent objects, and their manufacture may have begun before 4000 B.C., and must have continued for a long period after this time. But alloying was apparently not practised in the Balkans until the bronze age, from around 2500 B.C. in calendar years, at much the same time as it began in the Aegean and the Near East.

This gradual and logical development, which took at least a thousand years, from the first tentative use of copper and copper ore to the accomplished casting of the shaft-hole tools, clearly reflects considerable advances in pyrotechnology. But it is important to realize that, in the copper age at least, it was pottery rather than metallurgy which led the way in pyrotechnological innovation.

Already the very first neolithic farmers in Europe had ovens for parching grain and baking bread; examples of these were excavated at the very early neolithic site of Nea Nikomedeia in north Greece. And from the very beginning the Balkan farmers were accomplished potters. In the earlier Vinča culture temperatures as high as 700° or 800°C may have been reached for the firing of pottery. It is particularly significant that the attractive graphite-decorated pottery of the Gumelnitsa culture required even more exacting firing conditions. Graphite will burn off, if it is fired in oxidizing conditions where the supply of air is not limited, at a temperature above 700°C. Yet investigations by Mr Jay Frierman have shown that this handsome ware was fired to a temperature of almost 1,100°C, which in itself probably implies the use of a special potter's kiln. So either the graphite decoration was added as a separate exercise after the pot had been fired, and the whole fired again to a temperature below 700°C in order to fix the graphite, or the entire operation was done in a single firing to 1,100°C, in reducing conditions, with a carefully restricted flow of air. Frierman concluded that the pottery was fired under fairly sophisticated conditions which allowed the attainment of a high temperature with a careful control of the air flow.

All this had come about in Bulgaria and south Romania, where graphite decorated pottery was being produced, already before 4500 B.C. And the development of ceramic technology seems a logical one, for which no outside influence need be invoked. The exciting thing is that these conditions were precisely those needed for the smelting and casting of copper – a temperature of 1,100°C and the control of air to provide a reducing atmosphere. Seen purely in technological terms, the development of copper metallurgy in the Balkans was already made possible by the skills of the potter.

Technically, then, it is entirely possible that metallurgy developed independently in the Balkans. The natural resources were available, and so was the pyrotechnological skill. But this alone does not demonstrate that metallurgy was something worked out locally, without essential ideas from the earliest metalworkers of the Near East.

Other advanced developments

Two other remarkable features of the Vinča culture – art and symbolism – have been used by diffusionists, along with metallurgy, to suggest that it was inspired by the supposedly more 'civilized' lands to the south-east.

In some ways the most striking finds of the period are the small clay sculptures of 'figurines' which are very commonly found in the settlement debris of the period, in Jugoslavia, Bulgaria and Romania. They show similarities with the baked-clay figurines of the later neolithic of Greece, and impressive little art works of a similar nature are found at this time in Hungary also. The original excavations at Vinča revealed a whole complex of forms, one of the most common being a schematic figure of a standing woman with outstretched arms; little model animals were also found.

Quite recently some extremely impressive sculptures of the same period have come to light farther south, in the region of Priština. They form a distinct group, in what I have termed the Priština style, with their very carefully modelled heads, prominent noses and big, convex eyes. Some of these heads are almost life-size, and a complete bust from Alexandrovats (back endpaper), showing the head and shoulders, with the arms akimbo, is a masterpiece of prehistoric art.

The whole range of forms and the sophistication of some of them is exceedingly impressive. And it is clear that a number of designs are repeated again and again – for instance, the four-legged 'centaurs' with their almost human heads, or the seated ladies of the Priština style (front endpaper). Professor Marija Gimbutas, the leading American authority on the prehistory of eastern Europe, has argued forcefully that individual deities may be recognized among the figurines, and in some instances her arguments are convincing.

Another feature of the Vinča culture, which has recently attracted considerable attention, is the custom of marking pottery and other clay objects with incised signs. These, and the clay 'seals' of the period, were mentioned in Chapter 5, and they must now be considered more carefully.

The various marks on the pottery were detected many years ago, and they have been described more recently by the excavators of the important Vinča-culture settlement at Banitsa. More than 200 examples have been described from the important settlement of the Vinča culture at Tordos in Romania (Fig. 16). Some of them are very simple – just a few strokes on the base of a pot, or a straightforward cross; others show rather more complicated motifs.

The interest of these signs was very greatly enhanced by the discovery in 1961 of three clay plaques at the site of Tartaria in Romania, in the same region as Tordos (Fig. 38). The Tartaria tablets were published as belonging to the Vinča culture, but it has been claimed that the pit in which they were found is an intrusive one, dug down from the levels above, and consequently dating from many centuries later. The possibility cannot be excluded, therefore, that they have nothing at all to do with the Vinča culture or the Balkan copper age, but the similarities of some of the signs with those incised on the Vinča-period pottery at Tordos,

Banitsa and Vinča itself would suggest that they have. The Hungarian scholar Janos Makkay has recently presented this case in considerable detail, listing the comparable signs from no fewer than 37 sites of the period, and he makes it abundantly clear that such incised signs are a widespread feature of the period in Hungary and Romania.

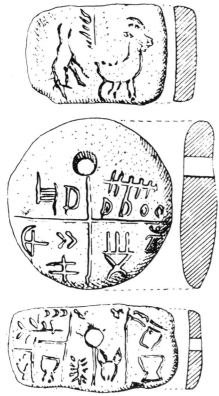

FIG. 38. The Tartaria tablets: three baked clay tablets from Tartaria in Romania. The signs have been interpreted by some scholars as showing early Near Eastern influence. The round tablet has a diameter of *c*. 6 cms.

His case has been greatly strengthened recently by two finds farther south, in Bulgaria. The more exciting is a small clay plaque, 12·5 centimetres in length, from the site of Gradeshnitsa in north Bulgaria, excavated in 1969 by Bogdan Nikolov. It has a number of incised lines which have been interpreted as signs (Pl. 6). The second is a circular plaque or 'seal' from the great site of Karanovo in the Maritsa valley. It is six centimetres in diameter, and again shows an arrangement of incised lines, interpreted by some scholars as signs, and an early form of writing (Pl. 7). However one interprets these signs, there can be little doubt about their context, for both finds came from properly conducted excavations in copper age deposits.

These three features discussed – metallurgy, art and symbolism – are all relevant to the question of innovation in Vinča society. For the central point which I wish to bring out is that these different innovations are related to each other, and each can be understood only by considering the society as a whole.

Recent work on the Vinča culture has revealed a large measure of continuity with its predecessor, the Starčevo culture, the first neolithic culture of Jugoslavia. There is evidence in the pottery for a steady development in some of the forms, and the Starčevo culture itself has yielded a large number of figurines which make a plausible starting point for the Vinča developments. Similar comments hold for the Gumelnitsa culture too. At Sitagroi in north Greece there is likewise an evolution: the figurines of the full Gumelnitsa phase are preceded by prototypes in the lower levels, and there is no need to suggest outside influences in order to explain the development.

The main point, however, is the remarkable evidence for prosperous permanent settlements in the Vinča and Gumelnitsa cultures. In northern and western Europe, discoveries of neolithic settlements are rare, and the depth of deposit is usually only a few centimetres. Except in special cases, such as Skara Brae on Orkney, where the houses were built of stone, little has been found to reveal the original plan of the houses, unless there are special conditions of preservation. Yet in the Balkans, good thick archaeological deposits indicate the locations of settlements. Vinča itself is a tell, built up of the debris of successive settlements so as to form a continuous sequence of more than nine metres of deposit. Large tells of this size are commoner on the very fertile soils of the lower Danube and the Maritsa valley of Bulgaria. One mound there, Djadovo, is fully eighteen metres high, and deposits of the copper age Gumelnitsa culture are sometimes found to a depth of seven or eight metres.

Several of these mounds have revealed complete village plans on excavation, and we may suppose that these tell settlements were often villages of up to thirty houses, with some 100 to 150 inhabitants. The floors and the lower part of the walls of many such houses were found at Tell Azmak and Karanovo in Bulgaria, complete with grain bins and bread ovens. They give a very vivid picture of settled peasant life.

In Jugoslavia the settlements may not have been in continuous occupation for such long periods, since tells with a depth of deposit like those of the Maritsa valley are not found. But some of the sites are very large, and Dr Alan McPherron has recently reported the discovery of a village with far more than the thirty houses, arranged regularly in rows with a space between them like a street.

The great depth of deposit at the Bulgarian tell sites is due in part, of course, to the use of house-building materials which on weathering give a thick layer of new soil and which have to be replaced every decade or so. The houses had timber frames, and the walls were of wattle plastered with mud in *pisé* technique; this mud was dried hard by the sun, but was evidently vulnerable to weathering. But the other important feature accounting for the great height of the tells is the long duration of occupation. The tells lie on very fertile plains, often the relict basins of lakes or the flood plains of rivers, and the lands around them were probably cultivatable with a relatively short fallow period, and in some cases perhaps without interruption – for it is possible that some crop rotation was practised already by the end of the copper age. At any rate the fallow was short enough for there always to be sufficient cultivatable fields within easy reach of the tell, probably within a kilometre or two. It has been suggested that the tells were periodically abandoned, the population moving on to a nearby one where the land had been lying fallow over a long period, and this is also possible. But it is in any case clear that each tell was occupied far longer, and far more frequently, than the settlements of the farmers of central Europe.

The tells in the Maritsa valley are said to be spaced some four or five kilometres apart, although further survey work is needed to document this. This would give each a territory of about fifteen square kilometres, if they were occupied simultaneously, and hence a population density of no more than ten persons per square kilometre. Ethnographic parallels suggest that no very intensive farming methods would be needed to support such a population density on the fertile plain.

The economy was one of mixed farming, based chiefly on wheat, barley and lentils, with cattle as well as sheep and pigs. Agricultural implements, including sickles, have been found. No doubt there were occasional local hostilities, but fortifications are not seen until they make their appearance in north-west Bulgaria late in the period.

All that we know of this society suggests that it could have been basically egalitarian. None of the artifacts, except perhaps the hoard of 44 annulets and pendants of gold from the tell site of Chotnitsa in northern Bulgaria, can be singled out as evidently suitable for display by a chief. Nothing compares with the magnificence of the burials in the Shaft Graves at Mycenae, or with the golden treasures of early bronze age Troy. This does not, of course, rule out the possibility that such finery existed in perishable materials: but we have no indication of this.

What we do detect, however, is something more modest. The great care lavished upon the figurines, and the imposing scale of some of them, does suggest that they were more than toys or frivolities: it invites us to imagine for them some more serious purpose – either social or religious, or a combination of both. Ethnographic parallels suggest a very wide range of possible functions for such images, as Peter Ucko, the British anthropologist, has reminded us; and to try, on present evidence, to invest them with any specific meaning – to identify them, for instance, as representing the Great Earth Mother, favoured by an earlier generation of archaeologists – would be incautious. Yet I think we can regard them as reflecting beliefs, and probably activities, centring upon entities which, if not necessarily superhuman (in the sense of deities), were at least suprahuman, relating, that is, to groups of men – age grades, brotherhoods or associations – or to tribal units and divisions.

We should note, too, that there is evidence for this in earlier periods. Figurines are found from the Starčevo culture, and a fascinating clue is afforded by the early neolithic settlement of Nea Nikomedeia in north Greece. Dating from around 6000 b.c. in radiocarbon years, this site is not directly relevant to the copper age Balkans of 2,000 years later. But the pottery and figurines found there are so similar to those found at early Starčevo sites farther north that it seems likely that similar finds will be forthcoming from the early neolithic of the Balkans. In the first phase at Nea Nikomedeia, four rectangular houses, about eight metres wide and between eight and eleven metres long, were found grouped around a slightly larger central building. (Only a small part of the settlement was excavated, and the original settlement certainly numbered many more than four houses.) The central structure measured twelve by twelve metres, and its special position is emphasized by the objects found within it. These include plump female figurines of clay, outsize greenstone axes, clay axes, flint blades and pottery vessels of a form not common on the rest of the site. The excavator, Robert J. Rodden, has referred to this building as a 'shrine', and the term is not inappropriate. Of course, it could be regarded as the house of the head man of the village, but at the same time the finds do hint at some further, cult function. If we regard it as a central building where members of the community, who did not all reside in it, met periodically for social and probably religious purposes, we may not be putting too heavy a construction upon the evidence.

It is here that we first begin to discern what must be the explanation both for the later wealth of figurines and for the appearance in the copper age of 'writing'. No evidence is found in these stable, permanent tell settlements to suggest that they were in competition with each other: there are no great megalithic monuments to boast the achievements of the community or to assert its territorial claims. Nor is there any evidence that individual village settlements were linked together in a chiefdom organization such as may be inferred for Malta or for late neolithic Britain (see Chapter 11). There is no evidence for a redistribution system like that of early bronze age Greece (Chapter 10), where the seals and sealings were functional objects of real economic significance. Instead the Balkan figurines do testify to a very real absorption in religious affairs: and it is in this context that the signs on the tablets and plaques have to be understood. I suggest, indeed, that this 'writing' emerged in a religious context, not an economic one. For there is no evidence that the signs formed part of a recognizable codified system, as would be the case for true writing designed to be understood by others who might read it. Probably they were meaningful only to those who were present when they were made. Yet that the signs were *symbols* cannot be doubted, and they may well have been made in the course of religious ceremonies. One thinks here of the famous sand paintings of the Navaho Indians of the American south-west. These elaborate designs, executed in accordance with strict convention and rich in symbolism, were made for a particular purpose during the ceremony, and destroyed when the ceremonial had ended. Had they been in a permanent medium they would have been – like the Balkan tablets – enduring repositories of symbolic information, indeed a form of writing.

Scanty, but I think convincing, indications that cult or meeting houses, perhaps like that of Nea Nikomedeia, existed in the later neolithic and copper age of the Balkans become very relevant at this point. They help to establish the ritual or religious context in which the other finds may be interpreted. At Chotnitsa in north Bulgaria, a small square building four metres long was discovered, which, unlike the other buildings on the site, contained no oven or grain bins or hearth or other indications of domestic activity. It contained, however, 44 ornaments of gold, of which four could be recognized as schematic representations of the human form, together weighing over 300 grams. Bulgarian scholars have suggested that this small building had some special cult significance, and that the gold adornments could have decorated a figurine or cult figure made of some more perishable substance. This cannot now be established, but the idea is supported by the practice of embellishing little bone figurines with miniature rings and annulets of copper, which could be diminutive versions of the gold rings of Chotnitsa.

The context in which the incised plaque from Gradeshnitsa (Pl. 6), described above, was found conveys a similar impression. It was in a building which, in the words of Bogdan Nikolov the excavator, 'was distinguished from the others so far brought to light by its larger size. It consists of two rooms separated by a dividing wall. The plaque was discovered in the southern part with a well preserved figurine of clay and two pottery vases. The base of one of these has an incised human figure with the hands on the belly. On the base of the second there are incised signs.'[71]

The cult associations are important because they connect the figurines and the plaques, and relate both these to buildings with a special function. They help to make intelligible the functional relationship between the figurines and the incised signs, and hence render unnecessary any explanation of them in terms of external influences.

Symbolism and writing in neolithic societies

The prehistoric Balkans were not alone, among simple farming societies, in enjoying an intense religious life with elaborate symbolism. Indeed, the 'mesolithic' village of Lepenski Vir, in the same area, had well-defined funerary conventions and a series of impressive sculpted heads of stone around 5500 b.c. in radiocarbon years. It seems that this was not a farming site, but dependent for fishing on the Danube, and the distinctly fish-like appearance of some of the heads hints at a system of beliefs related to the fish themselves. Here then, in a non-agricultural society, are indications of a rich religious life which can be compared with that of the Indians of north-west America in the last century – the Nootka, Kwakiutl and related tribes. They too had an economy based largely on fishing, and a wealth of symbolism reflected in their totem poles and other art.

Among farming communities, one of the most interesting parallels to the Balkan copper age is afforded by the pueblos of the American south-west. The Hopi villages, which are supported by agriculture, often irrigation agriculture, now average about 300 people, although originally many of them may have been larger. Although concentrated in fairly dense communities, the Hopi lack any centralized political organization – in the words of Marshall Sahlins, 'a society operating at tight quarters yet capable of only moderate formations of leadership and policy ... there is no organisation more inclusive than the village'.[72]

What particularly interests us here, however, is the ritual or ceremonial life of the Hopi, their 'intense ceremonialism'. The well-being of the people and crops is conceived as dependent on an elaborate cycle of rituals. Most of the ceremonies are held in *kivas*, separate buildings belonging to the clans or societies responsible for particular rituals, of which there are generally several in each village. They are specially decorated with paintings, and serve as places of retreat for priests and officials, and also as club rooms for the society members. The rituals themselves, in which the society members, wearing elaborate masks, impersonate the ancestors and animal spirits, are very complicated. There are separate rites for every stage in cultivation, and the Hopi have a precise calendar, based on the position of the rising sun on the horizon (Fig. 53).

Of course, no single element here is directly referable to the copper age of south-east Europe, although the Pueblo houses (Fig. 39), with their grain-grinding slabs set in a special area in the floor, are remarkably similar in plan to those of the Balkans, as is the handsomely decorated pottery. The point of the comparison is simply to emphasize how small and essentially egalitarian agricultural communities can develop an intense and formalized ritual, with its own explicit and concrete symbolism, and with special buildings and paraphernalia for its observance.

Only one element in the ritual assemblage of the copper age Balkans is of further note, for although the Pueblo Indians do not display the sculptural ability reflected in the Vinča figurines, they amply compensate for it in the mural decoration of the *kivas*. The Pueblo symbolism and artistic expression does not, however, involve the use of a script. But we have already looked at one agricultural society which did – that of Easter Island.

FIG. 39. The interior of a Hopi house in the south-western United States. With their mud construction, flat roof, separate area for grinding corn (with grinding slabs) and attractively painted pottery, Hopi dwellings are very similar to those of the Balkan copper age. (*After C. D. Forde*)

Certainly the society of Easter Island had a much more marked social hierarchy than either the Pueblo Indians or the copper age people of the Balkans, which is why it seemed profitable to compare its monuments with those of Malta. But the people who made and used the *rongo rongo* tablets there were not full-time specialists, any more than the priests and officials among the Pueblo Indians, or the cult leaders we imagine for the prehistoric Balkans.

Now despite the obscurity which unfortunately clouds the meaning of the *rongo rongo* writing (Fig. 40), certain things are fairly clear, and have been well expressed by the ethnologist Alfred Metraux. In the first place they were extremely sacred objects, surrounded by taboos. And early informants, placed in front of a tablet, intoned chants without trying to spell out the individual characters. Mrs Routledge, the last Western scholar to talk with someone who could still 'read' the tablets, observed that 'the signs were not to him, now at any rate, connected with particular words'. These and other considerations allowed Metraux to formulate an altogether plausible conclusion:

> The *rongorongo* or Easter Island bards used staves to augment the effects of their recitations. On these staves the engraved sacred symbols, like the notices on the staves of the Maori orators, may originally have been aids to memory; later the decorative or mystic aspect of the symbols gained over their pictographic significance ... We may suppose that the signs were arbitrarily associated with chants, each symbol representing a significant word, a phrase, a sentence, or even a verse.[73]

Now it would, of course, be absurd to suppose that one interpretation of the Easter Island *rongo rongo* tablets could have any very direct bearing

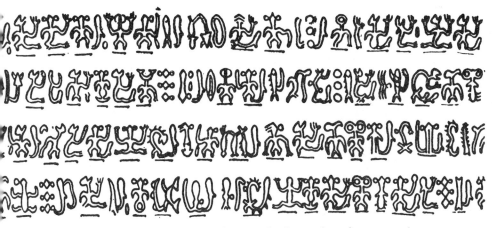

FIG. 40. The *rongo rongo* writing of Easter Island. Four lines from a wooden tablet showing the signs of this independently created script. (*After J. Macmillan Brown*)

upon the signs of the prehistoric Balkans. But the comparison is fruitful for two reasons. First, it reminds us that to call the Balkan signs 'writing' hints at functions which they may not have served. The pottery marks, like those at other places and times – for example, at Phylakopi in the Cyclades around 2000 B.C. – were perhaps a private code, significant only to the potter who made it. And the marks on the plaques or 'tablets', which can plausibly be associated with some ritual purpose, are likely to have had at most a mnemonic value, if indeed they were anything more than invocations, carrying a meaning only at the moment they were made.

Secondly the Easter Island tablets show us how a system of signs, much more elaborate than anything yet demonstrated for the Balkans, could develop in a relatively small society, which, despite its hierarchy, had no permanent central bureaucracy, and no full-time specialists.

To me, the comparisons made between the signs on the Tartaria tablets and those of proto-literate Sumer carry very little weight. They are all simple pictographs, and a sign for a goat in one culture is bound to look much like the sign for a goat in another. To call these Balkan signs 'writing' is perhaps to imply that they had an independent significance of their own, communicable to another person without oral contact. This I doubt. Even the *rongo rongo* tablets seem to have functioned essentially within an oral tradition, as mnemonic aids to a chant which had to be learned by other means. The writing of the Near East, like that of Crete, grew up in another context, that of the emerging palace economy, with the need to record in- and out-payments and to indicate ownership. So that, while we can agree with the Bulgarian scholar Vladimir Georgiev that these Balkan signs had an independent origin and held a real meaning for those who made them, to talk of writing, without careful qualification, may not be appropriate.

At any rate we now have a plausible social context for the art and signs of the copper age. The importance of the ethnographic parallels should not be exaggerated; they simply remind us of the elaboration in ceremonial of which technically simple, and in some cases rather egalitarian, societies were capable. The basic evidence for our reconstruction must come from the prehistoric remains themselves. It is not yet complete – but already it makes a fairly coherent pattern.

The acceptance of innovation

It is in this social context that we can now place the development of metallurgy in the Balkans. For the question of the early development of metallurgy is not solely a technological one, and other questions of craft skill and social organization must be considered. Here the development of real skill in modelling sculptures for purely ritual purposes is highly relevant. As we saw earlier, this was a culture with a sound agricultural basis, well documented by the tells of Bulgaria and Romania, and displaying a love of sophisticated and elegant products that is reflected in the pottery of the same area.

In general, any major technological innovation requires, as well as the technical means permitting its invention, circumstances in the society which favour its acceptance. Most pre-industrial societies are in many ways conservative. They function successfully by carrying out traditional procedures whose effectiveness has been tried and proved over many generations. These established patterns of behaviour – social and religious behaviour as well as traditions in agriculture and crafts – are very much what give a social group its individuality, and what, as preserved in the artifacts, serve to distinguish one archaeological culture from another. In order to survive, the society must to some extent function as a system which resists change, and all innovations, even potentially useful ones, tend to be viewed with suspicion. What needs explaining, therefore, in a prehistoric society is not so much why a useful innovation failed to catch on when it first became possible, but rather how innovations that were adopted in fact managed to overcome the inherent hostility and suspicion with which they were first regarded. A good example of this conservatism is afforded by the very early appearance of small copper objects in the Near East, well before 6000 B.C. There is some evidence from Çatal Hüyük that smelting was already practised at this time, and one might well have expected a fairly rapid development in metallurgy in the succeeding centuries, with the casting of larger and more useful tools, such as are seen in the Balkan copper age and the Aegean early bronze age. But instead there is no apparent development for nearly two millennia. The precise reasons for this are not yet clear, but evidently some failure or reluctance to exploit the new innovations was involved.

Two further features of the copper age cultures of the Balkans were important in facilitating an acceptance of innovation there: the emergence of an evident measure of craft specialization, and the development of a trade in luxury or prestige objects.

Craft specialization implies that an artisan spends part or all of his working time in the manufacture of a particular class of product which demands special skill. Already the complicated and special procedures required for the firing of the graphite-decorated pottery suggest this kind of skill. And there are one or two further indications of specialization. The clearest is the workshop for the manufacture of bone figurines which was found at Chotnitsa. These figurines are little flat representations of the human figure up to eight centimetres long, found at sites of the Gumelnitsa culture in the Danube valley. In one of the houses at Chotnitsa, which was otherwise an ordinary dwelling with hearth and querns for grinding grain, a whole series of these objects was found, from simple roughouts of flat bone to complete figurines. With them were a stone axe, delicate blades of flint, and larger stones and bone tools for polishing. There is no doubt that the house was occupied by a specialist carver of these objects, although clearly this would only be a part-time specialization.

Another workshop, this time of shell bracelets, was found at a tell on the Black Sea coast. Robert Evans is now studying this question of craft specialization in the Balkan copper age, and is following up other possibilities, including the specialist production of flint tools. But already we have enough evidence, even without that relative to metallurgy, to suggest that some craft specialization was developing at this time.

It is in just such a context that we would expect a somewhat complicated craft like metallurgy to develop. Indeed we should not overlook the possibility that the specialist in one craft might also be active in another. Pyrotechnological skill is something which the potter and the smith hold in common. As already mentioned, some of the little bone figurines have small metal rings as attachments, and again both could be the product of the same specialist craftsman.

The second feature of the culture particularly relevant to the growth of metallurgy is the development of a trade in attractive and desirable objects. No doubt the bone figurines already discussed, and perhaps some of the pottery, were in fact exchanged. But by far the clearest indication comes from shell bracelets and rings. These are commonly found in the copper age settlements of Bulgaria, Romania and Jugoslavia, as well as in such cemeteries as are known, and they occur farther north in the copper age cemeteries of Hungary and in the early neolithic of Germany. It has long been known that many of these were carved from the marine shell *Spondylus gaederopus*, which was thought to have come from the Black Sea and the Mediterranean. However, oxygen isotope analyses by Dr Nicholas Shackleton have shown beyond doubt that the shells in fact come from the Mediterranean – which in most cases implies the Aegean – so the Black Sea can now be ruled out. As mentioned earlier. Gumelnitsa culture levels at the site of Sitagroi in north Greece have yielded numerous examples of such bangles and annulets, and this may have been one of the starting points for the trade or exchange cycle.

Ethnographic parallels suggest that individual exchanges often occurred over a relatively short distance – perhaps no more than fifty kilometres at a time – but that the objects were handed on subsequently in a further exchange. The result of numerous exchanges of this sort over a long period of time would be the sort of distribution pattern observed archaeologically. It remains possible, however, that specialist craftsmen actually travelled to the Aegean to obtain suitable material.

This and other evidence suggests that there was already a demand for such prestige goods, that they were traded over considerable distances, and that in some cases they were manufactured by specialist craftsmen.

All of this can be demonstrated without direct reference to metal. But when we look again at the metal objects we find that many of them were more decorative than useful, at least until the more robust shaft-hole tools were developed. The first copper objects were beads, like those of Sitagroi II or the ore beads from Cernica, both before 4500 B.C. It is notable, too, that *Spondylus* shell beads are found in the same cemetery. Copper pendants and pins with double spiral beads are widely found, and many of the other early copper objects – fish-hooks or awls – were hardly of revolutionary utilitarian value.

In the regions where burial in cemeteries was common, especially in Hungary and southern Czechoslovakia, the graves often contain ornaments of copper. In an important cemetery in Slovakia, a copper shaft-hole axe was found in many of the graves, and this seems to have been one of the most valued of personal possessions. The proper interpretation of the social significance of such grave goods is a difficult problem, yet already it is clear that copper objects, including shaft-hole axes, were valued as prestige goods, and not merely as utilitarian tools.

Clear evidence that copper objects were in fact traded comes from the western U.S.S.R., where the finds are up to 200 kilometres from the nearest ore sources in the Carpathian Mountains to the west. One remarkable find there, the Karbuna hoard, contained over 400 objects of copper as well as stone axe-hammers, *Spondylus* shells and other objects.

We can now begin to discern how it was that, given the initial chance discovery of annealing, or smelting or casting or whatever – perhaps at first by accident during pottery manufacture – a demand for the new material grew up. Although at first the new objects of metal were not more efficient than those of other materials (for copper is much softer than stone), their novelty and attractiveness combined to make them highly desirable prestigious possessions. The Chotñitsa hoard suggests that they were used too for religious purposes.

No doubt it was several centuries before really effective tools were developed, like the shaft-hole axes and axe-adzes. But the importance of the industry in the later copper age and the level of specialization and investment it involved are dramatically documented for us by recent finds in 1970 at the prehistoric site of Rudna Glava in eastern Jugoslavia. There, several mineshafts have recently been explored that can be dated with confidence by pottery finds to the period of the Vinča culture, and hence several centuries before 4000 B.C. The shafts were dug to extract copper ore, and extend to a depth of 20 or 25 metres, following the veins of chalcopyrite. Nine of them have already been discovered, and there may be many more. The discovery has come as a considerable surprise, since it was generally assumed that the copper ores were dug out from more easily accessible exposed outcrops. Indeed, these are the earliest mines anywhere in the world, on the basis of present knowledge. Of course it is only to be expected that similar finds will one day be made in the Near East, but this exciting discovery brings home to us both how early the metallurgical developments in the Balkans took place and the scale of the enterprise in that flourishing 'copper age'.

Instead of the backward and 'primitive' society that, according to the diffusionists, the neolithic people of the Balkan world would, if left to themselves, have perpetuated, we now have a very different picture, tolerably well documented by the archaeological remains. Copper age society in the Balkans had an emerging craft specialization, a real system of trade and exchange (albeit based largely on the reciprocal exchange of gifts), and an intense ceremonialism, where new forms and, no doubt, new observances were continually evolving. At the same time, early developments in pottery firing had made metallurgy technically possible. It is in just such a situation that the new techniques would catch on, as they were developed, and innovations be accepted.

In the fifth millennium B.C. Balkan society was as complex and varied as any in the world, with its ritual, its art, its metallurgy and its 'writing'. It needed no aid mission from the Near East to develop these things; and we feel no surprise that some of them were first discovered in the Balkans, and that others were locally developed. These advances set the foundations for the European bronze age which was to follow and which itself can again only be understood in primarily European terms.

10 The Emergence of Civilization in Europe

The first real civilization of Europe came into being in the Aegean around 2000 B.C. First in Crete, in the culture known as Minoan, and then in mainland Greece, in the settlements termed Mycenaean, palaces are seen, with sophisticated products of skilled craftsmen, and numerous other indications of a complex and highly organized society which we term a civilization.

Inevitably the traditional view of these developments in Greece is that they were brought about either by migration or by diffusion from the Near East. And the tree-ring calibration of radiocarbon has itself virtually no effect on the dating of the Minoan-Mycenaean civilization. Its chronology, carefully built up using the dating evidence of numerous Egyptian imports as well as Mycenaean finds in Egypt, is firmly tied to the traditional chronology of Egypt. As we saw in Chapter 5, it is left essentially unchanged by the calibration, since the radiocarbon dates, when calibrated, harmonize with the traditional dating rather well.

But the collapse of the diffusionist framework elsewhere encourages us to examine again the origins of Aegean civilization, without some of those assumptions which in other instances have proved misleading. The supposed migrations, and the Near Eastern 'influences' about which the standard textbooks speak, should be looked at with a more sceptical eye. It cannot be doubted that there were indeed contacts between Crete and both the Levant and Egypt from about 3000 B.C., but a critical examination makes it doubtful whether they were of any great consequence to the society. I believe, indeed, that this first European civilization was very much a European development, and that most of its features can be traced back, not to the admittedly earlier civilizations of the Near East, but to antecedents on home ground, and to processes at work in the Aegean over the preceding thousand years.

'Civilization', like 'culture', is a word which is often used and rarely defined. In a very general sense one might apply it to the societies of Malta or Easter Island, with their great monuments and statues, or to the inhabitants of Vinča, with their elaborate cult figures and their metallurgy. But civilization, as here intended, and as defined by most archaeologists, suggests something more than this. It implies a more complex society, with a well-defined social stratification – usually with princes and priests, with full-time professional craftsmen producing a range of sophisticated goods, and with a permanent, central organization, often a literate one, based upon the prince's palace, or on the priest's temple or upon an urban community, living in a city. Man has created for himself a new environment which insulates him (or at any rate those well placed in the social hierarchy) from immediate contact with the world of nature and from the pressing concerns of the hunter or the simple subsistence farmer. As the American anthropologist Robert Redfield wrote: 'The turning point in the changes which mankind has undergone is the passage from precivilized to civilized life.'[74]

When deciding whether a specific early culture should be ranked as a civilization, archaeologists look for certain revealing features, including the following three: towns indicating a considerable concentration of population, monumental buildings such as temples or palaces, and writing. Most societies which we would wish to call civilizations can boast at least two of these. The Sumerian civilization of Mesopotamia, the earliest in the world, had all three. In early Egypt, as in the Maya civilization of Central America or in Crete, there were, however, no great cities; the Inca civilization of Peru lacked permanent written records. Yet despite this they must, by virtue of their social organization and technical attainments, certainly rank as civilizations. As we shall see, the society of the Minoans and Mycenaeans likewise represented a new and more sophisticated kind of life in the Aegean. An argument over the semantics of 'civilization' is useful only if it brings this out, while emphasizing that early Aegean civilization, lacking irrigation agriculture and major cities, was something different in many ways from that of Sumer.

The nature of the Minoan–Mycenaean civilization

The core of the Minoan-Mycenaean civilization was the palace. At Knossos, the principal centre of prehistoric Crete, Sir Arthur Evans found a most impressive complex of buildings, arranged round a paved central court fifty metres long (Fig. 41). He at once decided that this must have been the home of the legendary King Minos, and termed the hitherto unknown civilization which he had discovered 'Minoan'. Indeed, the dark and complicated passageways and storerooms which Evans revealed at once brought to mind the 'labyrinth' in which King Minos kept the monstrous Minotaur. Here, according to Greek legend, the hero Theseus slew the monster and found his way out of the maze with the clew of twine, conveniently provided for him by the Princess Ariadne.

This labyrinth of chambers and passages was in fact the basement area of the palace, the magazine area, with extensive storage space for grain,

FIG. 41. Ground plan of the Late Minoan palace at Knossos in Crete (after J. D. Pendlebury). Scale in metres.

and for olive oil, kept in huge jars up to 1·5 metres high. We can now see that this was the very hub of the palace economy, which worked in a much more systematically organized way, on the same principle that sustained the Polynesian chiefdoms – on the centralized redistribution of produce.

Above these dark little rooms were the spacious chambers of the first floor, the *piano nobile*, containing the magnificent apartments of the prince and the great public rooms (Fig. 42). Many of these were adorned with brightly coloured wall-paintings. With their decorative plants, their birds in flight and their sea creatures, the painting and the decorated pottery of the Minoans are evidence of a keen eye and a very lively appreciation of nature. They show, too, individuals and crowd scenes, and incidents in the ritual or sport of bull-leaping, where young men and women took a jump and performed a handstand on the back of the tossing bull.

The Cretan palaces – we know of four and of several villas, and there may have been more – clearly reflect a highly stratified society. And the

FIG. 42. Reconstruction of the courtyard of the Mycenaean palace at Mycenae itself. (*After A. J. Wace*)

complexity of the organization that was required to control the elaborate redistribution system is reflected in the inscribed tablets (Fig. 43) and sealings. Each commodity consigned to the palace was sealed with damp clay, and the mark of the sender's personal sealstone imprinted on it. Receipts and dues, as well as disbursements, were recorded by the palace scribes on clay tablets. They used both simple pictographic signs and a more complicated system where each syllable of the language had its own sign, in the Minoan script. The later version of this script was brilliantly deciphered by Michael Ventris, and the language successfully identified as an early form of Greek.

FIG. 43. The palace accounts: an inscribed clay tablet in the Minoan
Linear B script.

Finally, in outlining some salient features of Minoan Crete, one should stress the astonishingly high level of the craftsmanship. This is what makes such an overwhelming impression on the visitor to the Herakleion Museum in Crete. Already, prior to the foundation of the first Cretan palaces around 2000 B.C., the Minoans were accomplished workers in stone. Their bowls and vases in a variety of attractive stones, and the minutely carved gems and sealstones, reached their zenith in the Late Minoan period around 1500 B.C. The metalwork too was sumptuous, with elaborate and beautiful golden jewellery, richly embossed plate and finely embellished weapons of bronze. Imported ivory was most delicately worked. And all of this specialist activity centred upon the palaces which were themselves, with their grandiose conception, their carefully dressed stone, their channelled drains and their lively decoration, the very heart of Minoan civilization.

The corresponding civilization of the Greek mainland is termed Mycenaean, after the great walled citadel at Mycenae. Its emergence was later than the Minoan, since the first palaces in Crete are seen around 2000 B.C., and comparable craftsmanship is not seen on the mainland until about 1600 B.C. The citadels, which are the central feature of Mycenaean civilization, may have begun a little later. Obviously the Mycenaean civilization is a product of the same traditions as the Minoan, and it owed much to Crete. But it had its own special features. In Crete, for instance, there were no measures for defence, no great walls with huge blocks of masonry. A rather different, distinctly martial society is indicated by the massive fortifications of Mycenae, or Tiryns, and other of the mainland centres.

These were, like the Cretan palaces, focal points for the agricultural organization of the area, and for the redistribution of produce – something like the great chateaux of the Middle Ages, with their extensive terrains controlled by a powerful seigneur, skilled in war. A special feature of the Mycenaean civilization, also seen in Crete, was the stone-built corbelled tomb. We have already seen corbelled stone monuments in neolithic Europe, thousands of years earlier. The Mycenaeans, however, had the benefit of metal tools to dress the masonry, which surpasses in its finish even the finest of the neolithic tombs in the west. The 'Treasury of Atreus', for instance, has a central chamber thirteen metres high, whose walls curve upwards and inwards very smoothly (Fig. 5). It is a masterpiece of prehistoric architecture.

These tombs differed also from the stone age tombs of the west in the sumptuous magnificence of their contents. The 'Treasury of Atreus' (which was in fact undoubtedly a tomb) was robbed in antiquity. But undisturbed tombs have been found. Indeed at Mycenae itself, that determined and very fortunate excavator Heinrich Schliemann discovered the series of princely Shaft Graves, from a slightly earlier period than the corbelled tombs, whose contents, displayed today in the National Museum in Athens, are altogether dazzling. As well as weapons, beautifully worked vessels of metal and stone, gems and rings, there were several face masks of gold. The story is well known that when he found the finest of these Schliemann sent a telegram to the King of Greece: 'Today I have looked upon the face of Agamemnon.' We know now that these finds date from an earlier period than that of Agamemnon, the legendary victor at the War of Troy. But our wonder at these breathtaking treasures is in no way diminished.

The Aegean before civilization

Until Schliemann's great discovery in 1876, virtually nothing was known of this prehistoric civilization, which at once took the name Mycenaean. Several scholars indeed ridiculed Schliemann's claim that the finds were to be dated well before 1000 B.C., back in the prehistory of the Aegean, in the 'Heroic Age' portrayed in the epics of Homer. Underlying their disagreement was a reluctance to believe that such sophisticated objects could have been produced in prehistoric Europe at all. Yet obviously they were not in the style of classical Greece. Consequently, it was argued, they must be the work of Celts (who were barbarians, admittedly, but had supposedly learnt their great metallurgical skill from their Greek contemporaries) or of later barbarians – Goths, Avars or Huns – who were able to draw on many of the skills of the classical world. Ernst Curtius, the distinguished excavator of the great classical sanctuary at Olympia, went so far as to identify the 'Mask of Agamemnon' as a portrait of Christ dating from the Byzantine period. And to many archaeologists the finds were simply 'Oriental'.

These reactions were understandable, since little was known of the predecessors of the Mycenaeans, and the discovery of such sophisticated products in prehistoric Greece was altogether surprising. But Schliemann stuck to his view that these things had to be regarded as 'Mycenaean', and gradually his opinion was accepted. But neither he nor any reputable scholar at that time would have questioned that the skills which these objects reflected, and the general high level of culture, derived ultimately from the Near East.

The Mycenaean civilization, as understood today, shows several features that should be attributed to Minoan influence, and others that must be the result of earlier developments in the Aegean. Undoubtedly the palace organization, the focal point of both Minoan and Mycenaean civilization, did crystallize much earlier in Crete, and to understand its origins we must look at the preceding period in Crete.

Fortunately the site at Knossos is a tell – a mound built of the debris of successive occupations of the site. Beneath the impressive remains of the final palace were those of the first palace period, from around 2000 B.C. And beneath these again were deposits of what is known as the Early Minoan period, or early bronze age – a time when metal was in use, but the palace organization not yet fully developed. Below the Early Minoan levels were a further seven metres of deposit of the Cretan neolithic. Its excavator, Sir Arthur Evans, was thus able to reconstruct something of each phase of the prehistoric occupation of Crete, and this splendid sequence became the backbone, not only for Cretan studies, but for European prehistory as a whole. In Chapter 2 we saw how cross-dating between Egypt and Crete made possible a chronology for the Aegean. It depended, of course, on the sequence for Crete of three periods (Early, Middle and Late Minoan), each with three subdivisions. And, as we have seen, supposed contacts with Crete or the rest of the Aegean were used to date prehistoric Malta, Vinča, the megaliths of western Europe, and indeed European prehistory in general. Here, however, our interest is in the development of Cretan civilization itself, and what we can learn of it from the long sequence at Knossos.

The neolithic levels revealed a straightforward mixed farming economy, without the use of metal. The pottery was never painted, but the burnished brown surface might sometimes be decorated with incisions. Their art was apparently restricted to the manufacture of little figurines of clay (and, as we now know, of stone). Neolithic Crete, according to Evans, could be 'regarded as an insular offshoot of an extensive Anatolian province'. We would not quarrel with this too sharply today, although recognizing that the culture of neolithic Crete was a local adaptation, and no doubt different in many ways from its Anatolian predecessor.

To Evans, and to most Minoan scholars since, the succeeding, Early Minoan levels were so different as to suggest an almost complete cultural break. The pottery is now handsomely painted, and metal objects, especially daggers, are seen. Indeed, craftsmanship developed greatly in the Early Minoan period (which today we would date from before 3000 B.C. to shortly before 2000 B.C.). For the first time burial was in built tombs, and a great many of these, of circular plan, have been found in south Crete with very rich grave goods. Moreover, already at this early date there are positive signs of contact with both the Egyptian civilization and the Near East. Egyptian Early Dynastic stone vases have been found at Knossos, and sealstones of ivory are quite frequently found in the Early Minoan round tombs. There were, of course, no elephants in Crete, and the ivory was probably imported from Syria.

In the prevailing climate of archaeological thought, it was natural that these contacts with the civilized Orient were seen as decisive. As Evans saw it, a 'quickening impulse from the Nile permeated the rude island culture and transformed it' into the Minoan civilization. He suspected, indeed, an actual immigration of Predynastic Egyptians and assigned an Egyptian origin to most of the new features. Gordon Childe stressed also the debt of Early Minoan Crete to the Sumerian civilization.

This picture of an influx into Crete of a more advanced population at the beginning of the early bronze age was soon extended to the Aegean as a whole, where the 'Early Helladic' culture of mainland Greece and the 'Early Cycladic' of the Cycladic islands in the central Aegean likewise possessed painted pottery and practised metallurgy. The great Aegean archaeologists Wace and Blegen suggested in 1918: 'Further exploration and study will probably show that these three divisions, Early Helladic, Early Cycladic and Early Minoan, are all branches of one great parent stock which pursued parallel but more or less independent courses.'[75] Most later scholars have accepted this view. The standard textbook by Emily Vermeule sketches a similar picture: 'A variety of movements spread from Anatolia across the Aegean islands ... Crete perhaps received a group of Anatolian sailors, and Anatolians certainly settled the largely unexplored mounds of Macedonia and Thessaly. They were not all the same racial stock ... nor did they speak precisely the same language or make the same objects.'[76] For her a decisive new feature was the immigration of new people.

The subsequent course of events was then seen as a local evolution with very strong influences from Egypt and the Near East: the elements of civilization were diffused, but found local expression in Crete. In *The Dawn* (1925), Gordon Childe wrote: 'We have seen that Minoan civilization was deeply indebted both to Mesopotamia and Egypt. Now I must insist that it was no mere copy of either, but an original and creative force.'[77] In the same work, he also wrote: 'The early inhabitants of our continent were truly and remarkably creative and before the end of the second millennium had outstripped their masters and created an individual civilization of their own. But it was not the fruit of a miraculous birth, but the result of the diffusion and adaptation of the discoveries of the Orient ... '[78]

Ten years later Childe very compellingly elaborated this theory of diffusion and adaptation in the Aegean, setting it in economic terms in a form which is still almost universally accepted today. In his book *Man Makes Himself* he advanced his very original notion of an 'Urban Revolution' in the Near East. He pointed out that the three earliest civilizations in the Old World – in Sumer, Egypt and the Indus Valley – were centred in the flood plains of great rivers, facilitating irrigation. These civilizations, he felt, were built on the food surplus made possible by irrigation, concentrated in the hands of the king or priests. The surplus gave them the essential 'capital' to build temples and palaces, to support specialists and to undertake trading expeditions. This simple and convincing picture has formed the basis of nearly all later discussions of the origins of Oriental civilization, as well as the irrigation civilizations of the New World.

Childe very ingeniously extended his economic model to explain also what he believed to be the spread of civilization from these Oriental centres. His explanation indicates a mechanism, a reason, for the contacts and influences, and is a classic statement of diffusionist thinking at its most persuasive:

> But once the new economy had been established in the three primary centres it spread thence to secondary centres, much like Western capitalism spread to colonies and economic dependencies. First on the borders of Egypt, Babylonia and the Indus valley – in Crete and the Greek islands, Syria, Assyria, Iran and Baluchistan – then further afield, on the Greek mainland, the Anatolian plateau, South Russia, we see villages converted into cities and self-sufficing food-producers turning to industrial specialisation and external trade. And the process is repeated in ever widening circles around each secondary and tertiary centre ... The second revolution was obviously propagated by diffusion; the urban economy in the secondary centres was inspired or imposed by the primary foci. And it is easy to show that the process was inevitable ... In one way or another Sumerian trade and the imperialism it inspired were propagating metallurgy and the new economy it implies ... These secondary and tertiary civilisations are not original, but result from the adoption of traditions, ideas and processes received by diffusion from older centres. And every village converted into a city by the spread became at once a new centre of infection.'[79]

It is fascinating to note how appropriately, in many ways, this description of the propagation of a new economy might today be applied, with a few modifications, to the spread of cereal agriculture and the neolithic way of life to Europe. Instead of the excessively simple view of peasant migrants setting out from the Near East, taking all the elements of their peasant culture with them, we have here the notion of local adaptations in response to local conditions. And in the very last sentence Childe has clearly hit on the model of the spread of diseases, which is now influencing those studying the dissemination of cereal cultivation when they speak of a 'wave of advance'. But as a model for the origin of Aegean civilization, it is no longer acceptable. It overrates the intensity of contact between the Near East and the Aegean, misunderstands the nature of the trade which was taking place, and assumes that the economic and subsistence basis of Aegean civilization was analogous to that of Sumer. I believe that we can now present a different model which harmonizes more adequately with what we know of early Crete and the Aegean.

Processes towards civilization

The new explanation, like those advanced in earlier chapters, relies much more on the social and economic consequences of local developments. It is reluctant to accept resemblances between two different areas as indications of contacts or influences between them unless there is good, hard evidence for such contact. Nor are trading relations, even when demonstrated, necessarily assigned a governing role in the course of events. The originality of the native barbarians and their creativity under favourable conditions are instead valued more highly. The crux of the problem is to determine just what those 'favourable conditions' were. Overseas trade, and a flow of innovations from outside the Aegean, may, of course, have contributed to them, but they should not automatically be assigned a determining role.

Through the work of pioneers like Evans and Schliemann and their successors, we know more about the prehistoric Aegean than any other area of Europe, perhaps more than any region in the prehistoric world. This gives us a unique opportunity to examine the various factors and fields of human activity which govern culture change – population, for instance, and farming techniques, as well as social organization or craft technology. The real problem comes in understanding how these different factors interrelate – whether population pressures produced changes in agriculture, or farming developments governed population increase, and whether the development of metallurgy and weapons favoured the emergence of warlike chiefs, or vice versa.

The first point to emphasize is the great continuity between the late neolithic and the early bronze age in every part of the Aegean. For a number of reasons, it is only recently that excavators have begun to find stratified archaeological deposits from the period immediately before that of the Early Minoan, Early Helladic and Early Cycladic cultures, long ago discovered and studied by Evans, Blegen and other scholars. In Crete the reason seems to be that the builders of the first palaces levelled the land rather drastically, and at Knossos removed much of what was then the top of the tell – the final neolithic levels. This has led to something of a gap in the archaeological record. It was natural, therefore, given such a gap, that the Early Minoan finds should look very different from the neolithic ones of several centuries earlier, at the early end of the gap. But only recently, Professor John Evans, excavating at Knossos, has found stratified levels, lying between the 'late neolithic' and the beginning of Early Minoan I, which make the continuity much more apparent.

The same situation seems to hold on the mainland, where at Professor Caskey's important site of Lerna, there is a considerable gap at the same time. One or two sites, however, do now show what a long period elapsed before the beginning of what we term the 'early bronze age'. In fact it is possible to speak of a new, final neolithic period, lasting several centuries, between the old 'late neolithic' and the early bronze age. At the site of Sitagroi in north Greece, and at Emborio on the island of Chios in the east Aegean, there are long stratified sequences covering this period.

The radiocarbon dates are helpful too. And here the new calibration does make a difference. Of course, it sets all the dates earlier, but a date of 2400 b.c. is only set earlier by about 600 years, while one of 3100 b.c. might go as much as 1,100 years earlier, on the basis of Suess's calibration data. So a period of 700 radiocarbon years can become as much as 1,200 calendar years (cf. Fig. 14). In fact it looks as if one might identify a new final neolithic period some 800 years long, from around 4100 b.c. to about 3300 b.c. in calendar years.

Already in the final neolithic period, metallurgy had developed in every region of the Aegean: there are finds from Crete and the mainland, as well as from farther north. Indeed, as we saw in the last chapter, the earliest metal find so far made in Greece, dated around 3800 b.c. in radio-carbon years, equivalent to about 4700 B.C., is a copper bead from Sitagroi in north Greece. This site has very strong links with the Balkans, and it seems very probable that the new technique of metallurgy first reached north Greece from there. In other regions it could have been hit upon locally, and certainly in each the further development was a local one.

Other significant developments were clearly taking place in this dimly known period. Already at Dhimini, on the mainland of central Greece, we see a fairly complex system of fortifications. And at Knossos the late or final neolithic settlement was clearly very large – comparable in size with the first palace – and the buildings close together.

All of this leads us to question very closely the old idea of new arrivals in the Aegean at the beginning of the early bronze age – of immigrants from some more advanced land who supposedly produced a marked acceleration in the development of culture. The original notion of immi-grants from Egypt is no longer tenable, and very few would argue for a party of newcomers directly from the Near East. There is simply not the evidence in Crete or elsewhere in the Aegean which might match the Oriental finds sufficiently closely to sustain the idea. Admittedly Crete was already importing some stone bowls from Egypt, and very soon ivory from the Syrian coast, but that seems to have been the extent of the contact. It is certainly not seen in other areas of the Aegean.

The revised version of the immigration theory, as we saw earlier, was that the immigrants came from Anatolia. And since Turkey has an extensive Aegean coast this is clearly very possible. But again the actual hard evidence, when looked at in detail, is very scanty. Dr David French has looked at it carefully from the Anatolian standpoint and is not per-suaded. Moreover, even had there been such an immigration, it could have had only a limited bearing on the question of the origins of civilization, since Anatolia was hardly more advanced at that time than the rest of the Aegean. In the absence of good evidence to the contrary, it now seems as if the transition from neolithic to bronze age was everywhere in the Aegean a continuous one, only marginally influenced by Crete's few trading contacts with the Orient.

This conclusion, of course, puts the subsequent developments in the third millennium B.C., the Aegean early bronze age, in an altogether new light. For they were, as everyone has always acknowledged, very considerable. Indeed I think we can identify this as the formative period for Aegean civilization, when most of its distinctive features were taking shape. One site in each of the four chief regions will illustrate this.

In Crete, one of the very earliest archaeological excavations revealed at Vasiliki a handsomely laid-out 'mansion', which by its regularity and coherence of plan clearly foreshadows the palaces of the succeeding period. Metallurgy was practised on the site, and sealstones and jewellery from tombs in the same region of east Crete show the high level of crafts-manship which the Minoans had by then reached.

On mainland Greece Professor Caskey's excavations at Lerna yielded a comparable and precisely contemporary building, called the 'House of the Tiles', after the roofing material found there. This settlement was fortified by a wall with bastions. Inside the House of the Tiles was a large collection of clay sealings – imprints from sealstones – which testified to a high skill in engraving (as well as to important social developments, mentioned below).

In the Cycladic islands, sites such as Chalandriani on Syros were like-wise fortified. Metallurgy was practised there. And some of the graves in the cemetery reflected a considerable store of worldly wealth while others were very much poorer. It seems reasonable to see in this disparity in grave goods the development of some degree of stratification, contrast-ing markedly with the egalitarian tribal society which we imagine for the Greek neolithic.

And finally at Troy, in north-west Anatolia, the site of Schliemann's first triumphant excavations from 1870, we have a strongly fortified citadel, the contemporary of the other sites mentioned (Fig. 44). In it Schliemann found a splendid treasure of gold and silver drinking cups, jewellery, ceremonial battle axes, and other finery which could have belonged only to a chief of very considerable wealth and influence.

These four sites are sufficient to indicate the level of culture reached at this time in the Aegean, and the nature of the settlements which one might term 'proto-urban'. Their inhabitants could be numbered only in hundreds, not thousands, and yet with their fortifications, their specialized functions and their emerging complexity in social organization, these sites were beginning to show some of the features of an urban society. Moreover they were linked now by evident trading contacts. Already in the neolithic period there had been quite an extensive trade in raw materials of stone. Its sudden intensification is seen now in the very wide distribution of many local types. Each one clearly originated in a specific area: the little marble figurines in Crete and mainland Greece, for example, evidently imitate a Cycladic form, yet they are found in much of the Aegean (see Pl. 4). This is true particularly of metal forms, some of them uniquely Aegean ones. One may speak of an international spirit at this time in the Aegean, clearly the result of trade, itself stimulated by the development of bronze metallurgy. This intensified activity took place within the Aegean, not outside it – it was no 'quickening impulse from the Nile' permeating the 'rude island culture'.

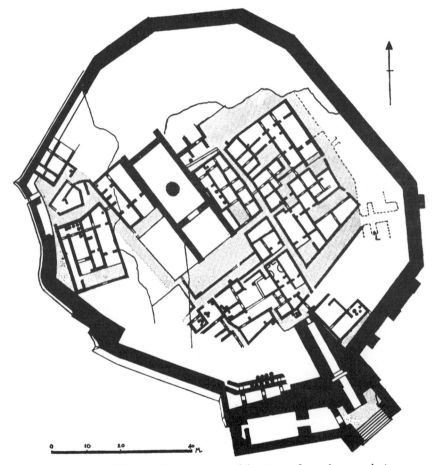

FIG. 44. Plan of the early bronze age citadel at Troy, from the second city, c. 2500 B.C. (*After J. Mellaart*)

The evidence is indeed sufficiently abundant to allow us to speak in more abstract economic and social terms. Surface surveys in several areas of the Aegean enable one to say something of the density of occupied settlements in each period, although statements based on surface finds can never be very accurate. We can see that in each region there are

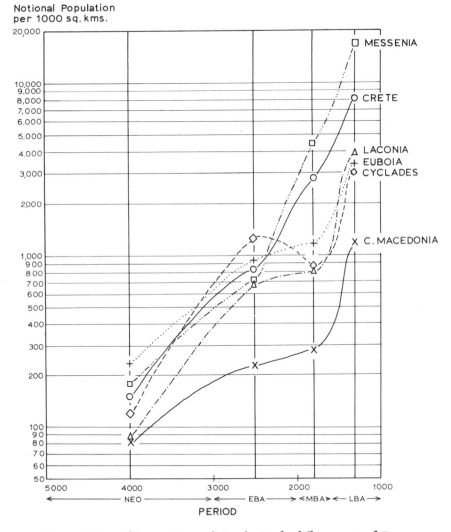

FIG. 45. Estimated increase in population density for different parts of Greece during the neolithic and bronze age periods. Population increase was a cause as well as a result of the emergence of Aegean civilization.

more early bronze age settlements known than neolithic ones, and it is reasonable to infer an increase in population. Figure 45 shows hypothetical estimates of the population density for the neolithic and early, middle and late bronze age periods in three regions, as calculated, using several assumptions, from the survey data. In south Greece (Crete and the Cyclades) the increase from neolithic to bronze age is much more marked than in Macedonia in the north.

It is tempting to relate this population increase in the south, and the absence of such a marked change in the north, to the further developments in farming at precisely this time. The specialist examination of plant remains and bones from neolithic sites has given us a very complete picture of the development of farming in neolithic times. In the early neolithic the chief cereal crops were the simple wheats, emmer and einkorn. Some leguminous plants, notably vetch, helped to provide protein. The most important stock animal was the sheep, which together with the goat accounted for 80 per cent or more of the livestock. Cattle and pigs made up the rest.

In the later neolithic period there was an increase in crop purity – that is to say, either one species or another would be grown in a given field, and not both at the same time. Improved cereal varieties developed: bread wheat, a hexaploid wheat, is now widely seen, for instance, instead of emmer. And a new range of plants was exploited, including beans and fruits, especially figs and grapes in the north.

All of these, and the greater flexibility and specialization in stock-rearing, were an improvement, and probably helped to support a larger population. But not until the crucially important domestication of the vine and the olive, for which we have evidence in the early bronze age, was the farming scene radically transformed.

With the early bronze age a new kind of farming became possible that did not depend on the traditional Near Eastern cereals alone. This was what the geographer calls Mediterranean polyculture, based on the 'Mediterranean triad' – wheat, olive and vine. The great advantage of these new tree crops is that they will grow on land not well suited to wheat or barley. Since they are not in competition for land with the original crops, they represent an absolute increase in the carrying capacity of the land. Moreover, they do not require attention at the busy time for wheat and barley, during sowing and particularly harvesting. So the farmer can maintain the same cereal production while producing also these new commodities.

I believe that in south Greece the development of this Mediterranean polyculture was as important for the emergence of civilization as was irrigation farming in the Near East. And this view is supported by the distribution of the Minoan-Mycenaean civilization, which corresponds closely with areas of true Mediterranean climate, where the vine and more particularly the olive will grow.

It is not easy to be sure that the increase in population in the neolithic set up population pressures on the available resources and led to increasing exploitation of wild tree crops, and ultimately to their domestication. The converse could also hold: that the exploitation of tree crops in late neolithic times, culminating in their domestication, raised the effective ceiling on population imposed by a limited food supply, and hence allowed population to rise. Probably both processes were happening at once, in a sort of feedback system, to use modern jargon: at one and the same time increasing population was encouraging experiment with tree crops, and the first successes with them were facilitating population increase.

The other great advance at about this time was the discovery of the alloying of copper to make bronze. Both arsenic and tin could be used to do this. Copper had, of course, been known in the Aegean for more than a thousand years, but it was used largely for trinkets and small tools. With the discovery of bronze, useful tools became possible, and more crucially, useful weapons. The dagger in the hands of one's neighbour offered only one course of action: to get a dagger oneself. Probably there was a sort of prehistoric arms race, where the possession of a dagger was as critical as the possession of automatic weapons or tanks today. In any case, daggers were very soon seen in every region of the Aegean. This was evidently one of the factors causing the widespread trade already mentioned. No doubt it helps to explain the great increase in fortified sites as well.

Perhaps, too, the development of metallurgy had something to do with the rise of chiefdoms in the Aegean, which we can discern at this time. Certainly the cemeteries in various areas have very suggestive indications of personal ranking reflected in the disparity of their grave goods. And many of the metal objects – the gold wine-cups, for instance, and the diadems – were very evidently status symbols. If the smith needed the wealth of the chieftain to finance his finer products, so the chieftain relied upon the smith for the display items with which to demonstrate and enhance his prestige and status.

An essential basis for a chiefdom society, as we saw in Chapter 8, is a system for the redistribution of goods, which is organized and controlled by the chief himself. This can, of course, function in a society where most people are producing the same crops, but it is much more useful economically when there is a diversity of production. Indeed, the kind of diversity resulting from Mediterranean polyculture – where one man has more olive oil than he can use, but little wheat, and another has plenty of grapes but would like more meat – virtually necessitates a redistribution system.

This is, of course, exactly the function fulfilled by the palaces of the Minoan-Mycenaean civilization, taking in and storing the produce from the very different fields, orchards and pastures which are found, even in quite a small area, in south Greece. The permanent organization of the palace was founded on the redistribution of goods in this way, controlled by the prince, and allowing him to keep a household of craft specialists.

Something of this sort was beginning already in the early bronze age, as is documented clearly by the clay sealings from the House of the Tiles at Lerna, and the sealstones of Early Minoan Crete, since the function of a seal is to put a personal mark on property which is leaving one's immediate possession. Such a procedure is not necessary in a barter transaction, but is clearly desirable if one is dispatching one's dues to the central authority.

Already, too, the excellence of the metalwork testifies to some craft specialization, no doubt sponsored by the chiefs of important settlements like Troy; indeed we do have some direct evidence for it. A clay hearth at Lerna bears the imprint of a decorative roll-seal, which was also used to decorate great pottery jars at two settlements within the same general area. Since the jars certainly did not move, the seal must have done, almost certainly in the hands of a specialist potter, who must have gone – like the potters of Crete today – from village to village in order to make these large jars.

There were, of course, many other developments and technological advances. One of these was the building of longships, perhaps with up to thirty oarsmen, resembling the war canoes of Polynesia (especially New Zealand). Indeed the period was almost certainly one of increasing hostility between rival communities. A rich plunder in metal goods was now to be expected if the enemy's defences could be overcome and his daggers and spears parried. This may be the explanation for the apparent recession in the all too accessible Cycladic settlements, indicated in the population figures for the middle bronze age (Fig. 45). Piracy may now have been rife, and just as in the Middle Ages, the pirates wrought terrible depredation. Crete, with its large, safe inland areas, could have escaped the worst of this. But small islands and exposed coastal areas must have become, as a result, more sparsely peopled even than in neolithic times.

Nearly everything which we see in the palace communities of the fully developed Minoan-Mycenaean civilization is foreshadowed in this crucial formative period in the third millennium B.C. The regularity of the Minoan building is anticipated at Early Minoan Vasiliki, and in the Early Helladic House of the Tiles at Lerna. The increasing abundance of bronze tools permitted the dressing of stone, so that the palace buildings could now be of ashlar. In the same way, the corbelled tombs of the Mycenaeans were built of handsomely dressed stone, and are perhaps the direct descendants of the round tombs of Early Minoan Crete.

The great wealth of the Mycenaean Shaft Graves, and the excellence of the palace craftsmanship, are foreshadowed already in the treasures found at Troy, and in the exquisite stone carving and lapidary work of Early Minoan Crete. Indeed, the use of seals incised with meaningful symbols is evidently a first step in symbolic communication, not far removed from the use of symbols in a pictographic script like that of Middle Minoan Crete. A case could in fact be made out for the local development of writing in Crete, and certainly the increasingly complex palace redistribution system made writing necessary. But this is not a necessary part of the argument. It is perfectly possible that the idea of writing and some of the skills of wall-painting were brought to Crete from the Near East, with which it enjoyed increasing trade in the early part of this period. Individual innovations were of course inspired from overseas. The argument here is that they were not central either to the economy or to the social system of Minoan Crete or Mycenaean Greece. It is therefore not correct to see Minoan-Mycenaean civilization as secondary, as derived or inspired from the Near East. It was a pristine and original creation in Greece, as much as the Sumerian civilization in Mesopotamia or the Olmec civilization of Mexico.

This alternative picture of the rise of Aegean civilization is, I believe, in better accord with the evidence than is Childe's model, which placed great emphasis on a trade where imperialist Sumer obtained raw materials in exchange for some of the luxuries of Mesopotamian civilization. In the early bronze age Crete was certainly receiving trinkets of ivory and stone from Egypt and Syria, but the volume of trade was very small. Whatever it meant in terms of personal contact and the flow of ideas and innovations (and I do not believe it meant much), in economic terms it can hardly have been of very great significance, even if we accept that the value of perishable goods imported was several times greater than that of the imperishable imports which have been preserved.

In the middle bronze age Minoan pottery is found on the Levant coast and in Egypt, and during the late bronze age (from 1600 B.C.) Mycenaean pottery is found in considerable quantity in the Near East. The pottery shape most frequently found is the 'stirrup jar' or the 'pilgrim flask', both vessels for liquid. Probably this liquid was olive oil, and the plausible suggestion has been made that it was often perfumed. Egyptian tomb paintings extend this picture, since they show Minoans bringing 'tribute' – which probably means, in economic terms, goods for exchange. These are chiefly textiles and finished products. In exchange the Aegean was receiving metal, although other imports are found. Large ingot bars of copper or bronze have been widely found in the Aegean, and a shipwreck at Cape Gelidoniya, at the south-east corner of the Aegean, helps to confirm that these were imported, together with tin, from Cyprus or the Near East. So we do have a picture of a thriving, if fairly limited trade.

But it is the very opposite of the one painted by Childe. To the best of our knowledge the Aegean was *importing* raw materials, chiefly metal. And it was the Aegean *exports* which were the manufactured goods – the pottery, the perfumed oil, the textiles. Indeed, far more Aegean pottery has been found in the Levant and Egypt than Near Eastern pottery in Crete. The evidence quite simply does not sustain Childe's idea of the Aegean as a rather backward and under-developed 'purveyor of raw material'. It suggests, on the contrary, that overseas trade was not of great economic significance to the Aegean until it itself experienced the need for a supply of raw materials which it obtained from the Near East, as well perhaps as from Italy.

Our conclusion, therefore, is that overseas contacts were not of crucial importance for the rise of Aegean civilization, although a number of new ideas doubtless came from overseas. J. W. Graham has reached just this conclusion about the genesis of Cretan palace architecture, and his words can be made to apply to Minoan civilization as a whole: '[There is] no good reason to see strong formative influences from a culture outside the island itself affecting the architecture of the palaces of Crete at any stage in their development ... But the imposition of isolated luxury trappings, such as details of decoration, or such splendid features as monumental reception or banqueting halls, is not only possible but likely.'[80]

Here, then, we see the whole development of the first European civilization as an essentially local, Aegean process, intelligible only in terms of the economy, technology and social organization of the time. Childe was right that we should not dismiss the process of its genesis as a miracle ('the fruit of a miraculous birth') and thereby circumvent the need to explain it further. But instead of thinking primarily in terms of diffusion and the adaptation of innovations from outside, we should consider increases in population density, changes in farming pattern, technological advance and developments in social organization, which can be studied and explained in Aegean terms. I am confident that in a few years, when suggestions of this kind have been tested through further excavation and research, we shall be able to give an account of the emergence of civilization in Europe at once more persuasive and in better accord with the evidence than the diffusionist one so widely accepted today.

11 Stonehenge and the Early Bronze Age

Stonehenge, the huge and problematic monument of great sarsen stones on the Salisbury Plain in southern Britain, has always held a particular fascination for the antiquary, and worked upon his imagination. The basic idea, of large upright stones supporting great horizontal lintel slabs, is a very simple one. And the very scale of the structure – over 30 metres in diameter and some 4·5 metres high – with the stark, uncompromising simplicity of the undecorated stones, gives it somehow a powerful and primitive appearance. Yet at the same time, the purely practical problem of getting the stones there, of shaping them, and above all of erecting them, all without the use of cranes, pulleys or comparable mechanical aids, would even today be a very daunting one. To the medieval eye the whole thing was miraculous, and the very name Stonehenge – 'hanging stones' – reflects something of the wonder it inspired. The twelfth-century chronicler Geoffrey of Monmouth believed indeed that the stones had been transported from Ireland and erected by the use of magic, employed by the great Merlin, official wizard at the court of King Arthur.

In more recent times it was suggested that the builders of Stonehenge were the early bronze-using people whose burial mounds cluster so thickly on the Salisbury Plain. A number of these barrows have yielded splendid decorations of gold, as well as beads of amber, and the chieftain buried under Bush Barrow had what looks like a mace of office. These finds, because of their distribution in Wiltshire and Dorset, are known archaeologically as the 'Wessex culture'.

It so happens that amber from the Baltic first makes its appearance in the Aegean around the time of the Shaft Graves of Mycenae. As we saw in Chapter 5, these Mycenaean finds, with their rich goldwork and their consummate craftsmanship, offered an obvious point of departure to any archaeologist seeking a Mediterranean origin for much of the finery of the Wessex culture. The theory was elaborated, and became one of the fundamental tenets of European prehistory, that the early bronze age of central and northern Europe was the result of influences from the civilized world of Mycenae. It seemed reasonable, therefore, to suppose that the final structure at Stonehenge might itself be the product of Mycenaean architectural skills. This was a more satisfactory response to the enigma of Stonehenge than an appeal to the magic of Merlin.

The tree-ring calibration of radiocarbon has made this diffusionist explanation for Stonehenge quite untenable: the corrected carbon dates for its construction are now set comfortably before the rise of Mycenaean civilization. As we shall see, the whole concept and its execution must have been of local, British inspiration. And although it might be argued that Stonehenge was completed prior to the time of the gold-loving Wessex chieftains, they too can have owed little to the Mycenaean world. This again is one possible inference to be drawn from the carbon dates in north Europe, although the question is at the moment being hotly contested.

Before attempting to assess the arguments and provide a new explanation, it is important to set the picture in its wider European context. For the rich dagger graves of south Britain, under their round tumuli, are indications of changes which were taking place much more widely. The dagger makes its appearance over much of Europe just before the time of the early bronze age Wessex, and it is now that bronze metallurgy develops, in place of the unalloyed copper of previous centuries. It is now too that burials, over much of central and northern Europe, are accompanied, for the first time, by rich grave goods. In Poland, north Germany and Brittany, as well as in Britain, there are graves with rich finds warranting the term 'princely burials'; in south Germany and Czechoslovakia, the territory of the Únětice culture, there are likewise rich burials; and similar customs are seen in southern France. Some generalizations, therefore, can be made which hold for much of temperate Europe. The explanation for these developments must be sought in demographic, economic and social processes of the kind discussed in the last two chapters. In this chapter, a first preliminary attempt will be made to do this for Britain.

Stonehenge and its date

The theories offered for the mysterious construction of Stonehenge in succeeding centuries are a mirror for the development of antiquarian thought. In the twelfth century Geoffrey of Monmouth could only appeal to magic. In 1620 the architect Inigo Jones was instructed by King James I to make a plan of the monument, and concluded that it was a Roman temple, no doubt thinking quite reasonably that only the Romans could have erected such a structure. The first serious fieldwork at Stonehenge was conducted forty years later by John Aubrey, who discovered the 'cavities' inside the bank, now known as the Aubrey Holes. His suggestion that it was a Druid temple was taken up with enthusiasm by the antiquary William Stukeley, who in 1740 published his *Stonehenge, a Temple Restored to the Druids*. These men triumphantly proclaimed the pre-Roman origins of the monument. Quite understandably they assigned it to the one religious organization in Britain at the time of the Roman conquest of which, through the writings of Julius Caesar, we have a direct record. Only in the later nineteenth century, when the division of the prehistoric past into neolithic age, bronze age and iron age became standard practice, was it widely realized that the original construction must have been long before the time of the iron age Druids.

It is only in the past twenty years that good, stratigraphic excavations have revealed the various stages in the construction of Stonehenge. Stuart Piggott and Richard Atkinson were able to show that the monument had grown and developed in late neolithic times from a much simpler affair of a type well known from other sites in Britain. It was not until phase II that the bluestones were erected in a double circle. And then in phase III this bluestone circle was dismantled and the great circle of sarsen stones with their 'hanging' lintels was set up (Pl. 12). Inside this circle a horseshoe arrangement of five free-standing 'trilithons' — each with two uprights supporting a lintel — was made. Later on, the bluestones were set up again in the positions they now occupy, forming a circle and horseshoe inside the main arrangement of sarsen stones (Fig. 46).

The phase I monument consisted primarily of a bank of earth and chalk forming a circle of nearly a hundred metres in diameter. Originally it was about two metres high, and was built of material quarried from a rather irregular ditch outside it. At the north-east side a gap was left in both bank and ditch to form an entrance causeway. Outside the perimeter of the ditch and circle, on the line of this causeway, stood the only three stones which are positively known to have formed part of this first Stonehenge. The most important of them is the Heel Stone, for seen from the centre of the circle it is obviously in rough alignment with the position of the sun when it rises on midsummer's day.

Four other stones, the Station Stones, may also have been erected at this

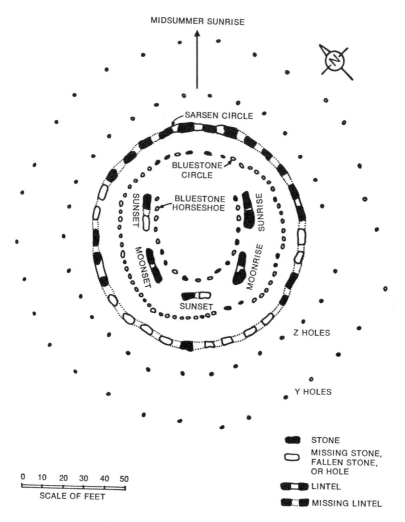

FIG. 46. Diagram of Stonehenge III, showing the sarsen circle and horseshoe of trilithons and the bluestone circle and horseshoe. (*After G. Hawkins*)

early stage. In themselves they are not imposing, but, as we shall see later, they may be of considerable significance.

The other important component of Stonehenge I is the series of 'cavities' or pits first observed by the antiquary, John Aubrey, in the seventeenth century. Excavation has now shown that there were 56 of these Aubrey Holes forming an accurate circle within the inner margin of the bank. They were up to two metres wide and sometimes more than a metre deep, with steep sides and flat bottoms. Most of them contained deposits of cremated human bones, which indicates that the site was being used as a cremation cemetery. Enough pottery was found during the excavations to set this phase of activity in the late neolithic period.

All of this ties in quite well with what we know of similar monuments in Britain of the same period, which likewise have a circular bank with an encircling ditch. In deference to Stonehenge, they are known as 'henge' monuments, and it is clear from the post-hole settings found at some of them that they often enclosed circular timber structures. Atkinson suggests that such a structure may have stood at the centre of Stonehenge at this period. The largest of these henges, at Marden and Durrington Walls, both (like Stonehenge) in Wiltshire, have diameters of more than 550 metres. The smallest known is only ten metres wide. Despite these disparities in size, they share a number of features in common, and are generally supposed to have had a ritual significance. The only thing special about Stonehenge I was the Heel Stone, and possibly the Station Stones, which have astronomical significance.

The main change in phase II was the transport of the bluestones, and their erection in two concentric circles in a position not far from where the bluestone circle now stands. Once again, arrangements of this very general sort are found at other henge monuments, from the great site at Avebury, in Wiltshire and 25 kilometres north of Stonehenge, right up to the Stones of Stenness and the Ring of Brodgar in the Orkney Islands, beyond the north tip of Scotland. Fragments of pottery of this period were found, from vessels known as beakers. These are very distinctive, the hallmark of a new cultural tradition in Britain at the very end of the neolithic period, serving to set Stonehenge II and a number of other henges in a clear cultural context.

It was in phase III that the sarsen stones were set up. They were probably quarried from a site near Avebury, and dragged to Stonehenge over a distance of nearly forty kilometres, although it may be that ice age glaciers had already brought them to the Salisbury Plain. The heaviest stones weigh about fifty tons, and the labour involved must have been colossal. Atkinson has calculated that the heaviest stones would require about 1,100 men to move them, hauling on twisted hide thongs, and using wooden rollers. The journey for a single stone coming from Avebury would have taken about seven weeks. The dressing of the stones, using only stone hammers and pounders, would have been a very lengthy enterprise, to be followed by the most impressive achievement of all: the erection of the standing stones and their 'hanging' lintels.

The uprights were erected by digging a hole of the appropriate dimensions, pulling the stone so that it projected over it, and then pulling on the far end, possibly with the aid of shear-legs. Up to 200 men would be needed for this task. The most difficult part was obviously the placing of the lintels on top of the uprights. One way of doing this would be to build an earth ramp. But Atkinson has described how a timber 'crib' could be used instead, more and more timbers being progressively inserted until the stone on its platform reached the required height (Fig. 27). This is indeed the same in principle as the method described in Chapter 7 which seems also to have been used for raising the statues of Easter Island, although the supporting structure there was of stone rather than of wood.

The dating of this remarkable structure presented problems, since there was no direct archaeological evidence in the form of associated pottery or other objects for phase III. For a long time the only relevant factor was the great cluster of round barrows in the neighbourhood. These, with their exotic grave goods, are assigned to the Wessex culture of the early bronze age, which, as we have seen, was conventionally dated by means of its link with Mycenaean Greece, to the period from 1550 to 1400 B.C. In 1953, however, very exciting supporting evidence was found for this dating, in the form of carvings on some of the upright stones, which had formerly escaped attention. There were daggers and axes, hollowed out of the stone, and one of the daggers, it was claimed, was of a well-known Mycenaean form. This was clearly carved after the erection of the stones, and was used to date this phase of the monument to 1500 B.C. or very shortly afterwards.

Finally, in 1959, the first radiocarbon dates for Stonehenge were announced. A date of 1720 b.c. ± 150 was obtained from a sample (an antler pick), dating the erection of one of the phase III trilithons. This was just a little earlier than had been predicted on archaeological grounds. It implies a 95 per cent probability that the radiocarbon date in question lies between 2020 b.c. and 1420 b.c., so that it did not necessarily conflict with the earlier suggestion of a date around 1500 B.C. We shall see below, however, that the tree-ring calibration seriously modifies these conclusions.

The unexpected discovery of the dagger carvings in 1953 was not, however, the last of the surprises which Stonehenge held in store. It had long been argued that the axis of Stonehenge was aligned on the point of midsummer sunrise (although there was doubt as to whether 'sunrise' implied the first gleam of light, or the appearance of half the sun's disc, or the full emergence of the sun – each occurring at a different point on the horizon). In 1963 Gerald Hawkins, an American astronomer, claimed in an article in the periodical *Nature* entitled 'Stonehenge Decoded', a further series of astronomically significant alignments amongst the stones of Stonehenge. His use of an electronic computer to calculate the position of the sun, moon and stars relative to the Salisbury Plain in 1500 B.C., and to produce bearings for each pair of stones, taken in turn, caught the popular imagination. His essential point was that the stones were aligned not only on the rising of the midsummer sun, but also on other significant solar and lunar events (Fig. 47).

The importance of midsummer's day, of course, is that the sun has then reached the northernmost point in its course. It then rises each day at a point which is, relative to the observer, farther south, until on mid-winter's day it reaches its southernmost extreme and then starts north again. To prehistoric man this cycle, and its correlation with the seasons, must have been of pressing interest, and it is not surprising that he should have wished to record the direction of the midsummer sun by setting up the Heel Stone.

The moon's wanderings are more complicated. It rises and sets progressively farther north, like the sun, until midsummer and then moves south again. But the extremes of its annual movement in this way are not the same from year to year. Instead they themselves shift, following a cycle of 18·6 years. The moon therefore has four extreme positions, rather than just two. There are northernmost and southernmost extremes for its midsummer rising, and corresponding ones for midwinter. Hawkins claimed that the four Station Stones were set up in such a way as to line up on the two extremes of the midsummer moonrise, sighting respectively along the long side of the rectangle which they form, and along the diagonal; the short side of this rectangle is aligned on the midsummer sunrise. These conclusions were reached earlier and independently by C. A. Newham, but his work was printed privately (in 1964) and did not receive the same widespread publicity as that of Hawkins.

Hawkins assumed that the Station Stones formed part of the phase I structure at Stonehenge, which is possible, although not certain. The

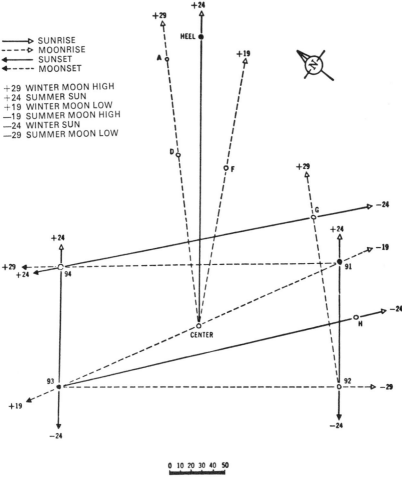

FIG. 47. Diagram of Stonehenge I, showing the solar and lunar alignments embodied in the stone settings. (*After G. Hawkins*)

great circular construction of phase III has no astronomical significance, although as architecture it is impressive; but Hawkins did suggest that the five great trilithons, forming the central horseshoe of the phase III monument, were each intended to frame the rising or setting of the sun and moon at the extremes of their journey at the winter or summer solstices. He was, in other words, giving the whole monument an astronomical significance, where previously archaeologists had thought of it rather in purely architectural terms.

Richard Atkinson wrote a splendidly trenchant review of Hawkins's book *Stonehenge Decoded*. Published in *Antiquity*, with the delightful title 'Moonshine on Stonehenge', it made some very telling criticisms of several inadequacies in Hawkins's arguments, as well as of the bumbling nature of his archaeology. Atkinson quoted a significant passage from the book: 'If I can see any alignment, general relationship or use for the various parts of Stonehenge, then these facts were also known to the builders. Such a hypothesis has carried me along over many incredible steps.' To which he rejoined: 'The epithet "incredible" is a most happy choice.'[81]

The whole matter has developed into one of those agreeably fiery little controversies to which archaeology seems particularly prone. In *Nature* Atkinson called Hawkins's book 'tendentious, arrogant, slipshod and unconvincing',[82] and in some ways he seems right: the presentation by Hawkins *was* sensational and slipshod, and did little to advance his case. However, his arguments for at least some of the alignments are now widely accepted, and it is clear that Stonehenge was used to observe the motions of the moon as well as the sun: it was indeed an observatory.

The Stonehenge controversy lives on. Our immediate interest, however, is in its date, because an early date would rule out the supposed civilizing influences from Mycenaean Greece. Since the conventional approach to the dating of Stonehenge is through that of the Wessex culture, with which Stonehenge III may have been contemporary, it is to this that we must now turn.

It was not until 1938 that Stuart Piggott, in a comprehensive study of the rich bronze age burials of Wiltshire and Dorset, defined what he called the 'Wessex culture'. He made out a good case for contacts between Wessex and the Mycenaean world. Amber from the Baltic is found in Greece from the time of the Shaft Graves of Mycenae, and in Crete a disc of amber mounted in a band of gold, and resembling two found in Wiltshire, has been found. Even the goldwork in Wessex, and a contemporary cup of gold from Rillaton in Cornwall (Pl. 9), suggested Mycenaean influence. As we saw in Chapter 5, Piggott concluded: 'Such resemblances may be individually fortuitous, but in their cumulative effect are too remarkable to dismiss.'[83] This, as we have seen, was the third important link for the traditional dating of prehistoric Europe.

Subsequent scholars greatly elaborated Piggott's idea, generally setting the span of the Wessex culture from around 1600 to 1400 B.C. As the only objects in the Wessex graves that could be regarded as direct imports to Britain from the Mediterranean, the curious little blue faience beads, of segmented form, were of special interest. With a view to establishing their place of origin, chemical analyses were carried out to determine the quantities of trace-elements (elements present at concentrations of less than one or two per cent) in them. Although the results, published in 1956, were not conclusive, this work represented an interesting application of modern scientific techniques to such material.

Piggott himself later became more cautious about the extent of direct contacts between the Wessex culture and the Mycenaean world. Yet in the prevailing climate of opinion, it was natural that the possibility of a Mycenaean contribution to Stonehenge III itself should be considered. The following speculative passage from Richard Atkinson's *Stonehenge* – still the best available description and discussion of the monument – exemplifies the general climate of thought in 1956 (of course, the author was aware that it was speculation, and separated it from the earlier discussion of the available evidence):

And yet were these Wessex chieftains *alone* responsible for the design and construction of this last and greatest monument at Stonehenge? For all their evident power and wealth, and for all their widespread commercial contacts, these men were essentially barbarians. As such, can they have encompassed unaided a monument which uniquely transcends all other comparable prehistoric buildings in Britain, and indeed in all Europe north of the Alps, and exhibits so many refinements of conception and technique. I for one do not believe it. It seems to me that to account for these exotic and unparalleled features one *must* assume the existence of influence from the only contemporary European cultures in which *architecture*, as distinct from mere construction, was already a living tradition; that is from the Mycenaean and Minoan civilizations of the central Mediterranean. Admittedly not all the refinements of Stonehenge can be paralleled in detail in Mycenaean or Minoan architecture ... But ... the architecture of the central Mediterranean provides the only outside source for the sophisticated approach to architecture exhibited at Stonehenge. We have seen that through trade the necessary contacts with the Mediterranean had been established. The Stonehenge dagger too may be seen, if one wishes, to point more directly at Mycenae itself ... Is it then any more incredible that the architect of Stonehenge should himself have been a Mycenaean, than that the monument should have been designed and erected, with all its unique and sophisticated detail, by mere barbarians?[84]

I am more optimistic about the possible achievements of 'mere barbarians', and take a different view, both of the Wessex finds and of Stonehenge. This is supported by some detailed arguments.

Other than the faience beads, there are no objects from the graves of the Wessex culture that can confidently be recognized as actual imports from the Mediterranean. The beads themselves are found throughout Britain (Fig. 48), although two shapes – the quoit bead and the star bead – are particularly numerous in the north. These cannot be matched so well in the Mediterranean as the segmented beads. But even the segmented beads are very scarce in central Europe, and arguing on the basis of dis-

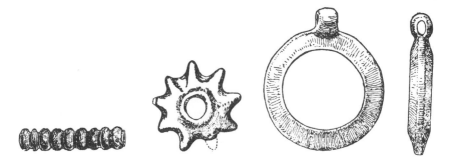

FIG. 48. Faience beads from the British early bronze age: the more common segmented form (*left*), and the star and quoit beads found chiefly in Scotland. (*After A. J. Evans* 1908; greater than original size)

tribution alone, one might suggest that they, as well as the quoit and star beads, were manufactured in Britain. A statistical study of the 1956 trace-element analyses recently reinforced this possibility. The British beads have a higher content of tin and of aluminium than is usual in the Mediterranean samples analysed. Of course, more analyses are needed – some are now in progress – and different interpretations have been made; but we can now suggest that these beads were locally made, by a process requiring no more advanced techniques than bronze smelting, widely practised at the time. Naturally, the initial idea – the technique of production, and the form of the beads – might have been learnt from the east Mediterranean. But even if this were so, prototypes are available in the Mediterranean by around 2500 B.C., so that this would present no difficulties in dating, if we were seeking to put the Wessex culture earlier than hitherto. In any case, it could be argued that the whole thing was an independent local invention.

There can be no doubt, on the other hand, that amber was exported from the Baltic down to the Mycenaean world. But I would argue that this amber trade was at its peak *after* the time of the early Wessex culture. If it is dated to 1650 B.C. at Mycenae, this only proves that the trade was under way by that date. It does not prevent the Wessex culture's beginning several centuries earlier.

Similar arguments apply to most of the Mycenaean features seen in Britain. Their association with the Wessex culture is not secure, and if they are indeed Mycenaean, they could indicate developing contacts in the middle or late bronze age. The carved daggers on Stonehenge, for instance, if they are really of Mycenaean form (which I frankly doubt), could have been carved there long after Stonehenge III was completed. And there is no need to connect the other finds in the Wessex graves with the Mycenaean world. The goldwork, for instance, is undoubtedly a superb development of a local tradition, already flourishing in the preceding Beaker period, as recent work by Joan Taylor has shown. Most of the other similarities can today be dismissed as fortuitous.

The tree-ring calibration of radiocarbon lends some support to these arguments. For while there are still no early radiocarbon dates for the Wessex culture barrows of Wiltshire and Dorset, there are clear and undisputed links between the finds in them and those of neighbouring lands, including Brittany and Germany, from which we do have dates.

A radiocarbon date from the Helmsdorf barrow in north Germany, for instance, which should be broadly contemporary with at least part of the Wessex culture, can be set around 1900 B.C. after calibration. And other similar dates are now beginning to form a pattern.

Using such evidence, which is admittedly indirect, I suggested in 1968, in a paper called 'Wessex without Mycenae', that the duration of the Wessex culture might have been from about 2100 to 1700 B.C. in calendar years. Radiocarbon dates from two dagger graves, quoted in Chapter 5, indicate now that rich burials of this kind must have continued until at least 1500 B.C. But they do not conflict with the early date suggested for the first of the Wessex dagger graves. We do not yet have enough dates from Wessex to give a final verdict on this question – and Christopher Hawkes, a leading scholar of the early Wessex bronze age, has argued with vigour against the early dating. But whatever the date, my own view is that the Mycenaean contacts with Wessex, if they existed at all, were of very marginal importance.

In any case, the radiocarbon dates which we have for Stonehenge now suggest that it was completed before Mycenaean times. Using the un-calibrated radiocarbon dates, Atkinson came to the conclusion that the main structure, Stonehenge III, was erected in the seventeenth century b.c., in radiocarbon years. If we accept this, using Suess's calibration curve, we would reach a date of between 2100 and 1900 B.C. in calendar years. Because of these early dates, some scholars, including Christopher Hawkes, now feel that Stonehenge III was actually built before the time of the Wessex culture. But of course, if the early Wessex dating is accepted, the construction date of 2100 to 1900 B.C. is in any case within the Wessex culture time-span.

The effect of the tree-ring calibration of radiocarbon upon the Wessex culture and Stonehenge is not so dramatic as it was for the megalithic tombs, or for the copper age in south-east Europe. This is partly because we have as yet rather few relevant radiocarbon dates. But it is also because the Wessex culture was rather later than these other cases. So that whereas a radiocarbon date of 2500 b.c. will be set 800 years earlier in calendar years, one of 1500 b.c. moves back by only two or three centuries (see Fig. 14). I believe, however, that the time shift is sufficiently drastic to make us look at Stonehenge and the wealth of the Wessex graves in their own right. For even if there were trading links with Mycenae – and the new chronology makes this very unlikely in the early Wessex period – they were probably at second hand and remote. They can have had little influence on developments in Britain.

In order to 'restore' Stonehenge, if not to the Druids, at least to the neolithic inhabitants of Wiltshire, we have to reconcile our minds to two different and local achievements. In the first place, there is the considerable sophistication of the whole concept of the monument as well as of its execution. Even setting aside the very ill-substantiated theory put forward by Hawkins, and later by the astronomer Fred Hoyle, that the 56 Aubrey Holes formed a prehistoric analogue computer for the prediction of eclipses, we have to accept that very high astronomical and geometrical skill was involved in setting out the Station Stones so that the diagonal of the rectangle as well as the sides was aligned upon one of the major moonrise turning points. The execution of the sarsen structure, with its tenon and mortice fixtures for the lintels and its careful dressing of the stones, also excites our admiration.

Even more than these, however, the level of organization needed for the construction of the monument is very impressive. Atkinson formulated this problem well, and despite his earlier suggestion, did not insist that the moving force had to be Mycenaean:

> Now in the rich and martially furnished Wessex graves we can admittedly see evidence for chieftainship, and the grouping of graves in cemeteries may imply whole dynasties of chiefs. Yet the pattern of society which they represent is surely that of so many other heroic societies, in which clan wars with clan, and rival dynasties carry on a perpetual struggle for power. Under such conditions, can the construction of Stonehenge, involving the displacement of so many hundreds of men from their homes for so long, have been attempted, still less achieved? Surely not; for such great works can only be encompassed by a society at peace within itself. And in such a society of conflicting factions, how is peace imposed except from above? ...
>
> I believe, therefore, that Stonehenge itself is evidence for the concentration of political power, for a time at least, in the hands of a single man, who alone could create and maintain the conditions necessary for this great undertaking. Who he was, whether native-born or foreign, we shall never know ... [85]

This social problem is, of course, related to the ones we have already tackled when discussing the temples of Malta and the megalithic tombs of western Europe. The construction of Stonehenge can be made more intelligible by reasoning along similar lines.

Chiefdoms in neolithic Wessex

One of the keys to our understanding of the remarkable early bronze age florescence of the Wessex culture of south Britain, and to the construction of the great sarsen structure at Stonehenge, must clearly be the society in Britain at a slightly earlier period. And it is indeed remarkably interesting that in the later neolithic it shows some clear signs of developing beyond the scatter of essentially egalitarian communities which we may imagine for the very early neolithic.

Settlement finds in the British neolithic are very rare, one possible explanation being that villages or clusters of houses did not stay at the same spot for several generations, as they clearly did on the tells of southeast Europe. The example of Bylany in Czechoslovakia may provide a better model. There shifting cultivation was practised, and the settlement was moved every ten or fifteen years. This periodic movement, and the construction of houses of wood rather than mud, prevented the accumulation of any great depth of settlement debris.

We do find in south Britain, however, the 'unchambered' or earthen long barrows discussed in Chapter 7. They are concentrated on the chalklands of the Wessex region (notably Dorset, Hampshire and Wiltshire). Earthen mounds up to 150 metres in length, sometimes covering a timber 'mortuary house', they were the principal monuments of the early neolithic of the area. In some areas their distribution and spacing suggest that each barrow may have been the chief monument of a single territory, the region occupied by the inhabitants of a farming community. If these people lived in a village, rather than in scattered houses, the village may have shifted its location within the territory. This suggestion, then, is very much like the one already made for the megalithic tombs of Rousay and Arran. Since the wooden chambers within the Wessex long barrows did not long remain open, when they existed at all, it is clear that the monument did not necessarily continue to serve as a communal burying place. But no doubt it did remain the central, symbolic monument of the community.

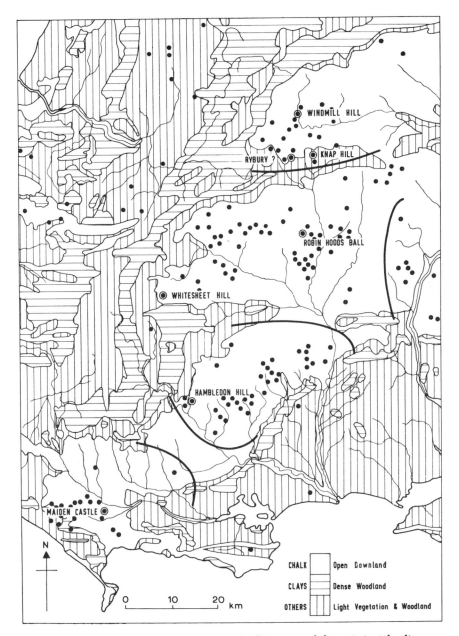

CHALK — Open Downland
CLAYS — Dense Woodland
OTHERS — Light Vegetation & Woodland

0   10   20 km

WINDMILL HILL
RYBURY ?   KNAP HILL
ROBIN HOODS BALL
WHITESHEET HILL
HAMBLEDON HILL
MAIDEN CASTLE

N

FIG. 49. The emergence of embryonic chiefdoms in neolithic Britain. The distribution of 'causewayed camps' (circles) in relation to the long burial 'barrows' of the first farmers (dots). In the later neolithic the 'camp' in each of the territories indicated was succeeded by a major henge monument.

These barrows of Dorset and Wiltshire have been divided by Paul Ashbee into five groups, and it is particularly interesting that each group has a single early neolithic monument of another kind located close to it (one group has two, or perhaps three). These are the 'causewayed camps', roughly circular banks, with entrances at several places, outside which are irregular ditches interrupted by 'causeways'. There may be up to four concentric circles, with a diameter of up to 400 metres. The function of these camps has been much discussed. They do not seem to have been permanently occupied, and it has been suggested that they were meeting places or rallying points for the population of a fairly wide area.

Their distribution certainly supports this suggestion, and each causewayed camp could be regarded as a 'central place' serving some twenty or thirty of the small farming groups documented by the long barrows (Fig. 49). The camps are not in fact centrally placed, with respect to the clusters of long barrows, but this need not prevent our regarding them as periodic tribal meeting places. It has been calculated that each 'camp' may have taken about 100,000 man hours to construct, as against 5,000 for the barrows. Therefore some inter-community co-operation must have been necessary for the camps, while the barrows were doubtless the work of the population of their own territories, even if this was as small as twenty to fifty persons.

In the late neolithic period a new class of monuments confirms this territorial pattern. For it is now that the 'henges' are seen. As described above, these are monuments with a circular bank enclosing a ditch. There are just four of these in south Britain with a diameter of more than 200 metres, and they are situated in four out of the five areas already recognized. It has been estimated by Geoffrey Wainwright that the digging of the ditch, and the construction of the bank, of these large henges may have taken something like a million man hours.

These considerable investments of labour pose a problem not unlike that set by the temples of Malta. And I believe we can answer it in the same way, by postulating the emergence of chiefdoms in the late neolithic period of Wessex, around 2500 B.C. in calendar years. The causewayed camps of the early neolithic already hint at some inter-community collaboration, and this may have developed in the late neolithic into a hierarchically ordered chiefdom society.

Admittedly we have no direct archaeological evidence for the chiefs themselves at this time, since burials, when they are found, are not accompanied by great quantities of pottery or impressive grave goods like those in some of the copper age cemeteries of south-central Europe. But there is already in the early neolithic an exchange in stone axes and no doubt other goods, over considerable distances. From quite an early date, flint was obtained from real mines, such as Grimes Graves in Norfolk, which can almost rival the copper mines of Rudna Glava as the earliest known anywhere. The mines do indicate a considerable degree of craft specialization. This, and the scale of the exchange needed to disseminate the products, could also be used to support the notion of some chiefly redistributive organization. Such a system was not proposed in Chapter 9 for the copper age villages of the Balkans, despite their developing technology and craft specialization, because they are quite without large communal monuments or public works of any kind. And the evidence from the distribution of settlements there, which is abundant, does not indicate any hierarchical organization in the society. In Britain we lack such settlement evidence, but the henges and also the curious 'cursus' monuments – long parallel banks sometimes running for several kilometres – suggest that the social organization was considerably more complex.

One important feature of some of the henges has emerged even more clearly from recent excavations by Geoffrey Wainwright at three of the large henges in our area (at Durrington Walls, Marden and Mount Pleasant). Timber buildings sometimes stood within these great enclosures. Already at Woodhenge, a very much smaller henge near Durrington Walls excavated in 1929, concentric circles of post-holes were found, and Stuart Piggott suggested how these might have supported a roof (Fig. 50). And now at Durrington Walls, six concentric circles of posts, the outer circle forty metres in diameter, have been interpreted in a similar way as supporting a roof. There may have been more such structures as yet unexcavated within the same enclosure.

There was much domestic debris at Durrington, suggesting that the site may have been permanently occupied. So one is tempted now to think of a full chiefdom stage of social organization, with the chief himself and his lineage occupying the territory near the principal monument – the henge – and other lineages occupying the remainder of the territory, the Salisbury Plain. Wainwright has calculated that the construction of the ditch and bank alone required some 900,000 man hours – at least 90,000

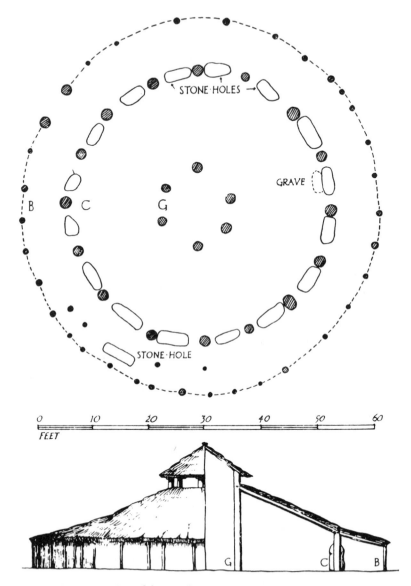

FIG. 50. Reconstruction of the circular wooden building, traces of which were found at The Sanctuary, near Avebury in southern England. Similar buildings stood within the enclosures at several of the henges. (*After S. Piggott*)

man days. This formidable investment of labour may not all have been expended at one go. But even if the henge was the result of periodic bursts of activity over a number of years, it involved a considerable labour force. Undoubtedly the workers were fed on resources which the chief could accumulate by virtue of his position, and redistribute to his workers.

We should remember too that Stonehenge, which is smaller in diameter but a far more impressive monument, lies within the territory which we are suggesting may have fallen within the province of Durrington Walls. And in the territory to the north, the Marlborough Downs, lie not only the great henge of Avebury, with its stone circles, but also Silbury Hill. Silbury, a huge man-made cone of earth, forty metres high, is now dated to around 2500 B.C. in calendar years. Richard Atkinson has calculated that its erection required some 18 million man hours of labour. His recent excavations there have shown that, once begun, the construction of this monument was continuous, so that the organization involved must have been prodigious.

A remarkable parallel to the round buildings inside the henges occurs among the eighteenth-century Creek and Cherokee Indians of the south-eastern United States. It is worth mentioning here, not merely because of the similarity in construction, but because the social organization there is a paradigm case—just as in Polynesia—for chiefdom societies in general.

The eighteenth-century naturalist William Bartram has left a graphic account of these Indians in his *Travels*. It is estimated that the total population of the Cherokee, one of the largest tribes occupying an area several times that of Wessex, was of the order of 11,000 persons. At this time there were sixty 'towns', whose average population was thus less than 200. They lived chiefly by agriculture (maize and kidney beans), supplemented by hunting deer and rabbit, and it is clear that the settlement was often very dispersed. At the centre of the larger 'towns' stood the circular council-house. The council of chiefs had at its head 'their mico or king, which signifies a magistrate or chief ruler ... yet when out of the council he associates with the people as a common man, converses with them, and they with him in perfect ease and familiarity'. Next to him in importance was the war chief and then the high priest or seer.

The redistributive nature of the society was well described by Bartram:

After the feast of the busk is over, and all the grain is ripe, the whole town again assemble, and every man carries off the fruits of his labour, from the part first allotted to him, which he deposits in his own granary; which is individually his own. But previous to their carrying off their crops from the field, there is a large crib or granary, erected in the plantation, which is called the king's crib; and to this each family carries and deposits a certain quantity according to his ability or inclination, or none at all if he so chooses, this in appearance serves as a tribute or revenue to the mico, but in fact is designed for another purpose i.e. that of a public treasury supplied by a few and voluntary contributions to which every citizen has the right of free and equal access, when his own private stores are consumed, to serve as a surplus to fly to for succour, to assist neighbouring towns whose crops may have failed, accommodate strangers, or travellers, to afford provisions or supplies when they go forth on hostile expeditions, and for all the exigencies of the state; and this treasure is at the disposal of the king or mico; which is surely a royal attribute to have an exclusive right and ability in a community to distribute comfort and blessings to the necessitous.[86]

This, then, was the economic reality behind the social reality of the social hierarchy.

Bartram described the circular building (cf. Pl. 10) which particularly interests us:

The council or town-house is a large rotunda, capable of accommodating several hundred people ... The rotunda is constructed in the following manner, they first fix in the ground a circular range of posts or trunks of trees, about six feet high, at equal distances, which are notched at top, to receive into them, from one to another, a range of beams or wall plates: within this is another circular order of very large or strong pillars, about twelve feet high, notched in like manner at the top, to receive another range of wall plates, and within this is yet another or third range of stronger and higher pillars, but fewer in number, and standing at a greater distance from each other; and lastly in the centre stands a very strong pillar, which forms the pinnacle of the building, and to which the rafters centre at top; these rafters are strengthened and bound together by cross beams and laths, which sustain the roof or covering which is a layer of bark neatly placed, and tight enough to exclude the rain ... Near the great pillar in the centre the fire is kindled for light, near which the musicians seat themselves, and round about this the performers exhibit their dances and other shows at public festivals.[87]

He gives a plan of such a rotunda (Fig. 51), and describes their use for social and religious purposes.

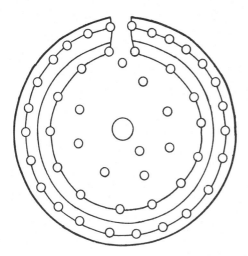

FIG. 51. Ground plan, by the eighteenth-century traveller William Bartram, of a rotunda of the Cherokee Indians 'capable of accommodating several hundred people'. The wooden rotundas of neolithic south Britain were of similar construction.

Another Creek round house, described by the traveller Hitchcock, was (like the structures in the henges) without a central pillar, and the central space was narrowed by a form of corbelling:

Upon the alternate couples of the twelve pillars are first placed horizontal pieces, then upon the ends of these are placed other horizontal pieces between the other couples of the pillars, then another series of horizontal pieces resting upon the second set, but drawn towards the centre of the circle a few inches [Fig. 52].[88]

On the slope so formed, the rafters were laid and tied, meeting at a central high point.

The wooden buildings inside the British henge enclosures may have been much like these, although apparently rather larger. Their function may have been similar too. By analogy with the central function of the earlier neolithic causewayed enclosures among their widely dispersed long barrows, it seems likely that the henges were meeting places for people who did not live permanently in one compact community.

The great henges now appear as the successors of the causewayed enclosures: periodic meeting places for all the members of the chiefdom, and perhaps the permanent home of the chief. These meetings were occasions of feasting and ceremony and no doubt of trade. (One nineteenth-century traveller said of the Indians of the south-eastern United States: 'They meet from all the towns within fifty or sixty miles round, where they buy and sell commodities as we do at fairs and markets.')[89] We imagine that the henge served as the focal point for a region up to forty or fifty miles in extent. The individual farming settlements — comparable with the smaller 'towns' of the Indians — may have had no communal houses or monuments, although some of the smaller henges

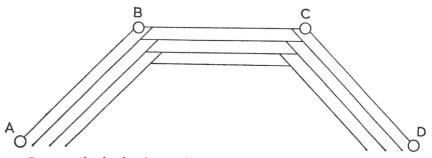

FIG. 52. Sketch plan by Hitchcock of the roofing of a Creek Indian rotunda. A, B, C, and D are upright stakes, forming a circle. Horizontal beams between these were the support for further horizontal beams set above and within them (as shown), so that the whole space was eventually covered by a corbelled vault of horizontal beams. A similar roofing system was probably used in neolithic Britain.

could have served such a purpose. Armed with such a picture of their function, the mobilization of resources involved in their construction seems less remarkable. As we saw in Chapter 8, mobilization of manpower for public works was a common feature of some of the Polynesian chiefdoms.

Of course, it would be absurd to make too much of the largely fortuitous resemblance between these buildings in the North America of the eighteenth century A.D. and those of neolithic south Britain in the third millennium B.C. It is not the superficial similarities in form which are important, intriguing as these may be, but the underlying social organization of a chiefdom society, with its supporting redistribution and the potential mobilization of manpower.

Two important features of chiefdoms are of considerable relevance to our understanding of Stonehenge and those other British monuments with a significance that was primarily religious or at least astronomical. In the first place, the religious and ceremonial activities of the society are often well developed in chiefdoms. As Elman Service, the anthropologist who has written most extensively about the social organization of chiefdoms, puts it: 'The shamanistic practices and local life-cycle rituals remain, but ceremonies and rituals serving wider social purposes become more numerous.' And secondly, the rise of chiefdoms is associated with the emergence of a specialist priesthood. In the words of Service: 'Whereas a shaman achieves his position by personal qualifications, a priest occupies a permanent office in the society. The differences between these two resemble the differences between the occasional leader of a tribal society and the true chief. Chieftainship and priesthood, in fact, seem to arise together as twin forms of authority ... Ordinarily priestly offices descend in the same family line as the secular offices; further, sometimes the priest and the chief are the same person.'[90]

Now three features of the British stone circles do imply some really sophisticated skills which could only have been accumulated through a good measure of such specialization over a long period of time. The sequences of astronomical observations needed to align the stones accurately clearly indicate that the traditional lore was passed on from one generation to the next, and the hereditary succession of experts in these matters is a very likely mechanism for this.

Firstly, the stone circles and other arrangements of stones are laid out with great geometrical precision. Professor Alexander Thom, who has spent years studying them, has demonstrated that some are true ellipses, and arrangements like that of the Station Stones at Stonehenge show that the builders were well capable of setting out right-angles. Secondly, Thom has shown, by a sophisticated statistical analysis of the many circles he has studied, that they were laid out in integral numbers of a unit, which he has termed the 'megalithic yard'. He suggests that the builders were anxious that the circumference as well as the diameter should be approximately equal in length to an integral number of these units, so

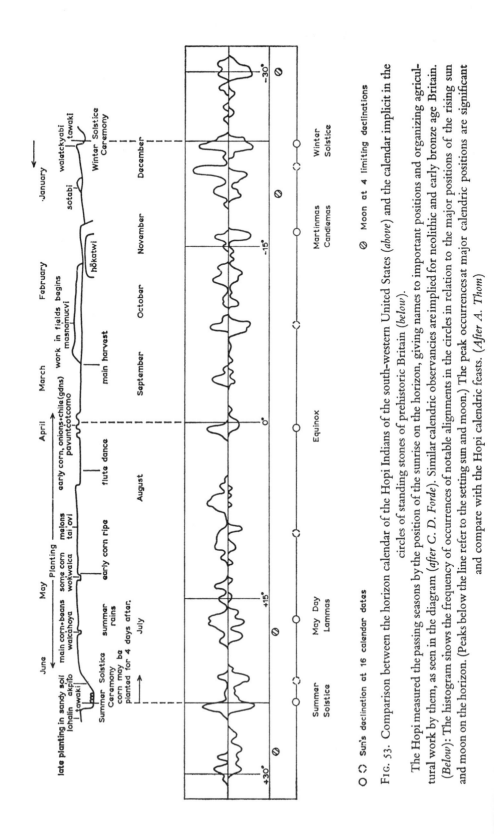

FIG. 53. Comparison between the horizon calendar of the Hopi Indians of the south-western United States (*above*) and the calendar implicit in the circles of standing stones of prehistoric Britain (*below*).

The Hopi measured the passing seasons by the position of the sunrise on the horizon, giving names to important positions and organizing agricultural work by them, as seen in the diagram (*after C. D. Forde*). Similar calendric observances are implied for neolithic and early bronze age Britain. (*Below*): The histogram shows the frequency of occurrences of notable alignments in the circles in relation to the major positions of the rising sun and moon on the horizon. (Peaks below the line refer to the setting sun and moon.) The peak occurrences at major calendric positions are significant and compare with the Hopi calendric feasts. (*After A. Thom*) that only certain values for the diameter could be used. Dr Max Hammerton has recently suggested that this rather uniform unit of length, which Thom has documented for the whole of Britain, may in fact be the human pace. This would be an agreeably simple solution, and make unnecessary the vision, which archaeologists were beginning to have, of priests travelling up and down Britain with yardsticks, checking the length of the local standard measure. But this does not detract from the interest of Thom's conclusion that great care, and possibly a symbolism of numbers, was involved in the layout of the monuments.

Their most striking feature, however, is that many appear to be aligned on the positions of the rising or setting sun or moon at the solstices. This point was, of course, made by Hawkins for Stonehenge, but had already been demonstrated far more convincingly by Thom on the basis of his study of many monuments. His histogram of observed declinations (Fig. 53) shows that many of the most prominent alignments of notable stones in these monuments cluster in the direction of the rising or setting sun at the summer and winter solstices, and the four standstill points of the moon's 18·6 year cycle. The stones were no doubt set in position partly as a record of an astronomical observation. Each monument was thus a symbolic artifact, a permanent record of some information about the world, just as sophisticated in its way as early writing. And at the same time, the alignments and circles formed a centre of observations and rituals which obviously were related to the seasonal cycle and the movements of the sun and moon.

These findings, as we saw, have created a great furore among British archaeologists, some of whom are reluctant to believe that the barbarian inhabitants of prehistoric Britain were capable of such ingenuity. But there are good ethnographic parallels for careful observation of the heavenly bodies, especially of the sun. The Hopi Indians, mentioned in Chapter 9, had a horizon calendar (Fig. 53), provided by the daily shifts of the sunrise on the horizon, which also served to determine the dates of the many ceremonies:

The smallest irregularities on the southern skyline are well known, and the more significant within the sun's path, probably some twenty or more, are named with reference either to their form, to ceremonial events or to agricultural operations, which fall due when the sun rises immediately behind them. For a well-educated Hopi such terms as *neverktcomo* and *lohalin* have as precise a significance as have for us May 3rd and June 21st, with which they correspond. The daily observation of these positions of sunrise is the duty of a religious official, the Sun Watcher, who forewarns the people of important dates, and announces them in due course; he also keeps a tally on a notched stick.[91]

The Hopi society is essentially egalitarian, and lacks public monuments, other than the meeting houses of *kivas* mentioned in Chapter 9. But the more hierarchical societies of Central America developed an astonishingly accurate calendar probably as early as 1000 B.C., and not long after that time devised a hieroglyphic writing to record it. The so-called Caracol at the great Maya ceremonial site of Chichen Itza records both solar and

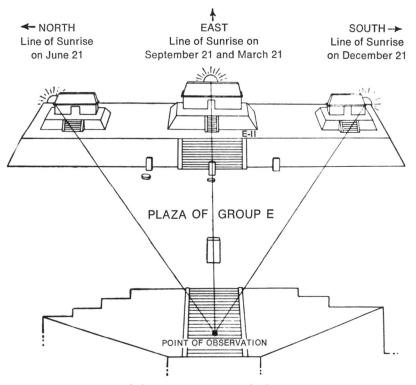

FIG. 54. Diagram of the Maya astronomical observatory at Uaxactun in Guatemala, showing accurate alignments for sunrise at solstices and equinoxes. (*After S. G. Morley*)

lunar positions at the vernal equinox, and Maya observatories, like that at Uaxactun in Guatemala (Fig. 54), are well known.

It seems likely that both the social organization and the calendrical expertise of the late neolithic and early bronze age inhabitants of south Britain lay somewhere between the different levels of competence documented in these two American examples.

Before leaving this question of priesthood, astronomical observation and ritual, it is worth returning to the Cherokee Indians of the south-eastern United States, who in the nineteenth century A.D., as well as building round houses like those found in the British henges, had quite a complex ceremonial cycle related to the annual change of the seasons. A graphic description by a contemporary traveller of the harvest celebration helps to remind us that the henges and other ceremonial sites were more than just observatories and meeting places. They were also the scene of elaborate rituals, the details of which we can only guess at. The date of the Cherokee festival described was fixed as the night of the full moon nearest to the period when the maize became ripe. Although it relates to another time and another continent, we can almost imagine this as the description of the celebrations at a neolithic henge:

But the harvest moon is now near at hand, and the chiefs and medicine men have summoned the people of the several villages to prepare themselves for the autumnal festival. Another spot of ground is selected, and the same sanctifying ceremony is performed that was performed in the previous spring. The most expert hunter in each village has been commissioned to obtain game, and while he is engaged in the hunt the people of his village are securing the blessing of the Great Spirit by drinking, with many mystic ceremonies, the liquid made from seven of the most bitter roots to be found among the mountains. Of all the game which may be obtained by the hunters, not a single animal is to be served up at the feast whose bones have been broken or mutilated, nor shall a rejected animal be brought within the magic circle, but shall be given to the tribe who, by some misdeed, have rendered themselves unworthy to partake of the feast. The hunters are always compelled to return from the chase at the sunset hour, and long before they come in sight of their villages they invariably give a shrill whistle, as a signal of good luck, whereupon the villagers make ready to receive them with a wild song of welcome and rejoicing.

The pall of night has once more settled upon the earth, the moon is in its glory, the watch-fire has been lighted within the magic circle, and the inhabitants of the valley are again assembled together in one great multitude. From all the cornfields in the valley the magicians have gathered the marked ears of corn, and deposited them in the kettles with the various kinds of game which may have been slaughtered ... The entire night is devoted to eating, and the feast comes not to an end until all the food has been despatched, when, in answer to an appropriate signal from the medicine man, the bones which have been stripped of their flesh are collected together and pounded to a kind of powder and scattered through the air. The seven days following this feast are devoted to dancing and carousing, and at the termination of this period the inhabitants of the valley retire to their various villages, and proceed to gather in their crops ... [92]

The henges of south Britain were the product of a social organization and an intensity of ceremonial and religious activity similar in many ways to this. The final structure at Stonehenge and the great mound of Silbury Hill are something more, both unique monuments; yet they emerged from this background of mobilization. The dressing of the sarsens at Stonehenge certainly shows an astonishing mastery and sophistication, but we must remember that it was only the beneficiary of a long tradition of monumental construction in stone. Indeed the great tomb at Maeshowe in Orkney, still in the mainstream of that funerary tradition, displays a skill and vision altogether comparable with that displayed by Stonehenge.

The development of metallurgy in society

It is in this general context that the developments of the British early bronze age must be viewed. In some respects they form a total contrast to those of the neolithic period, although many of the British stone circles and alignments are probably of bronze age date. The bronze age burials, for instance, display a considerable variety of rich and exotic objects. And while those objects made of metal were by definition not to be anticipated earlier, it would not be surprising to find others, like the handsome necklaces of amber, in neolithic contexts. But they do not occur in them.

At first it seemed possible that the appearance of these rich burials in south Britain around 2100 B.C. or a little later (in calendar years) might be explained in terms similar to those used for the Aegean early bronze age. For as we saw in Chapter 10, the appearance of bronze metallurgy in the Aegean is accompanied by the production of daggers and finery of gold and silver, by rich finds suggestive of high rank, by clear indications of a marked increase in population density, and by central structures – namely palaces – and seals, showing the beginnings of a redistributive system. The monumental constructions were not impressive – just a few fortification walls and granaries – yet the evidence seemed, and still seems, quite sufficient to recognize the emergence in the Aegean of chiefdoms.

The analogies in Wessex are obvious. In the first place, there is a very marked increase in the number of burial mounds, which in parts of Wessex are found in a density as high as six per square kilometre. These are now mounds for single rather than communal burial, and they can represent only a small part of the population; but clearly the total labour invested in building round barrows in Wessex, in the 500 or 600 years which the early bronze age may have covered, was materially greater than that involved in constructing long barrows over a rather longer period in the earlier neolithic. It does seem likely that, as in the Aegean, the population of the area increased in the early bronze age. Again, the rich finds clearly indicate a marked ranking in society. Also, the technological advances, with the use of bronze daggers, are comparable to those of the early bronze age Aegean. All of this makes it possible to propose that chiefdoms were emerging in Wessex at this time.

Already, however, the various monuments and finds of the neolithic can be interpreted as documenting a chiefdom society, albeit one of a very different kind. So we are led to suggest that what occurred in Britain in the centuries before 2000 B.C. was a *transformation* in what was already a chiefdom society, with less emphasis now on the mobilization of manpower for public works, and much more on the person and prestige of the chief and other sub-chiefs, upon the display of their wealth and upon its conspicuous consumption. Moreover, although the neolithic background was not the same in other parts of northern Europe, we can indeed suggest that similar transformations were taking place there.

There were other changes, too, which we can at present only begin to discern. For in eastern Europe, a new pottery style – corded ware – is widely associated with a new burial convention of inhumation in a single grave under a round mound, and with a new prestige artifact, the perforated stone battle axe. In much of central and western Europe, single burial under a tumulus is first seen accompanied by pottery vessels of the different type known as beakers, and by copper daggers that in some regions are the earliest metal artifacts known. It is conventional to explain these changes in terms of the migrations of 'Corded Ware People' (coming from the east) and of 'Beaker Folk' (coming from Iberia or perhaps from Hungary). Marija Gimbutas, indeed, regards all of this as the dispersion of a single group of people and their descendants, originating in south Russia. I do not believe that the migrations were as decisive or as great as they are sometimes painted, but clearly something was going on which we do not yet understand very well and which resulted in the widespread distribution of beakers and copper daggers, amongst other things.

For whatever reason, burials in single graves under round tumuli are found in Britain from about 2500 B.C. The graves contain beakers and often copper daggers as well – the earliest metal objects in Britain – and in one or two cases there are small objects of gold, including earrings. Dr Joan Taylor has recently argued persuasively that the handsome beaten-gold decorations known as 'lunulae' that have been found in Britain, were made at this time, although curiously enough they are not found in the graves. This, then, was the coming of metallurgy to Britain, and its ultimate origins can probably be traced back to the 'copper age' of south-east Europe, discussed in Chapter 9. The world's earliest daggers are seen in the 'copper age' of Hungary and tanged daggers very much like them occur in some of the Beaker graves in the same area and in the Vučedol culture of Jugoslavia towards the end of the 'copper age'.

What we perhaps see in the early bronze age is the impact of the new technology upon a society already to some extent stratified, and already showing a measure of craft specialization, as seen in the flint mines. It possessed an established network of exchange links, doubtless largely by gift exchange, documented by the distribution of stone axes from different and identifiable rock outcrops in western Britain.

The goods in the Wessex graves certainly reflect an extremely high level of craftsmanship which it is reasonable to associate with the further development of craft specialization. Some of the goldwork is exquisite, and Dr Joan Taylor believes that she is able to recognize in much of it the work of a single hand or workshop. Such a specialist or series of specialists is likely to have formed one of the household of a chief, and to have been supported by the chief's redistribution of produce.

Two trends are seen in this craft. The first is the employment of essentially neolithic skills, involving what Andrew Fleming has called 'fitting' – the ingenious production of objects each made of several different materials. Jet studs covered in sheet gold, beads and discs of amber encased in gold, dagger hilts decorated with tiny gold nails, and the bone inlay of the wooden handle of the Bush Barrow sceptre (Pl. 8), all reflect this skill. So do the beautiful pierced beads of amber, and the cups carved from the same material and from shale.

The second is a developing skill in pyrotechnology. For while the gold earrings and lunulae of the Beaker period required only hammering and some annealing, the beautiful gold cup from Rillaton required an altogether higher level of expertise, in hot working. The development of the daggers reflects this even more clearly, and it is perfectly possible that the alloying of copper with tin to make bronze was discovered independently in the British Isles. There seems no reason why the process should not have been discovered locally wherever tin was available. South-west Britain is one of the very few such regions.

In the same way, it may be that the smiths of Britain hit upon the technique of faience manufacture in the course of their metallurgical work. Once copper is being smelted and cast, the pyrotechnological means are there. I suggest that the use of seaweed as fuel may have led to its discovery, for bronze age cremations in Orkney often contain a glassy slag simply because seaweed was used as fuel for the fire. Seaweed in early Europe was one of the chief sources of alkali necessary for the manufacture of faience. And copper is the colouring agent used in the production of the faience beads. Copper smelting on sand dunes, with seaweed as fuel, offered an ideal situation for the natural discovery of faience. It is more than coincidence that so many of the Scottish beads come from the Culbin and Glenluce sands, and of course the star and quoit shapes produced there were a local speciality.

The high status of the chiefs, as well as making specialization possible, facilitated the other noted development of the time: the trade in luxury goods. For as well as metals and stones, and faience beads too, jet and considerable quantities of amber were traded. These movements were no doubt gift exchanges between persons of note, and towards the end of this period the exchange network extended right down to the Aegean, where, as we have seen, amber beads are found in burials of the early Mycenaean civilization around 1600 B.C.

All of this developed in a society where extravagant display had become usual. It may be that display and conspicuous consumption of wealth themselves brought prestige, just as among the Indians of the north-west coast of America with their competitive pot-latching. For the existence of a hierarchical chiefdom society does not exclude some social mobility of this kind. Perhaps there was competition, too, in the goods amassed for one's own burial, or offered on the death of a relative. This would help to account for the number of rich graves found in Wessex and much of north Europe (Fig. 55) containing gold and amber. Of course, these

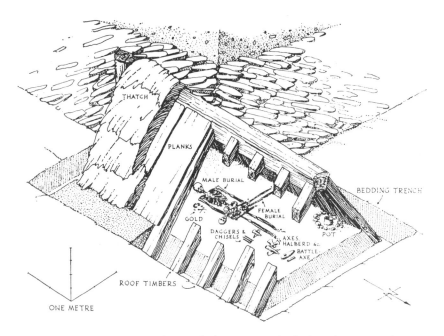

FIG. 55. Reconstruction of an early bronze age chiefly burial in a wooden mortuary house below a barrow at Leubingen in East Germany. The contemporary burials in Wessex were of comparable richness. (*After S. Piggott*)

burials represent only the more prominent members of society, whom it seemed appropriate to bury in this way.

Many of these comments are applicable to the society of the early bronze age in north-western Europe as a whole. At first, metal was used primarily for display and for daggers (Pl. 8), and the importance of the dagger for the development of metallurgy should not be underestimated. Much of the demand which stimulated the growth of this craft must have come from the need of almost every able-bodied male to be as well armed as his neighbour or rival.

And so it was throughout central and north Europe during the second millennium B.C. that the output of bronze objects increased, with an ever more useful range of artifacts. Axes, at first mere imitations of stone prototypes, were transformed into forms more economical of metal, and more useful. Metal vessels were produced, and ultimately agricultural tools, notably sickles. A large trade in both raw materials and finished objects grew up. Today only a few innovations, even in the later bronze age, are seen to have been of Mediterranean inspiration – shields perhaps, and possibly some varieties of sword. Contacts with the Mediterranean certainly became much more numerous at the end of the second millennium, in the late bronze age, and the diffusion of such innovations then becomes much more credible. Before this time they were infrequent and sporadic.

An interesting recent discovery, again based on radiocarbon determinations, is that some of our British hill forts, once thought to have been built solely during the iron age, were actually first constructed in bronze age times. Again these developments may be seen as a local response to local factors, including a rising population and the great improvements in weaponry during the bronze age, which made war a more serious business. As John Alexander has argued, the development in central and north Europe of the iron age hill forts and *oppida*, some of them in effect towns, may be seen as an authentically European development towards urban life, as natural and logical a response to local factors in the north as was the emergence of civilization in the Aegean.

Such discoveries open an entirely new perspective on the whole development of the European bronze age and iron age, and on European society in general. They now can be seen as the product of a continuous evolutionary process which can be traced back to the time of the Wessex early bronze age, to Stonehenge, and indeed beyond.

12 Prospect: Towards a New Prehistory

In the preceding chapters, an attempt has been made to look at some of the major developments of barbarian Europe in essentially local terms. Much more work is needed before these explanations can be taken seriously as satisfactory statements about the past, but at least they are plausible, in the light of current knowledge. They are constructions designed to demonstrate that a non-diffusionist explanation can be found for each of the major diffusionist episodes in the conventional prehistory of Europe. I would maintain that in each case the new explanation is as satisfying as the old one, and that it fits the present evidence better. It now becomes easier for us to jettison the shackles of the old diffusionist framework.

Moreover, in stressing the role of population densities and population growth, and of trade and exchange without markets or currency, these explanations may stimulate further work and suggest better models. For I certainly believe that little understanding will come of prehistoric societies, or at least of those beyond the subsistence level, without a serious consideration of their social organization, and the way it interrelates with the developing economy and technology.

At times, in order to be rid of the limitations of the conventional, diffusionist view, the first paradigm of prehistoric archaeology, the argument has become frankly anti-diffusionist. Perhaps this is reasonable in the circumstances, but it should not imply a necessary avoidance of diffusionist models. For there is no doubt that the development of trade with a civilized and technically accomplished neighbour can bring major changes in the technology and social structure of a 'barbarian' culture. It would be easy to build such a model, for instance, for the emergence of the salient hierarchical organization of the Celtic chiefdoms, which is reflected not only in the magnificence of the objects buried with the Celtic 'princes', but in the number of imports from the Classical world found with them. Certainly anthropologists are now using arguments of this kind to explain some of the very large chiefdoms described in Polynesia by some of the earlier travellers. A number of the features described, such as the institution of what was virtually a kingship in Hawaii, are now viewed as responses to contact with European traders. Similar arguments have been advanced for several features of Indian society in the eastern United States, which until recently were thought of as being entirely indigenous in origin.

Clearly the effects of culture contact must continue to play a major role in our thinking. But even if the pendulum swings again towards explanations of this kind, no valid meaning or explanatory power can again be ascribed to the term 'diffusion'. Henceforth its use can only be as an invitation to describe the nature of the contact and the mechanism of its influence. Movements and migrations of peoples are no longer acceptable as explanations for the changes seen in the archaeological record. And the very notion of discrete archaeological cultures as representing recognizable, socially related groups of people is increasingly coming into question. The notion, fashionable in archaeology a few years ago, that if only the data could be fed into a computer, they would divide themselves into a convenient taxonomy revealing valid cultural groups, is today seen as an oversimplification.

If we are searching for a new paradigm, a new theoretical framework appropriate for prehistoric archaeology, we cannot expect to hit upon it by intuition or pure ratiocination. Nor can we expect neighbouring disciplines to provide us with a ready-made answer, although they may offer various ready-made techniques. It is as vain to expect prehistoric archaeology to establish precise universal laws like those of physics, in a neat, deductive hierarchy, as to imagine that cultures and culture complexes will comport themselves like the species and genera of the biological sciences. The new paradigm will emerge gradually, through painstaking advance and uncomfortable error.

These strictures need not, however, prevent our discerning, or attempting to discern, some of its features. In the first place, any new framework requires new concepts, as well as the re-examination of those already in use, shaping problems into different configurations. The new methods of archaeology, recently developed or adopted, will help form these concepts. The limitations of a chronology based on radiocarbon, for instance, are only now beginning to be appreciated; for in the absence of more accurate methods it is almost impossible to distinguish events only a century or so apart. From the standpoint of the archaeologist they are effectively contemporary.

The distribution of artifacts in space is only now, through the application of locational analysis, undergoing systematic study. All the notions of random and regular spacing, of central place theory and settlement hierarchy, and of correlations among distributions, have yet to be assimilated to prehistoric archaeology. And the new ways of extracting information from the artifacts themselves, by chemical and other analyses, are far from exhausted.

As techniques of excavation improve, with more sensitive recovery and appropriate sampling techniques, with a more careful consideration of context and associations within the site, and of the site within its region, the flow of data increases. If the available sites are not wantonly destroyed by motorways, by urban expansion or by deep ploughing, this process must no doubt continue.

More fundamental than any of these techniques of data recovery, however, is the spirit of scepticism concerning assumptions and procedures of reasoning. The crucial problem lies in the interpretation of the variability seen in the archaeological record, rather than in the accumulation of more data concerning the variations themselves. Previously many of the explanations were felt to be self-evident: different assemblages of artifacts represented different groups of people. This may, of course, in many instances, remain true, but it can no longer be assumed.

It is a fundamental criterion of meaning in any scientific discipline that statements can, in certain circumstances, be shown to be wrong, and refuted. To some archaeologists, this means that no statements can be accepted until they have been rigorously tested against new data, which are not always immediately available. To others, the appropriate validation procedure is goodness of fit, against the existing data, which is not at all the same thing. Here, then, is a procedural problem which has yet to be resolved. But in any case, this self-critical concern with procedure, and with the precise meaning of basic assumptions, is a welcome antidote to the sometimes facile generalizations of the past. It represents the second important way in which the archaeology of today seeks to differ from that practised until recently.

The attempt to find and exploit new sources of information, and the wish that these should be used more critically according to recognized rules of procedure has led, as discussed in Chapter 6, away from a purely historical approach to the prehistoric past. Edmund Leach has even stigmatized the new outlook as 'behaviourist', and this is very much what Jacquetta Hawkes implied in her stricture that 'the scientific and techno-logical servant must not usurp the throne of history'. But whatever the dangers of behaviourism or scientism, they have also their more positive features.

This shift away from historical narrative, with its emphasis on unique events and its insights into individual human actions, has been accom-panied by an awakened interest in the underlying generalities which may hold for human societies in certain conditions, and which make the com-parisons between specific societies or cultures, widely removed in space and time, not only permissible but useful. This interest in generalization is perhaps the most important single feature of the new outlook in pre-history. It has made us realize how much the prehistorian still has to learn from a study of non-industrial societies.

This new interest is subtly different from the search for 'ethnographic parallels' conducted by the archaeologists of thirty and forty years ago. There, the procedure was to focus upon a specific feature of a prehistoric society – a tool-type perhaps, or a burial custom – and to find something closely similar in a living 'primitive' society. It was felt that the interpreta-tion of the prehistoric finds could well be closely similar to the interpreta-tion of the modern ones offered by the anthropologist's study of the society in question. Such one-to-one comparisons were long ago rejected as invalid, as highlighting superficial resemblances taken out of context. It was agreed that a comparative study of a number of living societies could offer a number of useful *possibilities*, of conceivable interpretations for the archaeological findings, but that these did not exhaust the range of valid explanations. For many years, indeed, the use of ethnography went out of fashion, and the archaeologist and the anthropologist went their separate ways.

Recently there has been an awakened interest in the use of ethnography. Peter Ucko wrote in 1969:

> The primary use of ethnographic parallels ... is simple. It is to widen the horizons of the interpreter ... I have tried to show with cave art,

figurines and rock art that without a widely oriented approach to archaeological interpretation, the date revealed by the archaeological material itself tends to become swamped by unitary and all-embracing explanation ... As far as I am concerned the use of ethnographic parallels can only in very exceptional cases suggest a one-to-one correlation between the acts of tribe A and the remains of culture B, but what they *can* do is to suggest the sorts of possible procedures which may result in the traits characterising culture B.[93]

Yet this may not go far enough. Ucko indeed refers to the comparative method practised by many anthropologists, but it is not really the specific characteristics of any individual modern society, their range, or even their frequency of occurrence, which really interest the prehistorian. Increasingly the interest focuses upon the organizational features which different living societies may hold in common, with the underlying hope and belief that these may reflect common human responses to similar environmental circumstances. The brief discussion in Chapter 8 illustrates one case in point. The role of gift exchange in many small and comparatively simple societies has been studied by anthropologists for many years, and it becomes possible to suggest that this reciprocal exchange may have been the principal form of trade among many early neolithic societies. A general concept is available which may prove of real value to the prehistorian.

There are two problems to appreciate here. In the first instance, the presence of such a phenomenon in a specific prehistoric society remains to be demonstrated by reference to the evidence. And secondly, it is we as observers who discern 'similarities' or 'analogies' between societies, whether living or dead. Comparative anthropology itself rests on the assumption that it can be useful to compare distinct and unique societies, and that the common elements which the anthropologist observes may indeed have some meaning.

Every society, like every event, may be studied in its uniqueness – for each is, in its own way unique – or, on the other hand, for what the scientist may decide it has in common with others. This generalizing approach is the first essential of a scientific method. And while some social anthropologists are pessimistic about reaching conclusions on the social and economic organization of prehistoric societies, generalization of this kind is at the root of all their writing, whether of the functionalist or structuralist or whatever school.

The shift in prehistoric archaeology, as I see it, is from talk of artifacts to talk of societies, and from objects to relationships among different classes of data. In the past, the most meticulous care has been lavished upon the classification and comparison and dating of artifacts, as if these inanimate relics were the principal object of study. The basic task was seen as one of artifact sorting. When this was completed the pieces of the jigsaw would fit into place. In other words, the task of reconstructing the past, given an adequate supply of suitable artifacts, was seen as an easy and fairly routine one. This was, of course, because, following the accepted, if not often explicitly stated, procedures of the diffusionist model, appropriate assemblages of artifacts indicated cultures, and changes in assemblages implied changes in cultures, generally by either migration or diffusion.

Today the aim is more ambitious. It is to talk meaningfully of the societies of which these artifacts are the relic. To discuss their environment and subsistence, their technology, their social organization, their population density and so forth, and from these parameters to construct a picture and an explanation of the changes taking place.

This rather glib statement of objective brings with it the various risks involved in generalizing and theorizing. For obviously the task of reconstruction begins with the artifacts: they are the basic material. And there is always the danger of reading into the prehistoric material structures and organizations observed or imagined in more recent societies. This is where all the scepticism, and concern with method and with testing – the second element we have identified in the new approach to prehistory – is so relevant.

Yet the objective is worthy. Even to state it in this way is to make clear at once why there is this quest for new kinds of evidence, itself the first distinguishable feature of the new archaeology. Artifacts alone are not enough. To study population, intensive surveys of whole regions and the careful consideration of land use, become necessary. This leads on directly to subsistence, and to the systematic recovery of prehistoric food remains, with a devotion which thirty years ago would have seemed ridiculous. The study of social organization is less easy, or at least has not advanced so far. But obviously settlement pattern is again a basic source of relevant information, and locational analysis, with its emphasis on central place theory, is one approach. Another is the more conventional interpretation of artifacts, but with renewed interest now in their precise distribution and association.

It is for this reason that living non-industrial societies are now of such relevance. Not that any individual society today can really serve as a suitable model for a given prehistoric society, but rather that the more general *processes* at work today in these small, living societies may serve as viable models for such processes in the past. Neither Richard Lee, who has carried out intensive study with the Bushmen of Africa, nor Lewis Binford, now working with the Eskimo of Alaska, would hold up these groups as recognizably very similar to specific groups of hunters or gatherers in the past. But the ways they utilize their resources, the way their life is geared to the seasonal changes in these resources, their population density and its relation to these same factors, the interrelations of both with the social organization—all these and many others offer potential insights not merely into the society under study but into any society which lived under comparable environmental restraints.

The new paradigm emerging in prehistoric archaeology will be written in terms of the interrelations of six or seven basic parameters which we can recognize as determining culture change. It will relate population growth and population density to the subsistence pattern, and the changes in it. It will link these with the social organization, and with the contacts, including trade and exchange, between neighbouring communities and adjacent regions. And ultimately it will analyse how all these have influenced and determined the structure of the perceptions and beliefs of the society, including their art and religion, and how these in turn have governed the exploitation of the environmental and the basic technology with which it was accomplished.

How prehistoric archaeology will relate these various factors is not yet very clear. Perhaps the systems model, where the culture or society is regarded with its environment as a system in equilibrium, will prove appropriate. I have tried to show elsewhere how the origins of civilization in the Aegean can profitably be considered in these terms. Or it may be that other approaches and models will prove more effective. Radiocarbon has helped to show the inadequacy of the conventional diffusionist picture built up by Worsaae, Montelius and Childe. The task now is to build up something demonstrably better to replace it.

APPENDIX

Radiocarbon Dating

The formation and properties of radiocarbon

Cosmic rays are radiation of very high energy reaching the earth from outer space. On arrival they strike some of the atoms of the air, notably nitrogen and oxygen, breaking these into tiny fragments, one of which is the neutron, itself one of the fundamental building bricks from which atoms are made. Balloon research shows such disintegrations to be most frequent at an altitude of about sixteen kilometres.

Radiocarbon is produced when a neutron collides with the nucleus of a nitrogen atom. (The nitrogen nucleus has the mass and charge equivalent to seven protons plus seven neutrons. The addition of a neutron leads to a nucleus of radiocarbon – carbon-14 – with six protons plus eight neutrons, and the loss of a proton.) Like nitrogen, it has an atomic weight of 14, but the properties, in chemical reactions, of carbon. The common, stable isotope, carbon-12, has an atomic weight of 12. There is also a further stable isotope, carbon-13, which forms almost one per cent of the carbon in the atmosphere, carbon-12 constituting the other 99 per cent. The proportion of carbon-14 in the atmosphere, formed in the manner described, is exceedingly small: one part for every 0·8 million million parts of carbon-12 (1 in 8 x 10^{11}).

This, then, is the process which is going on all the time in the atmosphere. Cosmic rays produce radiocarbon atoms at a steady rate of two per square centimetre of area of the earth's surface per second. The radiocarbon, as we have seen, combines with oxygen to give carbon dioxide and in this gaseous form is widely distributed in the atmosphere and dissolved in the oceans. It is assimilated also into living things in the same small proportion, since it behaves chemically in the same way as carbon-12. Only in a very few cases do the different atomic weights make any change in this constant proportion. When deviations from this

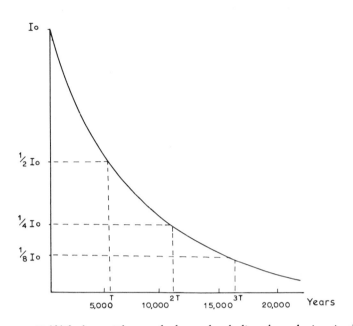

FIG. 56. Half-life decay. The graph shows the decline through time in the quantity of radiocarbon in a buried sample. Io is the initial concentration, T the half-life. After one half-life, the concentration falls to half its initial value.

proportion are observed, isotopic fractionation is said to have occurred.

Radiocarbon decays spontaneously, and after the death of the organism no more is taken into it. In the decay process a beta particle or electron – a particle of negative charge and negligible weight – is emitted, and the nucleus reverts to nitrogen. (The loss of negative charge from the electron shell is equivalent to the conversion of a neutron to a proton in the nucleus, thus leaving us with seven protons and seven neutrons. The atomic weight is unchanged [at 14], and the atom now behaves chemically as an atom of nitrogen.)

This decay process itself allows the remaining radiocarbon in the sample to be detected and estimated, since the intensity of beta radiation produced is dependent on the amount of carbon-14 present. The more atoms of carbon-14 there are, the more disintegrations will occur in a given time, giving off the electrons whose emission is detected in the laboratory.

A surprising feature of all radioactive decay processes is that, whatever the element concerned, they take place in the same, very regular way. The decay proceeds exponentially. That is to say, however much or little of the radioactive isotope one starts with, after a certain length of time which is an absolute constant for the isotope in question, half will have disintegrated radioactively, and half will be left in the original, radioactive form. This time interval is known as the *half-life*, the length of time required for one half of the given sample to undergo radioactive decay (Fig. 56). After two half-lives, half of the remainder (i.e. one quarter of the original quantity) will be left in the radioactive form; after three half-lives, one half of that – i.e. one eighth of the original quantity; and so on. Even after ten half-lives have elapsed there will still be some of the radioactive isotope left: the original amount $\times$ 2^{-10}, or one part in 1,024 of the original amount. The half-life of radiocarbon was originally determined by Libby as 5,568 years.

This regularity is crucial to the radiocarbon dating method. If, for example, measurement of the radioactivity in a sample shows it to be one quarter of that in a modern sample, we can set the age of the sample at two half-lives ($2 \times 5568 =$ about 11,150 years). This is the time elapsed since the death of the organism, when it stopped taking up radiocarbon, together with carbon-12, as food.

The exponential decay pattern also sets a limit on the age of samples which can be dated by this method. At an age of 70,000 years, samples have so little radioactivity left that they can scarcely be measured by present techniques. For earlier dates than this the method is not useful.

The regular decay rate of radiocarbon thus permits the calculation of the age of samples when their present remaining radioactivity has been measured. The application of the regularity to prehistoric chronology, by means of the radiocarbon method, is one of the most elegant contributions made by the natural sciences to archaeology.

The laboratory determination of radiocarbon

The laboratory determination of the radioactivity of the samples to be dated is a delicate matter. The amount of radiation to be measured is very small, even with a modern sample, so that very sensitive detection methods are needed. Moreover the task is greatly complicated by the background radiation always present in the laboratory. Part of this comes from the presence of small quantities of radioactive isotopes in metal and other materials, and this can be eliminated by using 'clean' materials. More troublesome is the cosmic radiation which has successfully penetrated the earth's atmosphere and reached the earth's surface. The radioactivity which has to be measured in a typical carbon sample is of the order of 50 counts per minute. Yet the radiation level in the laboratory, unless special precautions are taken, is of the order of 800 counts per minute. So the effects to be measured, namely the radioactivity in the sample itself, risk being swamped completely by all the extraneous 'noise' of this background radiation. Even with heavy shielding of lead around the counter, the background radiation still amounts to some 600 counts per minute.

Libby and his associates were all set to transfer their entire laboratory to the bottom of a deep mine, where cosmic radiation would hardly penetrate, when they hit on the solution: the anti-coincidence counter. The sample to be dated, in its own counter, is set in the middle of a ring of further counters. The passage of each electron from a disintegrating carbon-14 atom in the sample is detected by this central counter and recorded electronically.

In the anti-coincidence counter, the central counter containing the sample is surrounded by a complete series of further counters. They do not prevent the cosmic ray particle from penetrating to the central counter; but they do record its passage through the surrounding ring of counters, and automatically, for a tiny fraction of a second, shut off the recording mechanism of the central counter. The unwanted cosmic ray particle activates the shield counters, shutting off the recording equipment of the central sample counter for the instant that it takes the extraneous particle to pass the centre of the measuring device. In this way the equipment avoids recording cosmic ray intruders.

On the other hand the electrons originating from the radiocarbon are recorded normally by the central counter. Since their energy is less than that of the cosmic ray particles, they do not go beyond the wall of the central counter, and do not set off the surrounding anti-coincidence counters. In this way the unwanted and extraneous counts due to background radiation are cut down from 800 counts per minute to about 13 counts per minute. Libby and his associates used a Geiger counter, which is simply a hollow tube containing the sample, in which the electrical impulses, created by the electrons emitted in the disintegrations, are taken up. The archaeological samples, in the very early days, were simply spread in solid form on the inside wall of this cylindrical counter. Later it was found more accurate to convert the sample, by ordinary chemical means, into gas—usually carbon dioxide or methane. In both cases the electron produced in the disintegration of the carbon-14 atom allows an electrical impulse to pass in the counter, and this is recorded electronically. More recently, Harold Barker at the British Museum Research Laboratory found it possible to convert the gaseous sample, by simple chemical means, into liquid form—usually benzene or methyl alcohol. This is mixed with a liquid which has the property of emitting a flash of visible light when an electron from a disintegration passes through. The light-flashes are detected by photomultipliers, and again recorded electronically. This liquid scintillation counting has the added advantage that the samples can more easily be changed over, since the sample has less bulk than the corresponding amount of gas, and can be contained in a small glass vial.

The various improvements in these methods of measurement have greatly increased the accuracy. And where, in the early days, some 30 grams of pure carbon were required in a sample to be dated, today six grams or even three grams can be sufficient.

The problem of background radiation has not been eliminated entirely, however, and this is one of the basic limitations in the accuracy of the method. Some particles manage to get through the anti-coincidence counters, and are then recorded in the central counter as if they originated in the sample. The general magnitude of this problem can be gauged by using the set-up to measure without any sample in at all, and hence to

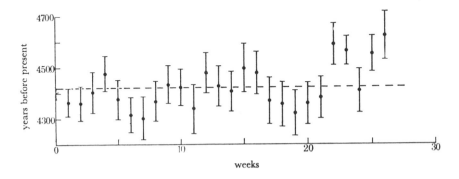

FIG. 57. Statistical variation in radiocarbon determinations. The results of repeated age measurements of a single sample over a period of six months. This variation is conventionally expressed by the standard deviation, the ± figure, which follows all radiocarbon dates. (*After H. Barker*)

record the background radiation which is getting through. But since the cosmic ray flux varies from moment to moment and from day to day in an unpredictable way, this is not an adequate answer. This continuous, fluctuating background radiation means that successive measurements of the radioactivity of the same sample give different readings (Fig. 57).

There is thus a counting error, due to the background radiation, which, while it can be reduced by successive measurements, cannot be eliminated. No way has been found of overcoming this problem, caused by the changing cosmic ray flux. Instead this basic counting error or uncertainty is publicly acknowledged. All radiocarbon dates are published with a 'plus or minus' figure attached, e.g. 3150 B.C. $\pm$ 130. The $\pm$ 130 refers only to the counting error; it does not include any estimate of other possible error sources in the date.

This 'plus or minus' term has sometimes caused confusion among ar-chaeologists. It does *not* mean that the error is precisely the amount quoted, nor that the correct reading has to lie within the limits set. It expresses instead a statistical concept: that the best estimate for the correct value (i.e. the mean for the correct value) is 3150 B.C. with a *standard deviation* of 130 years. This means that the correct value has a 66 per cent probability of lying within the limits specified (i.e. 3150 + 130 B.C. to 3150 − 130 B.C.). It has a 95 per cent probability of lying within the limits of two standard deviations (3150 + 260 B.C. to 3150 − 260 B.C.), and a 99·5 per cent probability of lying within three standard deviations. It has a finite but very small probability of lying outside even these limits.

In other words the 66 per cent confidence limits for the determination lie one standard deviation respectively above and below the quoted, mean value. The 95 per cent confidence limits lie two standard deviations above and below the quoted value.

There is nothing mysterious or puzzling about this. It just expresses neatly that we do not have a precise absolute figure for the determination – just a mean or best date, and a knowledge of the magnitude of the errors likely to arise from the counting problem. The standard deviation, or standard error, can be reduced by repeated measurements on the same sample. Obviously the most accurate dates are those with the smallest standard deviation. For most laboratories the standard deviation is of the order of 100 years. In some it has now been reduced below 50 years.

The four assumptions of the radiocarbon method

(1) *The half-life of radiocarbon.* The half-life of radiocarbon is an invariant constant of nature. Unfortunately, however, it is not a constant which can be calculated from first principles: it has to be measured in the laboratory. Consequently like all measurements it is subject to error. For this reason it has turned out to be, in practice, a somewhat variable constant! But the variation in the value accepted arises solely from these problems of measurement: it does not shake the view that carbon-14 has a single, fixed half-life, however difficult it may be to measure accurately.

The agreed value of the half-life is, of course, used to calculate all radiocarbon dates. For each sample to be dated, as we have seen, a measurement of its radioactivity is made in the laboratory. Knowing the original radioactivity at the time of death, and using the agreed half-life, the length of time since the death of the sample is obtained.

The half-life of radiocarbon has been measured several times in the laboratory in very carefully controlled experiments. The basic principle is easy: a known amount of radiocarbon (found by analysing a much more concentrated sample in a mass spectrometer, and then diluting it) is passed into a counter. The radioactivity of this known amount is measured in the usual way. Knowing both the quantity of radiocarbon present (from the mass spectrometer measurement) and the radioactivity associated with it (from the counter), the half-life can be calculated. The problem in establishing the half-life comes, in practice, in the performing of all these operations with sufficient accuracy.

In 1949, Libby decided to use the average value from three analyses conducted in different laboratories. This set the half-life of carbon-14 at what is now called the Libby value of 5,568 ± 30 years. Radiocarbon dates are thus calculated on the basis that over this period of 5,568 years a given sample of carbon will lose one half of its radioactivity. The ± 30 term indicates the counting error, for since it is based on laboratory measurement against a changing background radiation, the half-life has a standard deviation in the same way as any radiocarbon ages.

Since 1949, radiocarbon ages have normally been calculated on the 5,568 half-life. The calculation gives the age of the sample expressed in years *Before Present* (B.P.). To avoid confusion as to the precise year in which the measurement was made, the 'present' is taken, by international convention, to be 1950 A.D. Dates can be expressed in years B.C. by subtracting 1,950 years from the B.P. age.

More recent measurements of the half-life have suggested that the Libby value is too short, and the best available estimate is now 5,730 ± 30 years. This is, of course, 160 years (3·4 per cent) longer than the previous value. It means that radiocarbon takes longer to decay than had been thought, and consequently that the ages previously calculated should be increased by 3·4 per cent. So ages calculated on the old 5,568 half-life (in years B.P.) may be adjusted to the new 5,730 half-life through multiplication by 1·03. (Ages expressed in years B.C. can be adjusted through multiplying by 1·03 and adding 66 years.)

To avoid the confusion of having some dates expressed on one system and some on the other, it has been agreed that all dates should still at present be quoted on the old, Libby half-life of 5,568 years. In the future an international conference may agree to convert all dates, using a more accurate measurement of the half-life. At present it is important that all dates should be quoted using the same convention.

The difference between the half-lives is certainly not a trivial one – it amounts to nearly two centuries for a date around 4000 B.C. Indeed it had already been noticed that in areas, such as Egypt, with an independent calendrical chronology, the radiocarbon dates calculated on the 5,568 half-life were too young (i.e. not high enough, not early enough). For this reason some scholars have quoted two dates for each sample, one for each half-life. As we have seen in Chapter 6, however, the tree-ring calibration of radiocarbon manages to sidestep the problem of half-life, and indeed makes all the argument rather superfluous.

(2) *Absence of contamination.* The second fundamental assumption of the methods is that the sample has not been contaminated, since its death, with older or more recent material, whose isotopic composition would be different. Of course, when living things die they decay, and this chemical process reduces their weight, removing most of the water and soluble substances from the body. The skeleton which remains is rich in carbon, especially in the case of plants. Burning can prevent complete decay in plants, and if there is not too much air they will 'carbonize', and become

charcoal. Charcoal is, of course, almost pure carbon, and is ideal for radiocarbon dating.

There is always the risk that older carbon may penetrate the sample and dilute its radioactivity. More recent material – rootlets, or fungus growing on the sample – may add radiocarbon of recent origin, and make the sample appear deceptively young. Laboratory cleaning – a 'laundry job' – can sometimes eliminate such contamination. Washing in clean alkali will extract the humic acids, and washing in clean acid can remove mineral calcium carbonate.

Obviously great care must be taken in the collecting of samples. In the early days photographs were sometimes proudly published in archaeological reports with captions such as 'The Collection of Radiocarbon Samples'. In more than one of these, the 'expert' would be seen smoking a cigarette. Just a little cigarette ash, deriving of course from recent plant material, could seriously contaminate the sample.

Obviously the archaeologist has to be sure of the stratigraphic context from which the sample comes. Too often in *Radiocarbon*, the journal where all new dates are published, one reads the excavator's comment, 'too young'. Nine times out of ten this means that the excavator himself has submitted a sample which did not belong securely in the stratum to which he assigned it.

There is the risk too that the sample may not have been recently dead when buried. A beam of wood, for instance, can be re-used in a building, and in any case the heart of a long-lived tree is decades or centuries older than the outermost ring. There is even the risk of fossil wood being used, and 'bog oak' is a favourite explanation for archaeologists whose radiocarbon dates are very much earlier than expected. Dates obtained from samples of carbonized grain overcome this difficulty, since the grain is less likely to have been old at the time of its burial.

In practice, the actual contamination of samples turns out to be surprisingly rare. Confusion is introduced far more often through archaeological mistakes and uncertainties.

(3) *Uniform world-wide distribution of radiocarbon.* The assumption that the atmospheric level of radiocarbon is the same at a given time all over the world – Libby's principle of simultaneity – is not entirely correct,

but recent work has nonetheless established that fluctuations with latitude or longitude are small. This conclusion was originally reached by Libby's colleague, E. C. Anderson, who analysed samples of different plant and animal species from all over the world.

One problem is the earth's magnetic field, which affects the cosmic radiation reaching the atmosphere. Far more neutrons are produced at high latitudes than at the equator. Moreover, it is important to consider how the approximately 60,000 kilograms of radiocarbon in the world is distributed. Less than 2 per cent is in the form of free carbon dioxide, for the 'carbon exchange reservoir' includes the oceans, where much carbon dioxide is dissolved. And the mixing of the waters of the surface ocean and deep ocean is rather slow.

Fortunately, however, mixing in the atmosphere is much quicker. This has been demonstrated by the speed with which radiocarbon generated in H-bomb tests has become uniformly distributed about the world. More recent work has shown that there is no significant difference in the atmospheric concentration of radiocarbon with longitude. There is a small latitude effect, amounting to 0·4 per cent in recent samples. It causes samples in the Southern Hemisphere to appear about 40 years older than contemporaneous samples in the Northern Hemisphere. It is not a serious source of error.

An equally important question is whether all living plant and animal species do, in fact, contain the same proportion of radiocarbon to ordinary carbon-12 as does the atmosphere. Again the basic assumption is that they do, and again it is nearly but not exactly true in practice. One possibility is that plants living on calcareous soil might take up carbon from the mineral calcium carbonate, which would be very low in radiocarbon. This does not appear to be a serious problem for plants, which take up their carbon by photosynthesis, but is more trouble-some with shells. It is particularly acute for freshwater shells, where some of their material may originate from mineral carbonate in hard water. For this reason, freshwater molluscs are not generally considered ideally suitable material for reliable radiocarbon dating.

Plants and molluscs present a further problem. It was stated earlier that radiocarbon behaves chemically in precisely the same way as the stable isotopes of carbon, carbon-12 and carbon-13. In practice, however, just a little 'isotopic fractionation' does occur in the process of photosynthesis – that is to say, some plants do show a small but definite dis-inclination to take up the slightly heavier carbon-14 from the atmosphere; consequently they have a slightly lower proportion of radiocarbon than the atmosphere. The error in the date caused by this effect is, however, small – usually not more than 80 years. And fortunately a correction can be made by considering also the isotopic fractionation of carbon-13. The proportion of carbon-13 in the sample is determined by mass spectro-meter, and any variation from the normal level is noted. It is possible, then, to estimate and allow for the effects of the fractionation process on carbon-14.

These minor effects have all to be considered with care. But, as we have seen, none of them seriously affects the validity or the accuracy of the radiocarbon method.

(4) *Variation in the atmospheric concentration of radiocarbon with time.* The radiocarbon dating method originally made the important assumption that the proportion of radiocarbon to ordinary carbon-12 in the atmo-sphere has remained constant through time. This absence of secular variation of atmospheric radiocarbon seemed a reasonable assumption in 1949. The effects of cosmic radiation were not thought to have varied, and the only obvious change was the increase in the volume of the oceans as the ice caps retreated at the end of the last glaciation. This might have altered the balance of distribution of carbon dioxide in the earth's existing reservoir.

There were, in addition, two more recent effects. The first, the fossil fuel or 'Suess effect', arises from the industrial use of coal. Since the nineteenth century the burning of coal for fuel has released into the atmo-sphere considerable quantities of carbon dioxide which, originating in very ancient deposits, is without the usual proportion of radiocarbon. In effect this is diluting the radiocarbon with additional carbon-12, and over the past two centuries the proportion of carbon-14 to carbon-12 has fallen by about 3 per cent. But now that the deviation has been recognized and allowed for in the modern standard samples used, it presents no problem, being far too recent to affect archaeological samples.

The testing of atomic and nuclear weapons has had precisely the opposite effect: great quantities of radiocarbon have been produced and released into the atmosphere. The level in 1953 was more than 25 per cent

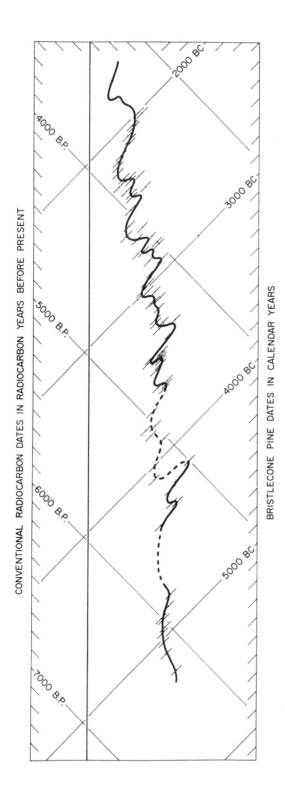

CONVENTIONAL RADIOCARBON DATES IN RADIOCARBON YEARS BEFORE PRESENT

BRISTLECONE PINE DATES IN CALENDAR YEARS

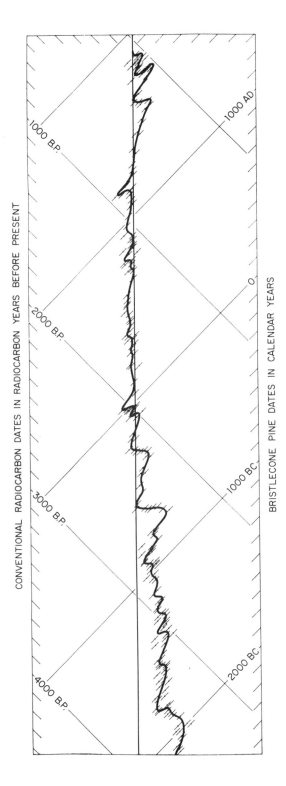

CONVENTIONAL RADIOCARBON DATES IN RADIOCARBON YEARS BEFORE PRESENT

BRISTLECONE PINE DATES IN CALENDAR YEARS

FIG. 58. Calibration curve published by Professor H. E. Suess in 1970, giving all the radiocarbon determinations of dendrochronologically dated bristlecone-pine samples determined at the La Jolla laboratory up to that time. (The curve itself is drawn by eye; other curves, differing slightly from this, could be drawn through the same data with equal validity.)

higher than it had been ten years earlier. But again this has little relevance for early samples.

It is now known, however, that the proportion of radiocarbon to ordinary carbon-12 has not remained precisely constant through time, and that before about 1000 B.C. the deviations are so great as to make radiocarbon dates significantly in error. As described in Chapter 4, the magnitude of this error has been established by tree-ring work, and this makes it possible to calibrate dates to give a value for the true date expressed in calendar years. The most recent calibration curve published by Suess is seen in Figure 58.

NOTES

1. V. Gordon Childe, 'Retrospect', *Antiquity, 32* (1958), 70.
2. Julian Steward, *Theory of Culture Change* (University of Illinois Press, Urbana, 1955), 209.
3. Rasmus Nyerup, *Oversyn over foedrelandets mindesmaerker fra oldtiden* (1806), quoted in Glyn Daniel, *A Hundred Years of Archaeology* (Duckworth, London, 1950), 38.
4. Sir Isaac Newton, *The Chronology of Antient Kingdoms Amended* (Dublin, 1728), 187.
5. John Evans, 1859, quoted in Daniel, *A Hundred Years of Archaeology*, 61.
6. Jacob Worsaae, *The Prehistory of the North* (1886), xxiv.
7. I. E. S. Edwards, 'Absolute dating from Egyptian records and comparison with carbon-14 dating', *Philosophical Transactions of the Royal Society of London, Series A, 269* (1970), 11–12.
8. Childe, 'Retrospect', 70.
9. James Fergusson, *Rude Stone Monuments in all Countries: their Age and Uses* (Murray, London, 1872), 454.
10. Ibid., 508.
11. Oscar Montelius, *Der Orient und Europa* (Stockholm, 1899), 2.
12. Ibid., 31.
13. Sir Grafton Elliot Smith, *The Migrations of Early Culture* (University Press, Manchester, 1929), 20–21.
14. Fergusson, *Rude Stone Monuments in all Countries*, 518.
15. Elliot Smith, *The Migrations of Early Culture*, 10.
14. Gustav Kossinna, *Die deutsche Vorgeschichte, eine hervorragend nationale Wissenschaft*, 8th edn (Berlin, 1941), 264.
17. V. Gordon Childe, 'The Orient and Europe', *American Journal of Archaeology, 43* (1939), 10.
18. V. Gordon Childe, *The Dawn of European Civilisation*, 1st edn (Routledge, London, 1925), 137.
19. V. Gordon Childe, *The Danube in Prehistory* (Clarendon Press, Oxford, 1929), 34.

20. V. Gordon Childe, *The Prehistory of European Society* (Penguin, Harmondsworth, 1958), 124.

21. Grahame Clark, *World Prehistory—a New Outline* (University Press, Cambridge, 1969), 139–40.

22. Sir Mortimer Wheeler, 'Crawford and ANTIQUITY', *Antiquity, 32* (1958), 4.

23. Kathleen Kenyon, 'Jericho and its setting in Near Eastern history', *Antiquity, 30* (1956), 184–97; F. E. Zeuner, 'The radiocarbon age of Jericho', ibid., 197.

24. Robert J. Braidwood, 'Jericho and its setting in Near Eastern history', *Antiquity, 31* (1957), 74.

25. Kathleen Kenyon, 'Reply to Professor Braidwood', *Antiquity, 31* (1957), 82.

26. Stuart Piggott, 'The radiocarbon date from Durrington Walls', *Antiquity, 33* (December 1959), 289.

27. Glyn Daniel, Editorial, *Antiquity, 33* (June 1959), 79–80.

28. Glyn Daniel, Editorial, *Antiquity, 33* (December 1959), 238–9.

29. Glyn Daniel, Editorial, *Antiquity, 34* (September 1960), 161–2.

30. Robert W. Ehrich, 'Geographical and chronological patterns in east-central Europe', in R. W. Ehrich (ed.), *Chronologies in Old World Archaeology* (University Press, Chicago, 1954), 439.

31. Colin Renfrew, 'Neolithic and Early Bronze Age Cultures of the Cyclades and their External Relations' (unpublished Ph.D dissertation, University of Cambridge, 1965), 187.

32. Willard Libby, 'The accuracy of radiocarbon dates', *Science, 140* (1963), 278–9.

33. Ibid.

34. H. S. Smith, 'Egypt and C-14 dating', *Antiquity, 38* (1964), 36.

35. E. H. Willis, H. Tauber and K. O. Münnich, 'Variations in the atmospheric radiocarbon concentration over the past 1300 years', *American Journal of Science Radiocarbon Supplement, 2* (1960), 4.

36. Willard Libby, 'Radiocarbon dating', *Phil. Trans. Roy. Soc., Ser. A, 269* (1970), 9.

37. Rainer Berger, 'Ancient Egyptian radiocarbon chronology', *Phil. Trans. Roy. Soc., Ser. A., 269* (1970), 32.

38. Glyn Daniel, *The Megalith Builders of Western Europe* (Hutchinson, London, 1958), 74.

39. V. Gordon Childe, 'The Middle Bronze Age', *Archivo de Prehistoria Levantina*, *4* (1953), 167.

40. Renfrew, 'Neolithic and Early Bronze Age Cultures of the Cyclades and their External Relations' (cf. n. 31), 186.

41. V. Gordon Childe, *The Dawn of European Civilisation*, 6th edn (Routledge, London, 1957), 315–16.

42. Childe, 'Retrospect' (cf. n.1), 70.

43. Childe, *The Danube in Prehistory* (cf. n. 19), 32–3.

44. Ibid., 35.

45. Vladimir Popović, 'Une civilisation égéo-orientale sur le moyen Danube', *Revue Archéologique*, *2* (1965), 56.

46. Vladimir Milojčić, 'Die absolute Chronologie der Jüngsteinzeit in Südosteuropa and die Ergebnisse der Radiocarbon- (C 14-) Methode', *Jahrbuch des Römisch–Germanischen Zentralmuseums Mainz*, *14* (1967), 9 and 15.

47. Childe, *The Prehistory of European Society* (cf. n. 20), 163.

48. Ibid., 164.

49. Stuart Piggott, 'The Early Bronze Age of Wessex', *Proceedings of the Prehistoric Society*, *4* (1938), 95.

50. Colin Renfrew, 'Wessex without Mycenae', *Annual of the British School of Archaeology, Athens*, *63* (1968), 277–85.

51. Childe, 'Retrospect' (cf. n. 1), 74.

52. V. Gordon Childe, *Piecing Together the Past* (Routledge, London, 1956), 154.

53. A. L. Kroeber, 'Stimulus diffusion', *American Anthropologist*, *42* (1940), 1.

54. Anthony Forge, 'Normative factors in the settlement size of Neolithic cultivators (New Guinea)', in Peter J. Ucko, Ruth Tringham and G. W. Dimbleby (eds), *Man, Settlement and Urbanism* (Duckworth, London, 1972), 375.

55. James Mellaart, *Earliest Civilisations of the Near East* (Thames and Hudson, London, 1965), 36.

56. V. Gordon Childe, *Prehistoric Communities of the British Isles* (W. and R. Chambers, London and Edinburgh, 1940), 46.

57. R. J. C. Atkinson, 'Neolithic engineering', *Antiquity*, *35* (1961), 293.

58. Tom Harrison, *World Within* (London, 1959), 111–12, quoted by Tom Harrison and Stanley O'Connor, *Gold and Megalithic*

Activity in Prehistoric and Recent West Borneo (Data Paper no. 77, Department of Asian Studies, Cornell University, New York, 1970), 107–8.

59. Harrisson and O'Connor, *Gold and Megalithic Activity in Prehistoric and Recent West Borneo*, 91–3.

60. T. G. E. Powell, 'Some points and problems', in T. G. E. Powell, J. X. W. P. Corcoran, Frances Lynch and J. G. Scott, *Megalithic Enquiries in the West of Britain* (University Press, Liverpool, 1969), 270–71; P. R. Giot (ed.), *Les civilisations atlantiques du néolithique à l'age du fer* (Actes du premier colloque atlantique, Brest 1961; published Rennes, 1963), 3.

61. Childe, *The Dawn of European Civilisation* (cf. n. 18), 133.

62. Ibid., 101.

63. J. D. Evans, *Malta* (Thames and Hudson, London, 1959), 133.

64. J. D. Evans, *The Prehistoric Antiquities of the Maltese Islands* (Athlone Press, London, 1971), 223–4.

65. R. C. Suggs, *Island Civilisations of Polynesia* (Mentor, New York, 1960), 224.

66. Mrs S. Scoresby Routledge, *The Mystery of Easter Island* (Routledge, London, 1919), 171.

67. Alfred Metraux, *Easter Island, a Stone Age Civilisation of the Pacific* (Deutsch, London, 1957), 159.

68. David Kaplan, 'Men, monuments and political systems', *Southwestern Journal of Anthropology*, *19* (1963), 407.

69. Theodore Wertime, 'Man's first encounters with Metallurgy', *Science*, *146* (1964), 1257.

70. Childe, *The Dawn of European Civilisation* (cf. n. 41), 122–3.

71. Bogdan Nikolov, 'Plaque en argile avec des signes d'écriture du village Gradeshnitsa, dép. de Vratsa', *Archeologiya*, *3* (1970), 9.

72. Marshall D. Sahlins, *Tribesmen* (Prentice-Hall, Englewood Cliffs, 1968), 43–4.

73. Metraux, *Easter Island, a Stone Age Civilisation of the Pacific*, 206.

74. Robert Redfield, *The Primitive World and its Transformations* (Cornell University Press, New York, 1953), ix.

75. A. J. G. Wace and C. W. Blegen, 'The Pre-Mycenaean Pottery of the Mainland', *Annual of the British School of Archaeology, Athens*, *22* (1918), 179.

76. Emily Vermeule, *Greece in the Bronze Age* (University Press, Chicago, 1964), 26.
77. Childe, *The Dawn of European Civilisation* (cf. n. 18), 29.
78. Ibid., 24.
79. V. Gordon Childe, *Man Makes Himself* (Watts, London, 1936), 169–70.
80. J. Walter Graham, 'Egyptian features at Phaistos', *American Journal of Archaeology*, 74 (1970), 238.
81. R. J. C. Atkinson, 'Moonshine on Stonehenge', *Antiquity*, 40 (1966), 215.
82. R. J. C. Atkinson, 'Decoder Misled?', review of Gerald S. Hawkins, *Stonehenge Decoded*, in *Nature*, 210 (1966), 1302.
83. Piggott, 'The Early Bronze Age of Wessex' (cf. n. 49), 95.
84. R. J. C. Atkinson, *Stonehenge* (Pelican Books, Harmondsworth, 1960), 165–6.
85. Ibid., 166–7.
86. William Bartram, *The Travels of William Bartram*, ed. Francis Harper (Yale University Press, 1958), 326.
87. William Bartram, *Observations on the Creek and Cherokee Indians* (Transactions of the American Ethnological Society, 3, 1879), 55–6.
88. Grant Foreman (ed.), *A Traveller in Indian Territory, the Journal of Ethan Allen Hitchcock* (Cedar Rapids, Iowa, 1930), 114–15; quoted in John R. Swanton, *The Indians of the Southeastern United States* (Smithsonian Institution Bureau of American Ethnology Bulletin, 137, 1946), 389–90.
89. J. Lawson, *History of Carolina, Containing the Exact Description and Natural History of that County* (Raleigh, North Carolina, 1860), 288; quoted in Swanton, *The Indians of the Southeastern United States*, 740.
90. Elman R. Service, *Primitive Social Organisation* (Random House, New York, 1962), 170–71.
91. C. Daryll Forde, *Habitat, Economy and Society* (Methuen, London, 1934), 227.
92. Charles Lanman, *Adventures in the Wilds of the United States and British American Provinces* (Philadelphia, 1856), 424–8; quoted in Swanton, *The Indians of the Southeastern United States*, 770–71.
93. Peter J. Ucko, 'Ethnography and archaeological interpretation of funerary remains', *World Archaeology*, 1 (1969), 262–3.

BIBLIOGRAPHY

CHAPTER I INTRODUCTION

Daniel, G. E., 'From Worsaae to Childe, the models of prehistory', *Proceedings of the Prehistoric Society, 38* (1971), 140–53.

Neustupný, E., 'Whither archaeology?', *Antiquity, 45* (1971), 34–9.

Renfrew, C., 'New configurations in Old World archaeology', *World Archaeology, 2* (1970), 199–211.

Sterud, G., 'A paradigmatic view of prehistory', in C. Renfrew (ed.), *The Explanation of Culture Change: Models in Prehistory* (Duckworth, London, 1973).

Trigger, B. G., 'Aims in prehistoric archaeology', *Antiquity, 44* (1970), 26–37.

CHAPTER 2 THE PROBLEM OF DATING

Burkitt, M. and Childe, V. G., 'A chronological table of prehistory', *Antiquity, 6* (1932), 185–205.

Childe, V. G., *The Dawn of European Civilisation*, 1st edn (Routledge, London, 1925).

Childe, V. G., 'Retrospect', *Antiquity, 32* (1957), 69–74.

Childe, V. G., *The Dawn of European Civilisation*, 6th edn (Routledge, London, 1957), 346–7.

Childe, V. G., *The Prehistory of European Society* (Penguin, Harmondsworth, 1958).

Daniel, G. E., 'From Worsaae to Childe, the models of prehistory', *Proceedings of the Prehistoric Society, 38* (1971), 140–53.

Edwards, I. E. S., 'Absolute dating from Egyptian records and comparison with carbon-14 dating', *Philosophical Transactions of the Royal Society, London, Series A, 269* (1970), 11–18.

Hayes, W. C., Rowton, M. B. and Stubbings, F. H., 'Chronology: Egypt; Western Asia; Aegean Bronze Age', *Cambridge Ancient History* I (1962), Ch. VI.

Gimbutas, M., *Bronze Age Cultures in Central and Eastern Europe* (Mouton, The Hague, 1965).

Hutchinson, R. W., *Prehistoric Crete* (Penguin, Harmondsworth, 1962).

Milojčić, V., *Chronologie der jüngeren Steinzeit Mittel- und Südosteuropas* (Archaeologisches Institut, Berlin, 1949).

Zeuner, F. E., *Dating the Past*, 4th edn (Methuen, London, 1958).

Montelius, O., *Die älteren Kulturperioden im Orient und in Europa, I. Die Methode* (Stockholm, 1903).

CHAPTER 3   THE FIRST RADIOCARBON REVOLUTION

The radiocarbon dating method

Barker, H., 'Radiocarbon dating, its scope and limitations', *Antiquity, 32* (1958), 253–63.

Barker, H., 'Critical assessment of radiocarbon dating', *Philosophical Transactions of the Royal Society, London, Series A, 269* (1970), 37–45.

Libby, W. F., 'The accuracy of radiocarbon dates', *Science, 140* (1963), 278–80; reprinted in *Antiquity, 37*, 213–19.

Libby, W. F., *Radiocarbon Dating* (University Press, Chicago, 1965).

Libby, W. F., 'Ruminations on radiocarbon dating', in I. U. Olsson (ed.), *Radiocarbon Variations and Absolute Chronology* (Proceedings of the Twelfth Nobel Symposium), (Wiley, London and New York, 1970), 629–40.

Libby, W. F., 'Radiocarbon dating', *Phil. Trans. Roy. Soc., Ser A. 269* (1970), 1–10.

Libby, W. F., Anderson, E. C. and Arnold, J. R., 'Age determination of radiocarbon content: world-wide assay of natural radiocarbon', *Science, 109* (1949), 227.

Waterbolk, H. T., 'Working with radiocarbon dates', *Proc. Preh. Soc., 37* (1971), 15–33.

Willis, E. H., 'Radiocarbon dating', in D. Brothwell and E. Higgs (eds), *Science in Archaeology*, 2nd edn (Thames and Hudson, London, 1969), 46–57.

Archaeological consequences:

Braidwood, R. J., 'Jericho and its setting in Near Eastern history', *Antiquity, 31* (1957), 73–81.

Bushnell, G. H. S., 'Radiocarbon dates and New World chronology', *Antiquity, 35* (1961), 285–91.

Clark, J. G. D., *World Prehistory – an Outline* (University Press, Cambridge, 1961).

Clark, J. G. D., 'Radiocarbon dating and the expansion of farming over Europe', *Proc. Preh. Soc.*, *31* (1965), 58–73.

Daniel, G. E., Editorials in *Antiquity*, 1958–60, notably *Antiquity*, *33* (1959), 80 and 238; and *Antiquity*, *34* (1960), 161.

Ehrich, R. W. (ed.), *Chronologies in Old World Archaeology* (University Press, Chicago, 1965).

Godwin, H., 'Radiocarbon dating and Quaternary history in Britain; the Croonian lecture', *Proceedings of the Royal Society, Series B*, *153* (1960), 287–320.

Kenyon, K. M., 'Reply to Professor Braidwood', *Antiquity*, *31* (1957), 82–4.

Mellaart, J., 'Anatolia and the Balkans', *Antiquity*, *24* (1960), 270–78.

Milojčić, V., 'Zur Anwendbarkeit der C14-Datierung in der Vorgeschichtsforschung', *Germania*, *35* (1957), 102.

Milojčić, V., 'Die absolute Chronologie der Jungsteinzeit in Sudosteuropa und die Ergebnisse der Radiocarbon-(C14)-Methode', *Jahrbuch des Römisch-Germanischen Zentralmuseums Mainz*, *14* (1967), 9–37.

Movius, H. L., 'Radiocarbon dates and Upper Palaeolithic archaeology in central and western Europe', *Current Anthropology*, *1* (1960), 355–92.

Thomas, H. L., *Near Eastern, Mediterranean and European Chronology* (Studies in Mediterranean Archaeology 17, 1967).

Waterbolk, H. T., 'The 1959 Carbon-14 Symposium at Groningen', *Antiquity*, *34* (1960), 14–18.

CHAPTER 4   THE TREE-RING CALIBRATION OF RADIOCARBON

Aitken, M. J., 'Dating by archaeomagnetic and thermoluminescence methods', *Philosophical Transactions of the Royal Society, London, Series A*, *269* (1970), 77–88.

Baxter, M. S. and Walton, A., 'Fluctuations of atmospheric carbon-14 concentrations during the past century', *Proc. Royal Soc., Ser. A*, *321* (1971), 105–27.

Berger, R., 'Ancient Egyptian radiocarbon chronology', *Phil. Trans. Roy. Soc., Ser. A, 269* (1970), 23–36.

Berger, R., 'The potential and limitations of radiocarbon dating in the

Middle Ages: the radiochronologist's view', in R. Berger (ed.), *Scientific Methods in Mediaeval Archaeology* (University of California Press, Berkeley, 1970), 89–139.

Bucha, V., 'Evidence for changes in the Earth's magnetic field intensity', *Phil. Trans. Roy. Soc., Ser. A, 269* (1970), 47–55.

Clark, R. M. and Renfrew, C., 'A statistical approach to the calibration of floating tree-ring chronologies using radiocarbon dates', *Archaeometry, 14* (1972), 5–19.

Damon, P. E., Long, A. and Grey, D. C., 'Fluctuations of atmospheric C14 during the last six millennia', *Journal of Geophysical Research, 71* (1966), 1055–63.

Ferguson, C. W., 'Bristlecone pine: science and esthetics', *Science, 159* (1968), 839–46.

Ferguson, C. W., 'A 7104-year annual tree-ring chronology for bristlecone pine, *Pinus aristata*, from the White Mountains, California', *Tree-Ring Bulletin, 29* (1969), 3–39.

Ferguson, C. W., 'Dendrochronology of bristlecone pine, *Pinus aristata*. Establishment of a 7484-year chronology in the White Mountains of eastern-central California', in I. U. Olsson (ed.), *Radiocarbon Variations* (cf. Olsson), 237–61.

Ferguson, C. W., Huber, B. and Suess, H. E., 'Determination of the age of Swiss lake dwellings as an example of dendrochronologically calibrated radiocarbon dating', *Zeitschrift für Naturforschung, 21A* (1966), 1173–7.

Michael, H. N. and Ralph, K., 'Correction factors applied to Egyptian radiocarbon dates from the era before Christ', in I. U. Olsson (ed.), *Radiocarbon Variations* (cf. Olsson), 109–120.

Olsson, I. U. (ed.), *Radiocarbon Variations and Absolute Chronology* (Proceedings of the Twelfth Nobel Symposium) (Wiley, London and New York, 1970). Among the very relevant contributions are those by Neustupný; Michael and Ralph; Stuiver; Ferguson; Lerman, Mook and Vogel; Suess; Damon; and Damon and Grey.

Ralph, E. K. and Michael, H. N., 'Problems of the radiocarbon calendar', *Archaeometry, 10* (1967), 3–11.

Stuiver, M., 'Origin and extent of atmospheric ^{14}C variations during the past 10,000 years', in *Radiocarbon Dating and Methods of Low Level*

Counting (International Atomic Energy Authority, Vienna, 1967), 27–40.

Suess, H. E., 'Secular variations of the cosmic-ray-produced Carbon 14 in the atmosphere and their interpretations', *Journal of Geophysical Research, 70* (1965), 5937–52.

Suess, H. E., 'Bristlecone pine calibration of the radiocarbon time scale from 4100 B.C. to 1500 B.C.', *Radioactive Dating and Methods of Low Level Counting* (cf. Stuiver), 143.

Suess, H. E., 'Bristlecone-pine calibration of the radiocarbon time-scale 5200 B.C. to the present', in I. U. Olsson (ed.), *Radiocarbon Variations* (cf. Olsson), 303–12.

Willis, E. H., Tauber, H. and Münnich, K. O., 'Variations in the atmospheric radiocarbon concentration over the past 1300 years', *American Journal of Science Radiocarbon Supplement, 2* (1960), 1–4.

Zimmerman, D. W. and Huxtable, J., 'Some thermoluminescent dates for Linear pottery', *Antiquity, 44* (1970), 304–5.

CHAPTER 5   THE COLLAPSE OF THE TRADITIONAL FRAMEWORK

Bakker, J. A., Vogel, J. C. and Wislanski, T., 'TRB and other C14 dates from Poland', *Helinium, 9* (1969), 3–27.

Blance, B., 'Early Bronze Age colonists in Iberia', *Antiquity, 35* (1961), 192–202.

Neustupný, E., 'Absolute chronology of the neolithic and aeneolithic periods of central and south-eastern Europe', *Slovenska Archeologia, 16* (1968), 19–56.

Neustupný, E., 'Absolute chronology of the neolithic periods of central and south-east Europe II', *Archeologické Rozhledy, 21* (1969), 783–808.

Renfrew, C., 'Colonialism and Megalithismus', *Antiquity, 41* (1967), 276–88.

Renfrew, C., 'Wessex without Mycenae', *Annual of the British School of Archaeology at Athens, 63* (1968), 277–85.

Renfrew, C., 'The tree-ring calibration of radiocarbon: an archaeological evaluation', *Proceedings of the Prehistoric Society, 36* (1970), 280–311.

Renfrew, C., 'Carbon 14 and the prehistory of Europe', *Scientific American 225* (1971), 63–72.

CHAPTER 6 BEYOND DIFFUSION

Diffusion and diffusionism

Binford, L. R., 'Some comments on historical versus processual archaeology', *Southwestern Journal of Anthropology*, *24* (1968), 267–75.

Childe, V. G., *Prehistoric Migrations in Europe* (Asheheoug, Oslo, 1950).

Daniel, G. E., *The Idea of Prehistory* (Watts, London, 1962).

Elliot Smith, G., *The Migrations of Early Culture* (University Press,
Manchester, 1929).

Hägerstrand, T., 'A Monte Carlo approach to diffusion', *European
Journal of Sociology*, *6* (1965), 43–67.

Harris, M., *The Rise of Anthropological Theory* (Routledge, London, 1968).

Naroll, R., 'Two solutions to Galton's problem', *Philosophy of Science*, *28*
(1961), 15–39.

Rowe, J. H., 'Diffusionism and archaeology', *American Antiquity*, *32*
(1966), 334–7.

Tylor, E. B., 'On a method of investigating the development of in-
stitutions applied to the laws of marriage and descent', *Journal of the
Royal Anthropological Institute*, *28* (1889), 245–69.

Recent approaches

Binford, L. R., 'Archaeology as anthropology', *American Antiquity*, *28*
(1962), 217–25.

Binford, L. R., 'A consideration of archaeological research design',
American Antiquity, *29* (1964), 425–41.

Binford, L. R., 'Archaeological systematics and the study of culture
process', *American Antiquity*, *31* (1965), 203–10.

Binford, L. R. and S. R. (eds), *New Perspectives in Archaeology* (Aldine,
Chicago, 1968).

Boserup, E., *The Conditions of Agricultural Growth* (London, Allen &
Unwin, London, 1965).

Braithwaite, R. B., *Scientific Explanation* (University Press, Cambridge,
1953).

Carneiro, R. L., 'On the relationship between size of population and
complexity of social organization', *Southwestern Journal of Anthropology*,
23 (1967), 234–43.

Clark, J. G. D., *Prehistoric Europe, the Economic Basis* (Methuen, London, 1952).

Clarke, D. L., *Analytical Archaeology* (Methuen, London, 1968).

Flannery, K. V., 'Archaeological systems theory and early Mesoamerica', in B. J. Meggers (ed.), *Anthropological Archaeology in the Americas* (Anthropological Society of Washington, Washington D.C., 1968), 67–87.

Haggett, P., *Locational Analysis in Human Geography* (Arnold, London, 1965).

Polanyi, K., 'The economy as instituted process', in K. Polanyi, C. M. Arensberg and H. W. Pearson (eds), *Trade and Market in the Early Empires* (Free Press, New York, 1957), 243–69.

Renfrew, C., *The Emergence of Civilisation, the Cyclades and the Aegean in the Third Millennium* B.C. (Methuen, London, 1973).

Renfrew, C. (ed.), *The Explanation of Culture Change: Models in Prehistory* (Duckworth, London, 1972).

Rowe, J. H., 'Diffusionism and archaeology', *American Antiquity, 32* (1966), 334–7.

Sahlins, M. D., 'On the sociology of primitive exchange', in M. Banton (ed.), *The Relevance of Models for Social Anthropology* (Tavistock, London, 1965), 139–238.

Service, E. R., *Primitive Social Organisation* (Random House, New York, 1962).

Smith, P. E. L., 'Agricultural land use and settlement patterns, a demographic perspective', in P. J. Ucko, R. Tringham, and G. Dimbleby (eds), *Man, Settlement and Urbanism* (Duckworth, London, 1972).

Steward, J. H., *Theory of Culture Change* (University of Illinois Press, Urbana, 1955).

Trigger, B. C., *Beyond History, the Methods of Prehistory* (Holt, Reinhart and Winston, New York, 1968).

Trigger, B. C., 'Major concepts of archaeology in historical perspective', *Man, 3* (1968), 523–41.

Ucko, P. J., 'Ethnography and archaeological interpretation of funerary remains', *World Archaeology, 1* (1969), 262–80.

Young, T. C., 'Population densities and early Mesopotamian urbanism', in P. J. Ucko, R. Tringham and G. Dimbleby (eds.), *Man, Settlement and Urbanism* (Duckworth, London, 1972).

CHAPTER 7   THE ENIGMA OF THE MEGALITHS

European megaliths

Ashbee, P., *The Earthen Long Barrow in Britain* (Dent, London, 1970).

Case, H., 'Settlement pattern in the north Irish neolithic', *Ulster Journal of Archaeology, 32* (1969), 3–27.

Childe, V. G., *Prehistoric Communities of the British Isles* (W. and R. Chambers, London and Edinburgh, 1940).

Daniel, G. E., *The Megalith Builders of Western Europe* (Hutchinson, London, 1958).

Daniel, G. E., 'Northmen and southmen', *Antiquity, 41* (1967), 313–16.

Fleming, A., 'The myth of the mother-goddess', *World Archaeology, 1* (1969), 247–61.

Giot, P. R., 'The impact of radiocarbon dating on the establishment of the prehistoric chronology of Brittany', *Proceedings of the Prehistoric Society, 37* (1971), 208–17.

Henshall, A. S., *The Chambered Tombs of Scotland* I (University Press, Edinburgh, 1963).

Piggott, S., *Neolithic Cultures of the British Isles* (University Press, Cambridge, 1954).

Powell, T. G. E. (ed.), *Megalithic Enquiries in the West of Britain* (University Press, Liverpool, 1969).

Renfrew, C., 'Colonialism and Megalithismus', *Antiquity, 41* (1967), 276–88.

Monument building in neolithic societies

Atkinson, R. J. C., 'Neolithic engineering', *Antiquity, 35* (1961), 292–9.

Bulmer, R., 'Political aspects of the Moka ceremonial exchange system among the Kyaka people of the western highlands of New Guinea', *Oceania, 31* (1960), 1–13.

Erasmus, C. J., 'Monument building: some field experiments', *Southwestern Journal of Anthropology, 21* (1965), 277–302.

Harrisson, T. and O'Connor, S. J., *Gold and Megalithic Activity in Prehistoric and Recent West Borneo* (Cornell University, Ithaca, New York, 1970).

Heizer, R. F., 'Ancient heavy transport, methods and achievements', *Science, 153* (1966), 821–30.

Kaplan, D., 'Men, monuments and political systems', *Southwestern Journal of Anthropology*, *19* (1963), 397–410.

Leach, E. R., 'Hydraulic society in Ceylon', *Past and Present*, *15* (1959), 2–26.

CHAPTER 8 THE WORLD'S FIRST STONE TEMPLES

(Several of the works listed for Chapter 7 are also relevant to this chapter.)

Malta

Evans, J. D., *Malta* (Thames and Hudson, London, 1959).

Evans, J. D., *Prehistoric Antiquities of the Maltese Islands* (Athlone, London, 1971).

Renfrew, C., 'New configurations in Old World archaeology', *World Archaeology*, *2* (1970), 199–211.

Renfrew, C., 1972, 'Malta and the calibrated radiocarbon chronology', *Antiquity*, *46* (1972), 141–5.

Trump, D. H., *Skorba* (Reports of the Research Committee of the Society of Antiquaries of London 22, 1966).

Chiefdoms:

Farb, P., *Man's Rise to Civilisation* (Secker & Warburg, London, 1969).

Renfrew, C., 'Beyond a subsistence economy: the evolution of social organisation in prehistoric Europe', in Moore, C. (ed.), *The Organisation of Complex Societies* (M.I.T. Press, Boston, in press).

Sahlins, M. D., *Social Stratification in Polynesia* (University of Washington, Seattle, 1955).

Sahlins, M. D., *Tribesmen* (Prentice-Hall, Englewood Cliffs, 1968).

Sanders, W. T. and Marino, J., *New World Prehistory* (Prentice-Hall, Englewood Cliffs, 1970).

Service, E. R., *Primitive Social Organisation* (Random House, New York, 1962).

Service, E. R., *Cultural Evolutionism, Theory in Practice* (Holt, Reinhart and Winston, New York, 1971).

Easter Island

Emory, K. P., 'Polynesian stone remains', in C. S. Coon and J. M. Andrews (eds), *Studies in the Anthropology of Oceania and Asia* (Papers of the Peabody Museum of American Archaeology and Ethnology, Harvard University 20, 1943), 9–21.

Heyerdahl, T., *Aku-Aku, The Secret of Easter Island* (Allen & Unwin, London, 1958).

Heyerdahl, T. and Ferdon, E. N. (eds), *Archaeology of Easter Island, I* (Monographs of the School of American Research and the Museum of New Mexico 24, Pt 1, 1961).

Metraux, A., *Ethnology of Easter Island* (Bernice P. Bishop Museum Bulletin 160, 1940).

Metraux, A., *Easter Island, a Stone Age Civilisation in the Pacific* (Deutsch, London, 1957).

Routledge, S., *The Mystery of Easter Island, the Story of an Expedition* (Sifton, Praed and Co., London, 1919).

Sahlins, M. D., 'Esoteric efflorescence in Easter Island', *American Anthropologist*, 57 (1955), 1045–52.

Suggs, R. C., *Island Civilisations of Polynesia*, New York, New American Library, New York, 1960).

CHAPTER 9   THE BEGINNING OF EUROPEAN METALLURGY

The copper age

Childe, V. G., *The Danube in Prehistory* (University Press, Oxford, 1929).

Childe, V. G., *The Dawn of European Civilisation*, 6th edn, (Routledge, London, 1957).

Coghlan, H. H., *Notes on the Prehistoric Metallurgy of Copper and Bronze in the Old World* (Pitt Rivers Museum, Oxford, Occasional Paper on Technology 4, 1951).

Forde, C. D., *Habitat, Economy and Society* (Methuen, London, 1934).

Jovanović, B., 'Early copper metallurgy of the central Balkans', in *Actes du VIII Congrès des Sciences Préhistoriques et Protohistoriques, I* (Belgrade, 1971).

Martin, P. S., Quimby, G. I., and Collier, D., *Indians Before Columbus* (University Press, Chicago, 1947).

Renfrew, C., *The Art of the First Farmers* (City Museum, Sheffield, 1969).

Renfrew, C., 'The autonomy of the south-east European copper age', *Proceedings of the Prehistoric Society*, 35 (1969), 12–47.

Renfrew, C., 'Sitagroi, radiocarbon and the prehistory of south-east Europe', *Antiquity*, 45 (1971), 275–82.

Tringham, R., *Hunters, Fishers and Farmers of Eastern Europe*, 6000–3000 B.C. (Hutchinson, London, 1971).

Wertime, T., 'Man's first encounters with metallurgy', *Science*, *146* (1964), 1257–67.

Signs and 'writing' in the prehistoric Balkans

Falkenstein, A., 'Zu den Tontafeln aus Tartaria', *Germania*, *43* (1965), 269–73.

Georgiev, V. I., 'Un sceau inscrit de l'époque chalcolithique trouvé en Thrace', *Studi Miceni ed Egeo – Anatolici*, *9* (1969), 32–5.

Hood, M. S. F., 'The Tartaria tablets', *Antiquity*, 41 (1967), 99–113.

Makkay, J., 'The late neolithic Tordos group of signs', *Alba Regia*, *Annales Musei Stephani Regis*, *10* (Székesfehérvár, 1969), 9–50.

Makkay, J., 'A chalcolithic stamps seal from Karanovo, Bulgaria', *Kadmos*, *10* (1971), 1–9.

Milojčić, V., 'Die Tontafeln von Tartaria und die absolute Chronologie des mitteleuropäischen Neolithikums', *Germania*, *43* (1965), 261–8.

Neustupuý, E., 'The Tartaria tablets', *Antiquity*, *42* (1968), 32–5.

Nikolov, B., 'Débuts de l'écriture du chalcolithique dans les terres bulgares', *Archeologiya*, *3* (Sofia, 1970), 1–9.

Schmidt, H., 'Tordos', *Zeitschrift für Ethnologie* (1903), 39–41 and 438–69.

Vlassa, N., 'Chronology of the neolithic in Transylvania in the light of the Tartaria settlement', *Dacia*, 7 (1963), 1–94.

CHAPTER 10   THE EMERGENCE OF CIVILIZATION IN EUROPE

Branigan, K., *The Foundations of Palatial Crete* (Routledge, London, 1970).

Childe, V. G., *Man Makes Himself*, 3rd edn (Watts, London, 1956).

Evans, A., *The Palace of Minos* (Macmillan, London, 1921–35).

Hood, M. S. F., *The Minoans* (Thames and Hudson, London, 1971).

Hutchinson, H. W., *Prehistoric Crete* (Penguin, Harmondsworth, 1962).

Marinatos, S. and Hirmer, M., *Crete and Mycenae* (Thames and Hudson, London, 1960).

Renfrew, C., *The Emergence of Civilisation, the Cyclades and the Aegean in the Third Millennium* B.C. (Methuen, London, 1972).

Taylour, W., *The Mycenaeans* (Thames and Hudson, London, 1964).

Vermeule, E., *Greece in the Bronze Age* (University Press, Chicago, 1964).

CHAPTER II STONEHENGE AND THE EARLY BRONZE AGE

ApSimon, A. M., 'The earlier bronze age in the north of Ireland', *Ulster Journal of Archaeology*, *32* (1969), 28–72.

Atkinson, R. J. C., *Stonehenge* (Penguin, Harmondsworth, 1960).

Branigan, K., 'Wessex and Mycenae, some evidence reviewed', *Wiltshire Archaeological and Natural History Magazine*, *65* (1970), 89–107.

Childe, V. G., *The Prehistory of European Society* (Penguin, Harmondsworth, 1958).

Coles, J. and Taylor, J., 'The Wessex culture: a minimal view', *Antiquity*, *45* (1971), 6–14.

Fleming, A., 'Territorial patterns in bronze age Wessex', *Proceedings of the Prehistoric Society*, *37*, Pt I (1971), 138–66.

Harper, F., *The Travels of William Bartram* (Yale University Press, New Haven, 1958).

Hawkins, G. S., *Stonehenge Decoded* (Souvenir Press, London, 1966).

Montelius, O., 'The chronology of the British Bronze Age', *Archaeologia*, *61*, Pt 2 (1908), 97–162.

Newton, R. G. and Renfrew, C., 'British faience beads reconsidered', *Antiquity*, *44* (1970), 199–206.

Piggott, S., 'The early bronze age in Wessex', *Proc. Preh. Soc.*, *4* (1938), 52–106.

Piggott, S., 'Mycenae and barbarian Europe: an outline survey', *Sbornik Narodniho Muzea v Praze*, *20* (1966), 117–25.

Renfrew, C., 'Wessex without Mycenae', *Annual of the British School of Archaeology at Athens*, *63* (1968), 277–85.

Renfrew, C., 'Monuments, mobilisation and social organisation in neolithic Wessex', in C. Renfrew (ed.), *The Explanation of Culture Change: Models in Prehistory* (Duckworth, London, 1973).

Stone J. F. S., *Wessex* (Thames and Hudson, London, 1958).

Swanton, J. R., *The Indians of the Southeastern United States* (Smithsonian Institution Bureau of American Ethnology Bulletin 137, 1946).

Thom, A., 1967, *Megalithic Sites in Britain* (Clarendon, Oxford, 1967).

Wainwright, G., 'Woodhenges', *Scientific American*, *223* (1970), 30–38.

INDEX

Abbeville, 22
adaptation, 200, 202
Aegean, 29–30, 39–42, 44–5, 47, 66–9, 84, 86–96, 98–103, 105, 107–8, 116–17, 151, 167, 169–70, 173–4, 187, 189, 192–3, 197–202, 203–7, 209, 212–14, 243, 246
agriculture, 114–15, 152, 161, 179, 208, 233; swidden, 132, 134–5, 228; see also farming
ahu, 160–62, 164–5
Ahu Vinapu, 161
Albania, 103
Alexander the Great, 27
Alexander, J., 247
Alexandrovats, 176
Ali Kosh, 173
Allan, W., 135
alloying, 172–4, 209, 245
amber, 42, 99, 103, 214, 222–3, 225, 243, 245–6
Anatolia, 63, 87, 200, 204–5
Anderson, E. C., 264
Antequera, 85
architecture, 120, 123, 145, 213, 224
Arran, 132–7, 140–42, 153, 228
art, 175–6, 178, 199
Ashbee, P., 137, 230
astronomical observation, 27, 237, 239, 241
Atkinson, R. J. C., 129–31, 216, 218–19, 222–3, 226–7, 233
Aubrey, J., 216, 218
Aubrey Holes, 216, 218, 227
Australia, 60–61, 116
Avebury, 218, 232–3
Azmak, Tell, 178

Balkans, 16, 39, 41–2, 66–9, 88, 91–2, 94–5, 97, 103, 107–8, 116, 167–71, 173, 175, 178, 180, 182, 184, 186–7, 190–91, 204, 231
Banitsa, 176–7
barbarians, the, 17, 108, 198, 202, 223, 224, 239, 248
Barker, H., 259
Barnenez, 90
Bartram, W., 233–5

Beg an Dorchenn, 144
Berger, R., 79, 81–3
Binford, L. R., 142, 254
Blance, B., 87
Blegen, C., 30, 66, 200, 203
Borneo, 138–40, 142
Boserup, E., 114–15
Boucher de Perthes, J., 22
Braidwood, R., 55–6, 113
Breuil, H., 60
bristlecone pine, 69, 71, 81, 82, 83, 266–7
Britain, 58, 64–6, 69, 85, 93, 101, 107, 120, 122, 123, 127, 129, 137, 141, 154, 158, 181, 215, 224, 225
Brittany, 40, 58, 66, 68, 85, 89–90, 122–4, 127–9, 143, 215, 225
Brückner, E., 24
Bucha, V., 76
Bulgaria, 96, 98, 103, 167, 169, 171, 174–5, 177–9, 180, 187–8
Burkitt, M., 44
Bush Barrow, 100, 214, 245
Bylany, 228

calendar, 20, 27, 43, 72; civil, 27, 28; horizon, 183, 238–9
calibration, see tree-ring calibration
Can Hasan, 173
Caracol, 240
Carapito, 91
carbon-14, 49–50; see also radiocarbon dating
Carpathian Mountains, 171, 190
Case, H., 127, 143, 145
Caskey, J. L., 203, 205
casting, 167, 170–73, 175, 187, 190
Çatal Hüyük, 66, 173, 187
causewayed camp, 229–30, 235–6
Çayönü, 173
cemetery, 189, 209, 227, 231; cremation, 218
Censorinus, 27
Cernica, 173, 189
Chalandriani, 87, 205
chambered tomb, 86, 125, 130, 131, 132, 141, 143, 145; see also megalithic tomb

Charles, J. A., 174
Cherokee Indian, 233, 235, 241
Chichen Itza, 240
chiefdom, 154, 155–9, 181, 195, 209, 210, 227, 228–42, 243, 246, 248, 249
Childe, V. G., 17, 31, 36, 39–47, 59, 63, 66, 86, 88–9, 93–5, 99, 103, 105–6, 108–9, 113, 123, 134–5, 143, 150, 167, 170, 200–202, 212–13, 254
China, 61
Chotnitsa, 174, 180, 182, 188, 190
Clark, J. G. D., 46, 62, 64, 65, 113, 141
Clark, M., 78, 83
cold hammering, 172, 245
collective burial, 67, 85, 87, 122, 126, 128, 129, 137
Cook, Captain, 160, 164
corbelled vault, 40, 89, 122–3, 128, 131–2, 197, 211, 235
cosmic radiation, 255, 258, 260
craft specialization, 114, 116, 118, 157, 162, 163, 166, 188, 189, 191, 196, 210, 231, 244, 245
Crawford, O. G. S., 48
Creek Indian, 233, 235, 236
Crete, 24, 29–30, 37, 40, 44, 45, 66, 69, 86, 93, 99, 151, 186, 192–3, 196–200, 202–6, 208, 210–13, 222
cross-cultural survey, 111
cross-dating, 28, 29, 30, 84, 86, 106, 199
Cueva de la Pastora, 132
Cueva del Romeral, 120
culture change, 110, 112–14
Curtius, E., 198
Cyclades, 93, 200, 208
Czechoslovakia, 101, 189, 215

dagger grave, 42, 103, 215, 226
Daniel, G., 18, 35, 36, 46, 57, 59, 86, 122, 124
Danube, 40, 63–4, 91–8, 134, 144, 178, 182, 188
Darwin, C., 19, 22
dendrochronology, 70, 71, 73, 80
Denmark, 40, 66, 89, 93, 99, 120, 123, 126, 129
De Vries, Hl., 74
Dhimini, 204
diffusion, 18, 30–37, 39, 40, 46–7, 85–6, 90, 93–5, 109–11, 192, 247
diffusionism, 17–18, 36, 103–4, 109, 123, 145, 150, 159, 168–9, 201, 215, 248, 253

Djadovo, 178
dolmen, 39, 85, 123, 126–9
drystone technique, 122, 128, 131, 132
Durkheim, E., 157
Durrington Walls, 57, 58, 218, 231, 233

Earls Barton, 103
Easter Island, 159–66, 184–6, 193, 219
Edwards, I. E. S., 27
Egypt, 15–16, 24, 26, 28–30, 33–5, 37, 40, 42, 44, 53, 61, 63, 72, 83, 84, 86, 92, 107, 123, 147, 156, 192, 193, 199, 200, 201, 204, 212, 262
Ehrich, R., 66
Elliot Smith, Sir Grafton, 33, 34, 35, 36, 61
Emborio, 203
Er-Mane, 131
Essé, 124, 128
ethnographic parallel, 116, 135, 137, 138–9, 140, 141, 142, 160–64, 179, 180, 181, 183–6, 189, 219, 233–6, 237, 239–42, 251–2
Euphrates, 32
Evans, Sir Arthur, 24, 29, 41, 45, 151, 193–4, 198, 199, 202, 203, 224
Evans, Sir John, 22
Evans, J. D., 89, 148, 151–2, 203
Evans, R., 188
evolution, 18, 111; local, 86, 125, 127, 129, 132, 145, 151; parallel, 37
exchange, 116–17, 189, 191, 212, 231, 244; gift, 140–41, 144, 156, 252
explanation, 109–11, 119, 145, 202, 248, 250

faience, 42, 44, 45, 101–2, 223–4, 245–6
Falkenstein, A., 67
farming, 55, 58, 60–64, 113, 119, 142–3, 165, 179, 199; see also agriculture
fault-line, chronological, 103–6
Ferguson, C. W., 74, 76, 79, 80
Fergusson, J., 31, 33, 39, 121, 127
figurine, 60, 86, 92, 93, 152, 153, 170, 175, 178, 180–82, 184, 188, 198, 206
Flannery, K. V., 154
Fleming, A., 245
Forde, C. D., 184, 238
Forge, A., 115
fortifications, 88, 197, 204, 205
France, 42, 107, 120, 122–3, 126, 137, 215
French, D. H., 204
Frierman, J., 175, 176

Fussell's Lodge, 137

gallery grave, 122–4, 128
Galton, F., 111
Gavrinnis, 86
Geer, G. de, 25
Geiger counter, 258, 261
Gelidoniya, Cape, 212
Geoffrey of Monmouth, 214, 216
Georgiev, G. I., 98
Georgiev, V., 186
Germany, 99, 120, 189, 215, 225
Ggantija, 147–9, 155
Gimbutas, M., 98, 176, 244
Giot, P. R., 143
Godwin, H., 59
Gradeshnitsa, 177, 182
Graham, J. W., 213
grave goods, 101, 122, 189, 199, 205, 209, 215, 219, 231, 244
Greece, 16, 29–30, 33, 37, 39, 41, 42, 63, 79, 87, 103, 175, 181, 189, 192, 198, 204, 206–11, 219, 222
Grimes Graves, 231
Gumelnitsa, 41, 44–5, 96, 97, 171, 174, 178, 188–9

Hacilar, 66
Hagar Qim, 148–9, 155, 161
half-life, 77, 256–7, 261–2
Hal Saflieni, 149, 151, 165
Hammerton, M., 239
Harrisson, T., 138, 139
Hawkes, C. F. C., 103, 226
Hawkes, J., 251
Hawkins, G., 217, 220–22, 227, 239
Heel Stone, 217–18, 220
Helmsdorf, 102, 226
henge, 57, 218, 230–32, 235–6, 242
Heyerdahl, T., 35, 159
hierarchy, 156, 193, 195, 205, 230, 234
Hissar, Tepe, 170
Hitchcock, E. A., 235–6
Hoëdic, 143–4
Hole, F., 154
Homer, 41, 198
Hood, S., 29, 66
Hopi, 183–4, 238–40
House of the Tiles, 205, 210
Hove, 103
Hoyle, F., 227

Huber, B., 79
Hungary, 170, 175, 177, 189, 244
Huxtable, J., 82

Iberia, 39–40, 45, 67–8, 85–91, 103, 105, 107, 124, 128–9, 143, 169, 244; see also Spain and Portugal
Île Carn, 90
Île Gaignog, 90
Île Longue, 40, 85, 128, 132
immigration theory, 204
Inca, 193
incised signs, 176, 177, 182
independent invention, 33, 110, 169–70, 211
India, 31, 33, 111
Indus valley, 201
innovation, 111–12, 178, 187–91, 202; individual, 89; local, 88; technological, 187
inscribed tablets, 196
Iran, 63, 154
Ireland, 40, 85, 120, 129, 141, 143, 145, 214
irrigation, 154, 158, 166, 201, 209
isotope, 49, 189, 257, 262, 265
Italy, 33, 38–9, 47, 102, 122, 212

Jarmo, 55–6
Jericho, 55–6, 117
Jones, Inigo, 216
Jordhoj, 90
Jugoslavia, 94, 167, 171, 174–5, 178–9, 188, 244

Kahun, 29
Kaplan, D., 166
Karanovo, 68, 98, 177, 178
Karbuna, 190
Kelabit, 138
Kenyon, K., 55–6
Kercado, 89–90
kiva, 183–4, 240
Knockiveagh, 145
Knossos, 24, 41, 193–4, 198–9, 203–4
Knowth, 85
Kossinna, G., 35–6
Kroeber, A. L., 110–11

Lascaux, 60
Leach, E., 251
Lee, R., 254
Leki Male, 102
Lepenski Vir, 182

Lerna, 203, 205, 210
Leubingen, 246
Levant, 63, 192, 212
Libby, W. F., 48, 53–4, 60, 70, 72, 76–7, 81, 257–8, 261–3
local development, see evolution, local
long barrow, 127–8, 137, 145, 228, 230, 236, 243
Los Millares, 85–7, 90–91, 128

Macedonia, 200, 208
Macmillan Brown, J., 185
McPherron, A., 179
Maeshowe, 85, 120, 132, 137, 242
Makkay, J., 177
Malta, 16, 107–8, 118, 122, 147, 149, 151–6, 158, 159–66, 169, 181, 184, 193
Mané Karnaplaye, 90
marae, 160
Marden, 218, 231
market, 99, 100, 116–17
Martin, G., 82
material culture, 152–3
Maya, 20–21, 193, 240–41
Mediterranean polyculture, 208–9, 210
megalithic tomb, 16–17, 31, 36, 39, 44, 46–7, 65–6, 69, 85–91, 108, 118, 120–46, 162, 181; see also chambered tomb
Melanesia, 160
Mellaart, J., 66, 206
menhir, 139
Mesopotamia, 16, 26, 28, 42, 67, 193, 200, 211
metallurgy, 16–17, 35–6, 39–41, 67, 86–8, 91, 93, 108, 167–91, 200, 203, 205–6, 209, 215, 242–7
Metraux, A., 162, 164, 185
Mexico, 20, 62, 166, 211
Midhowe, 137, 141
migration, 34, 36, 42, 109, 192, 244, 249
Milankovitch, M., 25
Milojčić, V., 56–7, 59, 65–8, 94–7
mines, 190, 231, 244
Minoan, 24, 29, 40, 44, 86, 151, 192, 193–7, 198–200, 203, 205, 210–13, 224
Mnajdra, 147, 155, 161
mobilization, 158, 237, 243
models, 113, 169, 202, 248; economic, 201; social, 124, 158
Montelius, O., 18, 32–3, 36–41, 45, 86, 91, 105, 126, 254

monumental building, 158, 160, 193
Mortillet, G. de, 18
mother goddess, 47, 85, 86, 180
Mount Pleasant, 231
Movius, H., 61
Munnich, K. O., 73
Mycenae, 29, 40, 42, 99, 102, 150–51, 180, 195–7, 214–15, 222, 226
Mycenaean, 16, 29, 41–2, 69, 86, 98–103, 128, 151, 192, 193–7, 198, 210–12, 224–7, 246

Nea Nikomedeia, 174, 180–81
Needham, J., 110
neolithic revolution, 142
Netherlands, 58, 120
Neustupný, E., 76, 95
New Archaeology, 15, 142
Newgrange, 85–6, 89–90, 121, 132
New Guinea, 140–42
Newham, C. A., 221
Newton, Sir Isaac, 21, 26
Nikolov, B., 177, 182
Nyerup, R., 20
Nympsfield, 128

observatory, 16, 20, 222, 241
obsidian, 152, 155
O'Connor, S., 139
Olmec, 62, 211
Olympia, 198
Orca dos Castenairos, 91
organization: agricultural, 197; central, 158, 193; economic, 113, 115, 116–17, 156, 211; social, 113, 115, 117–18, 137, 153, 155–6, 160, 162, 164–5, 205, 211, 231, 237, 242
Orkney, 132, 137, 141–2, 245

palace, 192, 194–8, 201, 204, 210, 211, 243
Palermo Stone, 27
Palestine, 33, 39, 63
paradigm, 19, 233, 248, 249, 254
passage grave, 39–40, 44–6, 85, 89–90, 122, 131, 143–4
Penck, A., 24
Pendlebury, J. D., 194
Petrie, Sir W. Flinders, 29
Phylakopi, 186
Piggott, S., 57–9, 64–5, 101, 216, 222–3, 231–2, 247

Pinus longaevia (formerly *Pinus aristata*), 74
plaque, 177, 182, 186
Poland, 215
Polanyi, K., 117
pollen analysis, 58–9
Polynesia, 33, 159, 164, 233, 249
Popović, V., 95
population, 113–16, 118, 135–7, 143, 153, 155, 158, 161; density, 115–16, 134, 143–4, 154, 164, 179, 207–8, 243; growth, 115; pressure, 114, 209
Portugal, 39, 120, 128; *see also* Iberia
potassium/argon method of dating, 60
pottery, 29, 92–3, 98, 152, 174–6, 178, 180, 188, 191, 199–200, 210, 212, 218, 231, 244
Powell, T. G. E., 143
Praia das Macas, 91
Prasklice, 102
Prestwich, J., 22
priesthood, 158, 237, 241
Priština, 176
Pyramid, 15, 69, 123, 147
pyrotechnology, 174, 188, 245

radiocarbon dating, 48–54, 255–68
Redfield, R., 193
redistribution, 116, 118, 156–8, 162–3, 181, 195–7, 210–11, 231, 233, 237, 243, 245
religious activity, 181–3, 190, 242
rich burial, 215, 222, 242–3
Rillaton, 101–2, 223, 245
Ring of Brodgar, 137, 218
Rodden, R. J., 181
Romania, 67, 96, 167, 169, 171, 175, 177, 187, 188
rongo rongo tablets, 162, 184–5, 186
rotunda, 234–5
round barrow, 219, 243
round house, *see* rotunda
round tomb, 46, 69, 86, 129, 199
Rousay, 132, 135–6, 140–41, 153, 155, 228
Routledge, E. Scoresby, 161–3, 185
Rudna Glava, 190, 231

Sahlins, M. D., 157, 161, 183
Scandinavia, 25, 40, 127, 137
Schliemann, H., 197–8, 202, 205
Schmidt, H., 92, 93
Schuchardt, C., 151
Schulman, E., 74
Scotland, 40, 143
script, 93, 184–5, 211

sculpture, 94–5, 187
seal, 97, 176–7, 199, 210–11, 243
Sept Îles, 90
Sequoia, 73–4
Service, E., 237
Shackleton, N., 189
Shaft Graves, 42, 99–102, 150, 180, 197, 211, 214, 222
Sicily, 102, 152, 155
Silbury Hill, 233, 242
Siret, H. and L., 86, 92–3
Sitagroi, 79, 98, 171, 178, 189, 203–4
Skara Brae, 178
Skorba, 151, 152
smelting, 167, 171–2, 175, 187, 190, 225, 245
Smith, H. S., 73
Spain, 39, 41–2, 44–5, 67, 120, 122–3, 126, 132; *see also* Iberia
spirals, 149–50
Spondylus, 189–90
standard deviation, 54, 78, 259–60, 265
Starčevo, 178, 180
Station Stones, 217–18, 220–21, 227, 237
statue, 149, 160, 164
Steward, J., 19
Stonehenge, 16–17, 20, 42, 69, 101–3, 107, 122, 129, 214–47
Stones of Stenness, 137, 218
strategy of research, 113
stratigraphic method, 23, 41
Stukeley, W., 216
Suess, H. E., 69, 71, 75–9, 203, 226, 267, 268
Suggs, R., 159
Sumer, 67, 95, 107, 156, 186, 193, 201–2, 212
Sweden, 120
symbolism, 175, 178, 182–6, 239
Syria, 39, 100, 199, 212

Tahiti, 160, 163
Tarxien, 148–52
Tartaria tablets, 67, 95, 176–7, 186
Tauber, H., 73
Taylor, J., 225, 244–5
Tell Azmak, 178
temples, 15–16, 108, 118, 147–66, 201
Tepe Hissar, 170
territory, 135, 137, 141, 144–5, 155, 179, 228
Téviec, 143–4
thermoluminescence dating, 82
Thom, A., 237–9
Thomsen, C., 23, 32, 39

Three Age System, 23–4, 39, 113
Tinkinswood, 131
Tiryns, 197
Tordos, 92–3, 176
trade, 40, 99, 113, 155, 166, 188–9, 191, 201–2, 205–6, 209, 211–12, 224–6, 236, 246–8, 252; commercial, 116–17
Treasury of Atreus, 40, 86, 197
tree-ring calibration, 57, 68, 69–83, 84, 106, 192, 215, 225–6
Troy, 30, 41, 44–5, 66, 69, 92–4, 96, 98, 167, 169, 171, 180, 205–6, 211
Trump, D., 151–3
Turin Royal Canon, 27–8
Tustrup, 90
Tylor, E., 111
typological method, 37, 39, 61

Uaxactun, 241
Ucko, P. J., 180, 251–2
Urban Revolution, 42, 200
U.S.S.R., 174, 190, 244
Únětice, 100, 102, 106, 215
Ussher, Archbishop, 21

Valdbygaards, 127
varve dating, 25, 59, 82
Vasiliki, 205
Vassits, M., 91–3
Venta, La, 62

Ventris, M., 196
Vermeule, E., 200
village, 55–6, 178, 179, 228
Vinča, 41, 44–5, 66–7, 92–8, 167, 169, 171, 173–8, 184, 190, 193

Wace, A. J., 195, 200
Wainwright, G., 230–31
warfare, 164–5
Warren, P., 29
Waterbolk, H. T., 59
Wertime, T., 167, 171
Wessex, 42, 44–5, 101–3, 108, 214–15, 219, 222–6, 228–42, 243, 246–7
West Kennet, 128
Wheeler, Sir Mortimer, 48
Willis, E. H., 73
Windmill Hill, 59
Woodhenge, 231
Worsaae, J., 18, 23–4, 26, 32, 39, 254
writing, 35, 111, 120, 177, 181, 182–6, 193, 211, 240
written records, 99

Xanthoudides, 86

Zagros, 63
Zimbabwe, 36, 159
Zimmerman, D., 82

A NOTE ON THE TYPE

THE TEXT of this book has been set on the Monotype in a type face named Bembo. The roman is a copy of a letter cut for the celebrated Venetian printer Aldus Manutius by Francesco Griffo, and first used in Cardinal Bembo's *De Aetna* of 1495—hence the name of the revival. Griffo's type is now generally recognized, thanks to the researches of Mr. Stanley Morison, to be the first of the old face group of types. The companion italic is an adaptation of a chancery script type designed by the Roman calligrapher and printer Lodovico degli Arrighi, called Vincentino, and used by him during the 1520's.

Bound by The Haddon Craftsmen, Inc.,
Scranton, Pennsylvania. Binding design by Susan Mitchell.

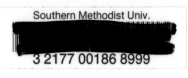